Palgrave Studies in Prisons and Penology

AF803658

Series Editors
Ben Crewe
Institute of Criminology
University of Cambridge
Cambridge, UK

Yvonne Jewkes
Social & Policy Sciences
University of Bath
Bath, UK

Thomas Ugelvik
Faculty of Law
University of Oslo
Oslo, Norway

This is a unique and innovative series, the first of its kind dedicated entirely to prison scholarship. At a historical point in which the prison population has reached an all-time high, the series seeks to analyse the form, nature and consequences of incarceration and related forms of punishment. Palgrave Studies in Prisons and Penology provides an important forum for burgeoning prison research across the world.

Series Advisory Board
Anna Eriksson (Monash University)
Andrew M. Jefferson (DIGNITY - Danish Institute Against Torture)
Shadd Maruna (Rutgers University)
Jonathon Simon (Berkeley Law, University of California)
Michael Welch (Rutgers University).

More information about this series at
http://www.palgrave.com/gp/series/14596

Matthew Maycock • Rosie Meek
James Woodall
Editors

Issues and Innovations in Prison Health Research

Methods, Issues and Innovations

palgrave
macmillan

Editors
Matthew Maycock
Universtiy of Dundee
Dundee, UK

Rosie Meek
Royal Holloway University of London
Surrey, Berkshire, UK

James Woodall
Leeds Beckett University
Leeds, UK

Palgrave Studies in Prisons and Penology
ISBN 978-3-030-46403-5 ISBN 978-3-030-46401-1 (eBook)
https://doi.org/10.1007/978-3-030-46401-1

© The Editor(s) (if applicable) and The Author(s), under exclusive licence to Springer Nature Switzerland AG 2021
This work is subject to copyright. All rights are solely and exclusively licensed by the Publisher, whether the whole or part of the material is concerned, specifically the rights of translation, reprinting, reuse of illustrations, recitation, broadcasting, reproduction on microfilms or in any other physical way, and transmission or information storage and retrieval, electronic adaptation, computer software, or by similar or dissimilar methodology now known or hereafter developed.
The use of general descriptive names, registered names, trademarks, service marks, etc. in this publication does not imply, even in the absence of a specific statement, that such names are exempt from the relevant protective laws and regulations and therefore free for general use.
The publisher, the authors and the editors are safe to assume that the advice and information in this book are believed to be true and accurate at the date of publication. Neither the publisher nor the authors or the editors give a warranty, expressed or implied, with respect to the material contained herein or for any errors or omissions that may have been made. The publisher remains neutral with regard to jurisdictional claims in published maps and institutional affiliations.

Cover illustration: © alamy G246X4

This Palgrave Macmillan imprint is published by the registered company Springer Nature Switzerland AG.
The registered company address is: Gewerbestrasse 11, 6330 Cham, Switzerland

Foreword

It is an extraordinary time to be writing and thinking about prison health. Sometimes only a cliché will do: this book could not be more timely. I write during Easter 2020 when the Corona virus or Covid 19 is raging throughout the UK, and prisons and the health of those who are held and work there are one of the most acute areas of concern.

I hope that by the time this book is read the crisis will have passed but I hope too that what we have learnt about prison health in this period, and that this book illuminates and confirms, is not forgotten. The central theme of this book is that prison health cannot just be seen as 'an absence of disease' but must be understood as 'the attainment of positive health and well-being'. We are so very anxious about prison health now not because the facilities and care provided in prison health centres are poor but because we know that the total environment of the prison undermines prisoners' health and well-being, making them especially vulnerable to disease.

The current health crisis may have brought these issues to the fore but some of us have been concerned about them for a long time. They have been a preoccupation of the inspectorate of prisons for many years including during my time as Chief Inspector from 2010 to 2016. Even prior to the current epidemic, prisons were suffering what the House of Commons

Justice Committee called an 'enduring crisis',[1] and in my last Annual Report for 2014–2015 I described how staff shortages, a lack of purposeful activity and squalid conditions undermined improvements in health care.[2] The health of men and women locked in shared cells for many hours every day, often fearful and anxious, with little to occupy them physically or mentally must be compromised. For the growing population of elderly prisoners, children in youth custody and the disproportionate number of prisoners whose health was compromised by their circumstances prior to custody, health deficits will be even greater. I am no health expert but I remember now how one of my strongest impressions as I first began to immerse myself in prisons as Chief Inspector was simply how unhealthy prisoners looked. I recall being struck by how many prisoners had poor teeth—and understood even then that this must be an indicator of much wider health problems and I am pleased one chapter addresses this. I too talked to men and women working in prison gardens, as did the authors of two chapters in the book, and saw how this could support prisoners' well-being. When I walked into an arts project in an otherwise chaotic prison I saw, as another chapter describes, the therapeutic value these activities can have.

This book therefore rightly calls for more research into prisoner health in its widest sense and how health outcomes can be improved. The great contribution of this book is not just that it examines a variety of innovative interventions in prisoner health and well-being but also examines in detail the research methodologies used to explore them. Conducting research in prisons in fraught with practical and ethical difficulties. Simply obtaining access is difficult enough and then there are big questions about what 'informed consent' means in a prison context and how the relationship between the prisoner and the researcher can be ethically managed. These issues take a different form in women's prisons and I am pleased that a significant section of the book takes a gendered approach.

The position of the researcher is critical too. I found visiting prisons on a regular basis physically and emotionally demanding. It challenged my

---

[1] House of Commons Justice Committee (29 October 2019, HC 191: para: 5).

[2] HM Chief Inspector of Prisons for England and Wales (2017) *Annual Report 2014–15*. Williams Lea Group on behalf of the Controller of Her Majesty's Stationery Office. pp. 7–11.

own preconceptions and values. Another theme of the book across many of its chapters is the importance of reflective research, and the authors' self-aware responses to the work they were doing offer important insights for future prison researchers.

Most importantly the book addresses—how do we know? How do we know what is happening behind prison walls and within the prison walls, behind the personal walls that prisoners like us all erect around the very personal information and feelings that their health involves? As my period as Chief Inspector progressed, my understanding of the limits of what we could know from our inspections grew. I came to understand that none knows more about what is happening in prison than prisoners themselves. So in addition to a rich description of different technical research methodologies, the book returns repeatedly to themes of co-production and enabling the prisoner voice to be heard. Indeed, the book had its origins in a seminar at HMP Barlinnie in Scotland and echoes of the voices of prisoners and prison staff that informed that seminar are heard in this book, which eventually followed.

The book is in effect a call to prison and health researchers to turn their attention to prison health. The corona virus has taught us that the health of one of us can quickly become an issue for the health of all of us. It is not just prisoners and prison staff who would have cause to be grateful for a greater understanding of prison health—it is a matter that affects us all.

Royal Holloway University of London — Nick Hardwick
HM Chief Inspector of Prisons 2010–2016
9 April 2020

Contents

Notes on Contributors

Laura Abbott is a senior lecturer in Midwifery at The University of Hertfordshire and a fellow of the Royal College of Midwives. Laura's doctorate examined the experiences of pregnant women in prison: 'The Incarcerated Pregnancy: An Ethnographic Study of Perinatal Women in English Prisons'. Laura volunteers with the charity Birth Companions and has co-authored The Birth Charter for pregnant women in England and Wales, published by Birth Companions in May 2016. She has been publicly recognised as one of the Nation's 'lifesavers' from 'Made at Uni' for the impact of her research. Laura hopes to continue to highlight the issues facing women, campaigning for the recommendations arising from her research to be actioned, meaning change on the ground for pregnant women and new mothers in prison.

Elizabeth Bos is Research Fellow, Centre for Business in Society, Coventry University. Elizabeth is a geographer with an interest in the concepts of participation and reconnection. She holds an undergraduate degree in Human Geography, an MSc in Urban Regeneration Research and Practice, and her PhD thesis is entitled 'Reconnections in the City: Exploring the Drivers of Community Garden Participation'. Her work particularly focuses on the activities of food growing and community gardening, the outcomes these produce for individuals and communities, and the processes that are needed to enable successful and meaningful participation in such activities. She has a keen interest in the way partnership working can promote participation, especially for those who currently experience societal marginalisation and exclusion. With 10 years' experience of working with a range of communities, third sector organisations and partners to deliver small- to large-scale projects, Elizabeth is focused on producing high-quality research that promotes sustainable change.

Geraldine Brady is Associate Professor in Social Work, School of Social Sciences, Nottingham Trent University. Brady's research focuses on understandings of contemporary social issues, exploring the ways in which individuals and groups can become socially excluded and stigmatised. She has an interest in the development of socially just policy and practice approaches, with a particular focus on: children, young people and young adult's marginalisation and inequality in the fields of health, social care, education and criminal justice; experiences and responses to CSA/E; third sector interventions in prisons; creative methodologies. Geraldine began researching criminal justice interventions (with Geraldine Brown) in 2013. She has co-led four studies (Brown et al. 2015, 2016, 2018; Bos et al. 2016; Brady et al. 2018), contributing to a body of interdisciplinary research in this field. She also reflects on the ethics and politics of participatory and creative research methods in her aim to influence change.

Gavin Breslin, PhD is a senior lecturer in Sport and Exercise Psychology at Ulster University. Gavin's research and teaching interests explore the psychology of performance and mental health. He is a member of the Sport and Exercise Science Research Institute (SESRI), and The Bamford Centre for Mental Health and Well-being at Ulster University. He is a British Psychological Society (BPS) Chartered Sport and Exercise Psychologist, a registered practitioner of the Health Care Professions Council (HCPC), fellow of the Higher Education Academy, and Chief Assessor for the BPS Stage 2 Qualification in Sport and Exercise Psychology in the UK. Gavin has led on policy development and has consulted with national and international athletes and teams in sport and exercise psychology. His research was instrumental in establishing the national Action Plan for Well-being in Sport in Northern Ireland

(2019–2025) and an international consensus statement on mental health awareness interventions in sport.

Geraldine Brown is an assistant professor in Centre for Agroecology, Water and Resilience, Coventry University. Geraldine's background is in Sociology and Social Policy and the focus of her research includes exploring individuals' and groups' experiences of public policy and practice, community engagement and community action. A key aspect of her work is to consider factors which contribute how individuals and groups experience exclusion or marginalisation and, in so doing identify ways of bringing about 'change'. Geraldine takes a community development approach to her work and has undertaken research with 'criminalised men and women', 'pregnant teenagers and young parents', 'Black and Minority Ethnic communities', 'older people with a mental health need'. Geraldine's doctoral thesis focused on understanding the relationship between African Caribbean community activism and 'urban gun crime'. Geraldine is an experienced qualitative researcher and has a long-standing history of working collaboratively with third sector and community organisations and public bodies.

Alan Farrier is a qualitative researcher working in the Healthy and Sustainable Settings Unit (HSSU) based at the University of Central Lancashire, which he joined in 2014. Over the past 15 years he has worked on a variety of health and well-being research and evaluation projects, mainly with an arts or nature focus. In particular, he has worked with people in prison, young offenders and young people excluded from mainstream education, and people with mild to moderate mental health issues. His current work concerns prison and university settings. Alan is interested in a range of psychosocial research methods, including narrative-based interviewing and analysis, visual and mobile methods. He takes a whole system approach to research and evaluation in a variety of public health contexts, in order to understand challenges and produce work which has real-world applicability.

James Fraser is a registered general and mental nurse and nurse teacher and has held a number of nursing posts within general and psychiatric hospitals in the NHS in Scotland. He was also a lecturer in Nursing before studying at Abertay University, Dundee, Scotland for a PhD thesis entitled "An exploratory study of male ex-prisoners' experiences of health and healthcare in prison and the community" and graduated in November 2017.

Alison Frater Chair of the National Criminal Justice Arts Alliance (NCJAA), a visiting professor at Royal Holloway University of London and a consultant in public health, Alison Frater is an experienced director of public health and a senior leader with a record achievement in effective advocacy: addressing health inequalities, improving access to health and health care. She has published widely in health policy and public health research most recently on arts, health and justice in the *International Journal of Forensic Psychotherapy*, on deaths in custody in the BMJ and jointly edited a book of essays on crime and justice; she is currently the public health lead for UCL-based randomised trial, MOAM (Mentalisation for Offending Adult Males). Convinced of the need for an interdisciplinary approach to improve social justice, she has just completed a Master of Arts and is committed to research on the impact of arts in health and justice.

Ruth Freeman is Professor of Dental Public Health Research and Honorary Consultant in Dental Public Health. She is Director of the Oral Health and Health Research Programme, where she leads a multi-disciplinary team of inclusion oral health researchers, and Co-Director of the Dental Health Services Research Unit at the University of Dundee. She is Member of the British Psychoanalytic Council and Fellow of the Faculty of Public Health, Royal College of Physicians (UK).

Cindy M. Gray is an interdisciplinary professor of Health and Behaviour in the School of Social and Political Sciences and Institute of Health and Well-being at the University of Glasgow. Her research interests focus on: using multiple perspectives and approaches to develop in-depth understandings of people's attitudes, beliefs and values in relation to different health behaviours; and using the information gained to inform the development of health behaviour change interventions. With Kate Hunt and others, Cindy led the development of the Football Fans in Training intervention and of the Fit for LIFE intervention. She is particularly interested in working with high-risk and/or hard-to-reach populations: these include obese men, inactive older women and people in prisons among others. More recently, Cindy has developed a programme addressing the growing prevalence of non-communicable diseases (NCDs) in low- and middle-income countries in sub-Saharan Africa. This work includes using creative, arts-based methods: to explore local communities (often unspoken) beliefs and values about NCDs (and their risk factors); and as a basis for the development of socio-culturally competent NCD prevention interventions.

Jamie Grundy is an independent educator, trainer and researcher in the fields of crime prevention, higher education, community development and prison education. He has been Widening Participation Manager with Cardiff Metropolitan University, UK, where he created an education and training template between local prisons and the university.

David Honeywell is an associate research assistant at the University of Manchester, currently working on a project on prison suicide. David began his academic career in 2013 at the University of York where he worked as an associate lecturer in criminology and has since taught criminology at Durham and Hull universities. In 2018, he completed his PhD in sociology about ex-prisoners and the transformation of self through higher education, which was inspired by his own personal journey as an ex-prisoner who escaped a dysfunctional life through learning. While in prison in the 1990s, he gained an Open University qualification which later led to degrees in criminology, social research methods and sociology.

Kate Hunt is Professor in Behavioural Sciences and Health, and Interim Director of the Institute for Social Marketing and Health. Kate graduated in Human Sciences and undertook her masters at the University of Oxford, and her PhD at the University of Glasgow. She has a longstanding interest in inequalities in health and in Gender and Health (moving from an early interest in women's health to a focus on men, masculinities and health). More recently, her research has focused on the development and evaluation of public health interventions and policy, including culturally sensitised interventions delivered through professional sports clubs to engage people in long-term positive behaviour change, and on the health of people living and working in prisons. Kate is President of the UK Society for Social Medicine and Population Health and an Honorary Professor at the University of Glasgow, and Curtin University, Australia.

Nasrul Ismail is a social scientist with research interests in the fields of prison health, political economy, criminology and law. His current research investigates the impact of macroeconomic austerity on prison health in England. It is funded by the Economic and Social Research Council (ESRC). To date, Nasrul has published more than 40 papers in leading academic journals, including the BMC Public Health, Journal of Public Health, and Journal of Medical Ethics. He also teaches MSc Public Health and BA Criminology at the University of the West of England (UWE Bristol) and Bachelor of Medicine and Bachelor of Surgery (MB ChB) at the University of Bristol. Nasrul read law and public health at the University of Bristol and UWE Bristol, respectively. Prior to his academic career, Nasrul was a Public Health Commissioner for various public-sector organisations (with a total budget of £25.3 m) for nearly a decade.

Alice MacLean worked as an investigator scientist at the Social and Public Health Sciences Unit, University of Glasgow, until June 2019. MacLean was one of the grant holders on the Fit for LIFE project between 2012 and 2016.

Matthew Maycock is a Baxter Fellow in the School of Education and Social Work, University of Dundee, and visiting fellow at the Centre for Gender Studies, Karlstad University. He previously worked at the Scottish Prison Service undertaking research, often on gender and transgender issues in prison, as well as facilitating staff development across a range of areas. He was previously an investigator scientist within the Settings and Organisations Team at SPHSU, University of Glasgow. He undertook a PhD at the University of East Anglia that analysed modern slavery through the theoretical lens of masculinity. Throughout various studies, Maycock has consistently worked on gender issues with masculinity being a particular focus.

Rosie Meek is Professor of Psychology and Criminology and was founding Head of the Law School at Royal Holloway University of London, where her teaching and research expertise is in Criminal Justice and in particular, prisons, prison education and prison healthcare. As well as writing widely on the role of the voluntary sector in prisoner rehabilitation, Meek is best known for her work on the role and impact of sport and physical activity in prison settings: together with dozens of chapters, journal articles and evaluation reports on the topic, her 2013 book *Sport in Prison* was published by Routledge, and in 2018 she led a national review on behalf of the Ministry of Justice into sport in youth and adult prisons, which resulted in a number of policy recommendations and reforms.

Anita Mehay is a research fellow and Health Psychologist, based at University College, London. Her academic base is interdisciplinary, spanning critical psychology, social work, and criminology, and focuses on community development and participatory approaches to achieve change at individual, social and structure levels. Anita completed her doctoral research at Royal Holloway, University of London and practitioner psychology training at the University of Surrey, which both focused on supporting the health and well-being of young adults in prison. Since her doctoral research, Anita has worked on a number of large national studies evaluating approaches to supporting the health and well-being of young people and families from some of the most deprived areas in the England. She has also been awarded consultancy and research grants including from the Prisoners' Education Trust, Greater London Authority, Prostate Cancer UK and the Ministry of Justice (UK).

Jane Ogden is Professor in Health Psychology at the University of Surrey where she teaches psychology, vet, nutrition and dietician students to think more psychologically about health. Her research focuses on eating behaviour, behaviour change and weight management, symptom perception and communication. She has published over 200 research papers and 8 books and her most recent book shows students how to think more critically about research. She is also passionate about getting psychology out of the ivory tower and is a frequent contributor to the media.

James Woodall is Reader and also Head of Subject in Health Promotion at Leeds Beckett University. James' research interest is the health-promoting prison and how values central to health promotion are applied to the context of imprisonment. He has published widely on health promotion and its application to prison settings. James has published more broadly on health promotion matters, including empowerment in health promotion and the contribution that lay people can make to the public health agenda.

David Woods, PhD is a teaching fellow in the School of Sport at Ulster University, with specific teaching expertise in the psychology of high performance and mental well-being. David is also a member of the Sport and Exercise Science Research Institute (SESRI). David initially specialised in Organisational Psychology, before moving to a focus on Sport and Exercise psychology, which led to his research programme exploring the impact of sport and exercise on the mental well-being of people in prison. David is a member of the British Psychology Society, Division of Sport and Exercise Psychology.

List of Figures

List of Boxes

1

Introduction

Matthew Maycock, Rosie Meek, and James Woodall

Prison contexts often have profound implications for the health of the people who live and work within them. Despite these settings often housing people from extremely disadvantaged and deprived communities (Houchin 2005), many with multiple and complex health needs (Senior and Shaw 2007), health research is generally neglected within both criminology and medical sociology. This neglect is significant given that multiple studies have illustrated not just that there is a direct relationship

M. Maycock (✉)
Universtiy of Dundee, Dundee, UK

R. Meek
Department of Law and Criminology, Royal Holloway University of London, Surrey, UK
e-mail: r.meek@royalholloway.ac.uk

J. Woodall
Leeds Beckett University, Leeds, UK
e-mail: J.Woodall@leedsbeckett.ac.uk

© The Author(s) 2021

M. Maycock et al. (eds.), *Issues and Innovations in Prison Health Research*, Palgrave Studies in Prisons and Penology, https://doi.org/10.1007/978-3-030-46401-1_1

between health and offending (Social Inclusion Unit 2002) but that people who have served custodial sentences have higher mortality rates from all causes compared to those with no custodial experience (Binswanger et al. 2007, 2013; Farrell and Marsden 2008; Graham et al. 2015; Paanila et al. 1999; Phillips et al. 2017; Spittal et al. 2014; Verger et al. 2003; Zlodre and Fazel 2012). Moreover, there has been a marked increase in the population of older people in prison (Baidawi et al. 2011; Ginn 2012; Williams and Abraldes 2007), partly driven by longer average sentence lengths (Millie et al. 2003). In England and Wales, we now have as many people aged 50 and over in prison (16% of the prison population) as we have young adults aged under 25, and the percentage of over 50s in custody is even greater in Scotland, at 22% (Sturge 2019).

The authors agree that prison health is a key public health concern with research being fundamental to inform policy and practice in addressing the significant health and social issues faced by this group. The concept of 'prison health' has, in the main, been clearly aligned to a biomedical perspective (Sim 1990). Morris and Morris (1963, p.193), in their study of Pentonville prison, encapsulated the predominant discourse which surrounded prison health:

> *For the prison, health is essentially a negative concept; if men are not ill, de facto they are healthy. While most modern thinking in the field of social medicine has attempted to go further than this, for the prison medical staff it is not an unreasonable operational definition.*

Such a view has notable implications, as health is defined by the absence of disease and not the attainment of positive health and wellbeing. The authors adopt a far broader view of prison health, which is reflected throughout the chapters in the book. Indeed, our stance on 'prison health' is embedded in a social model that moves away from a reductionist, biomedical focus to a viewpoint whereby health is influenced by a range of factors that can be structural and environmental in nature. Our position is supported more widely by an international systematic review (which included studies from Australasia, Europe, USA and Africa) conducted by Herbert et al. (2012) which concluded that prison health services fail to fully exploit public health and 'upstream' health promotion work. This has been echoed in England and Wales where critical reviews of prison health services described a reactive and inefficient service, underpinned by a medical model that was largely blind to the social determinants of health and thus failed to exploit public health opportunities (HMIP 1996).

This book constitutes the first publication to utilise a range of social science methodologies to illuminate diverse and new aspects of health research in prison settings. Through the fourteen chapters of this book, a range of issues emerge that the authors of each contribution reflect upon. The ethical concerns that emerge as a consequence of undertaking prison health research are not ignored, indeed these lie at the heart of this book and resonate across all the chapters. Foregrounding these issues necessarily forms a significant focus of this introductory chapter.

Alongside explicitly considering emerging ethical issues, our contributing authors also have considered diverse aspects of innovation in research methodologies within the context of prison health research. Innovative research practice is challenging in this setting, given the myriad of practical issues that prison researchers face. Many of the chapters are innovative through the methodologies that were used, often adapting and utilising research methods rarely used within prison settings. By incorporating a range of perspectives on methodological and ethical issues, innovations in health-focused social science research before, during and after a period in custody, this book constitutes an opportunity to explore continuities and disconnections in people's health and well-being as they move through (and in and out of) the prison system. Chapters from a wide range of disciplines and engagements with the prison systems of England, Northern Ireland, Scotland and Wales are incorporated within this book, including people with lived experience of prison, and those who work in custodial settings. It is hoped that the book will provide a starting place for on-going discussion around health research within prison settings in the UK, but also beyond. The book brings together chapters from students, scholars, practitioners and service users from a range of disciplines (including medical sociology, medical anthropology, criminology, psychology and public health).

The Initial Symposium in Glasgow in May 2016

The starting place for this book was a symposium held in Glasgow in May 2016, from which some of the researchers who are featured in this book began to discuss challenges and opportunities for innovation within prison health research. The initial symposium, which considered the methodological and ethical dimensions of conducting health-focused social science research through and beyond prison settings, was supported by funding from the Foundation for the Sociology of Health and Illness, Royal Holloway University of London, and the Social and Public Health Sciences Unit at the University of Glasgow. It was held over two days, one at the Social and Public Health Sciences Unit, University of Glasgow, and secondly at HMP Barlinnie, Glasgow. The second day was of particular significance as this allowed symposium participants to get an insight into Scotland's largest prison. Additionally, this setting enabled prison staff and people serving custodial sentences to participate in the symposium and contribute to what was at that point an emerging discussion. The contribution of people in custody was particularly insightful, through critiquing a number of the presentations at the symposium from a reflective perspective grounded in the lived experiences of custody. This points to a wider limitation with prison research and what it can and can't tell us about life in prison (Drake et al. 2015), and the emergence of convict criminology within this space (Earle 2016; Ross and Richards 2003).

The symposium included 24 presentations and keynote addresses, including research from a wide range of international jurisdictions (including, Poland, Denmark and the USA). However, given the richness of the studies included in this chapter, it was decided to focus on the UK prison context in this book, in order to provide a consistent context for comparison and contrast between diverse studies. We are hopeful that this book reflects the dynamism and critical engagement of the initial symposium and more widely represents a number of new connections and collaborations between a previously disparate body of scholarship.

The Unique Contribution to the Field of Prison Health Research

Prison health research remains in its relative infancy, although there are a number of pre-existing contributions on prison health that are relevant for the focus of this book (Anonymous 2013; Cinar et al. 2017; Elger et al. 2017; Hammersley 1990; Hatton and Fisher 2011; Holligan 2016; Malloch 1999; Meek 2014; Paton et al. 2002; Phillips et al. 2017; Pope et al. 2007; Pratt 2016; Read and Mccrae 2016; Ross 2013; Scott 2014). Of these, *Emerging Issues in Prison Health*, edited by Elger et al. (2017), has particular resonance. This book consists of 16 chapters examining a wide range of health issues in prison (e.g., older prisoners, diet and drugs in prison). This in many ways reports findings from a range of health studies conducted in prisons and with former prisoners. We see our publication as having a different orientation, taking an explicitly eclectic (reflecting the growing diversity of prison health research) and reflective approach in which the methodological and ethical aspects of conducting health research in prison are foregrounded. This book does not only entail the reporting of study findings, but goes further to reflect on some of the opportunities and challenges of conducting health research in prisons—this we feel is sometimes not explicit in the writing of those researching prison settings. Furthermore, this book incorporates a wider range of perspectives on health research in prison, including chapters from people with lived experience of prison and those working within prison systems. Additionally, *Health and Health Promotion in Prison* by Ross (2013) bears some initial similarities. However, this is a historically orientated book considering the policy and legal context of health in prisons. Throughout there is a focus on UK and US prison populations and the practical application of the UN Health in Prisons model. The distinctiveness of this book over the Ross (2013) book is that the latter does not consider some of the more practical issues associated with conducting health research in prison, so there is little focus on methods or the ethics of conducting health research in prisons. Furthermore, innovative approaches to health research, focusing on particular groups of prisoners (such as male prisoners, pregnant prisoners, etc.) are not considered. Ultimately, we suggest that our text is more process and less policy focused and therefore ultimately contributes to quite a different and distinct perspective on prison health research. We hope that this first book to explicitly focus on issues and innovations associated with prison health research also contributes to a small but important literature on ethics in prison research (Arboleda-Flórez 2005; Brewer-Smyth 2008; Crighton 2006; Fine and Torre 2006; Freudenberg 2007; Gostin 2007; Hornblum 1997; Moser et al. 2004; Overholser 1987; Pope et al. 2007; Shaw et al. 2014; Ward and Bailey 2012). Ethical issues are at the forefront of any research study, but arguably require more careful consideration in a prison context where notions of informed consent, for example, are more complicated. Additionally, we hope that this edited collection can lead to a more nuanced and carefully framed debate about the potential issues and scope for innovation in relation to undertaking health research in prison settings.

Prisons as an Opportunity to Reduce Health Inequalities

It is important to recognise abolitionist positions in relation to academic exploration of prisons (Feest and Paul 2020), as these question the extent to which is it either possible or desirable to undertake health research within prisons at all. The editors of this book—as well as the authors of the subsequent chapters—as a consequence of undertaking research in these contested and complex social spaces, are situated within what might be loosely framed as a revisionist position in relation to prisons. This has profound implications for the book since as opposed to debating whether prisons should exist or not, the chapters that follow explore and analyse possible improvements that can be made in the provision of healthcare in prison, as well as considering the implications of a wide range of health interventions in prison. While we have already identified that in relation to mortality, prisons have negative implications, prisons can also provide an opportunity for health services to engage with hard-to-reach sections of society who experience health inequalities and yet often don't engage with services in the community (Bridgwood and Malbon 1995; Marshall et al. 2001). Furthermore, despite issues with the evidence base around prison health governance (Mcleod et al. 2020), there is a well-established mandate for both supporting and improving the health needs of people in prison (World Health Organisation 2007). We hope that this book constitutes a strengthening of this position, and further evidences the possibilities of improving the health of those in prison. The book therefore foregrounds a range of associated innovations and issues that have not been explicitly focused on in this form previously.

Issues and Innovations in Prison Health Research

The book has an eclectic combination of chapters. However, three key thematic areas, which are salient throughout the book, and which link the chapters together, are: the issues of ethical and reflective practice and working innovatively to generate research data.

Ethical Considerations of Prison Health Research

Within the wide range of literature exploring aspects of ethical considerations associated with prison health research (Arboleda-Flórez 2005; Brosens et al. 2015; Brewer-Smyth 2008; Crighton 2006; Eldridge et al. 2011; Freudenberg 2007; Gostin 2007; Lazzarini and Altice 2000; Pope et al. 2007; Simpson et al. 2017; Silva et al. 2017; Ward and Willis 2010; Weijer et al. 2011), a number of themes emerge that resonate with the subsequent chapters of this book. For example, the literature relating to consent specifically in relation to prison health research is relatively thin with the following study aside (Waldram 1998). This is, however, a wider issue as there has been a longstanding debate about the extent to which people in custody can give informed consent in the same ways that people in community settings are able to (Roberts and Indermaur 2003; Moser et al. 2004; Ward and Bailey 2012).

Reflective Prison Health Research and the Implications for Undertaking This Research for Researchers

Each of the chapters included in this book embody diverse reflections of those contributing researchers into prison health research, resonating with a small pocket of prison health literature (Ramluggun et al. 2010; Walsh 2005). Through these reflections, it is evident that undertaking health research in prison is demanding and difficult, and requires a lot of both the researcher and participants (as well as staff facilitating the research). This raises issues about the impacts of health research within prisons, not only on research participants but also on those undertaking research in prison settings. Within this context, the health of researchers tends to be overlooked, even in health-focused studies (with a number of notable exceptions, including: Hek 2006, Liebling 1999, Sloan and Wright 2015). Through including often overtly reflective chapters, we hope to illuminate some of the issues that undertaking health research in prison has for researchers, something that needs to be carefully considered in the design, funding and implementation of prison studies.

Innovations in Prison Health Research

Each of the thirteen chapters that follow are innovative in some way, either in the methodology utilised, through the reflections of the researchers undertaking the research or through the focus of the research. Consequently, each of the chapters examine often overlooked aspects of prison health research, that we hope are thought-provoking and insightful.

Overview of the Book

Following this introduction this book is composed of thirteen further chapters exploring a diverse range of issues and innovations in prison health research, utilising diverse methods and theory. These are written by people with lived experience of prison as well as those working within prison systems, alongside a wide range of researchers from multiple disciplines. The contributors range from practitioners to PhD students, and professors with international reputations in relation to prison health research. Taken together, the chapters provide a unique insight into the opportunities and challenges associated with undertaking health research in English, Northern Irish and Scottish prisons.

Chapter 2 by Dr James Woodall (Leeds Beckett University), is titled *Participatory Research in Prison: Rationale, Process and Challenges*. In this chapter, Dr Woodall reinforces the principle of co-produced research—a term growing in importance in health research *per se*, but less so in prison health research. The chapter argues that research in prison should also concern working with and alongside, not 'on', people and communities. The innovation and added value of participatory methods within prison research is be discussed before some associated challenges, and ways in which they can be managed, are outlined. This chapter provides important insights into an underutilised methodology within prison contexts.

Similarly, to Chap. 2, Chap. 3, *Promoting Health Literacy with Young Adult Men in an English Prison* by Dr Anita Mehay, Prof Rosie Meek and Prof Jane Ogden (UCL, Royal Holloway University of London and the University of Surrey), outlines an innovative approach within prison settings, through a focus on health literacy. It outlines a health literacy framework to explore the prison as a place for supporting health and well-being and draws upon findings from a doctoral research project within a single English prison for young adults. Health literacy describes the "cognitive and social skills which determine the motivation and ability of individuals to gain access to, understand and use information in ways which promote and maintain good health" (World Health Organisation 2009). Through a series of mixed-methods studies, the chapter highlights the numerous individual, social and structural barriers faced by young men in prison to develop their health literacy but also reveals the ways they attempt to reclaim some control over their physical, mental and emotional needs. Finally, the chapter presents a group-based model for strengthening health literacy, highlighting what could be achieved to support more health literate environments.

Continuing the focus on innovative health research in prison, Chap. 4, *Challenges and Practicalities in Adopting Grounded Theory Methodology When Conducting Prison Research*, by Dr Nasrul Ismail (University of the

West of England) considers another underutilised methodology within prison health research, grounded theory. Using an interdisciplinary, large-scale methodology, this research investigates the impact of austerity from the perspective of 87 prison health governance actors in England. In so doing, this chapter articulates the challenges and demystifies the practicalities of adopting grounded theory in prison research. It underscores the importance of implementing an appropriate grounded theory typology which will orientate the epistemological, ontological and subjectivity alignments of the research. Furthermore, this chapter evaluates the ways in which researchers can tolerate the fluidity and ambiguity presented by the intertwined data collection and analysis process. Finally, it critically appraises how grounded theory methodology reinforces good research skills, such as resilience, persistence, perseverance, patience and reflexivity, throughout the research project.

Chapter 5, *The Research Experience from an Insider Perspective*, by Dr David Honeywell (University of Manchester) reflects on the implications of a researcher with lived experiences of custody returning to prison to conduct health research. At the time of writing Dr Honeywell was working towards his PhD, and through an overtly reflective methodology during this process, Dr Honeywell learned as much about himself as the research participants he was interviewing. This chapter discusses the complexities of research through the shared lived experiences of both himself and his respondents. Through a series of discussions with several ex-prisoners, Dr Honeywell discovered there were many parallels between his participants' experiences of self-transformation and his own. As a result of this approach, this study became more emotional than Dr Honeywell had expected and psychologically difficult, which in social science research is rarely discussed. Despite many attempts to re-integrate during the late 1990s, Dr Honeywell found himself trapped between his old world and the new world he was attempting to transition towards, which he later learned is called liminality. This is because the former identity of being an ex-prisoner can never be erased and therefore carries stigma which then creates barriers. Even the transformative benefits of education, employment, relationships and friendships weren't fully able to shield Dr Honeywell from the painful and prolonged experiences of social and psychological liminality. The research resulted in a 'looking glass self' experience, whereby the interviews became a two-way mirror image narrative which made the author question why such experiences are rarely talked about. It caused Dr Honeywell to question if being an ex-prisoner gave him access to some of the more complex aspects of research through his own insight into what was not being said as well as what was being said. The chapter reiterates that there is no real end to the desistance process, but that it is in fact an endless journey of re-negotiating identities, stigmatisation, rejection and identity conflict which results in a series of existence between two worlds.

Chapter 6 by Dr James Fraser (Abertay University) analyses *Prisoner Experiences of Prison Health in Scotland*. This chapter outlines a study that aimed to investigate prison- and post-prison-related healthcare experiences of male prisoners in order to better inform future policy. The study was a qualitative, phenomenological study using interpretive phenomenology. Between April 2014 and April 2015 narrative data was gathered from semi-structured interviews with 29 males within six weeks of their release from prison. Interviews were audio-recorded and transcribed ($n = 9$), or detailed field notes were made ($n = 20$) dependent on participant preference. Data was analysed using inductive phenomenological analysis. The analysis revealed four themes: (1) Meaning of health (2) Access to healthcare (3) The obfuscatory organisation (4) Vulnerability and hope. This chapter concludes by considering whether the effectiveness of policy changes that were intended to ensure equity of access to NHS services for prisoners is questionable. The author stresses the need for a renewed commitment to, and tangible progress towards, providing equivalency in healthcare for people in prison.

Chapters 7 and 8 use quite different methods to explore aspects of horticultural interventions adapted for the prison context. Chapter 7: *Building Health and Wellbeing in Prison: Learning from the Master Gardener Programme in a Midlands Prison*, by Dr Geraldine Brown, Dr Elizabeth Bos and Dr Geraldine Brady (Coventry University) presents the findings from an evaluation of the Master Gardener Programme, a horticultural intervention with substance-misusing men in prison, undertaken by an inter-disciplinary research team from Coventry University. The Master Gardener Programme, led by Garden Organic, 'the UK's leading organic charity', was initially launched nationally as a pilot community programme in 2010. The extension of the programme from a community to a prison setting was in recognition of research evidence (national and international) that showed a range of positive outcomes associated with the role of horticulture in supporting physical, emotional, behavioural and social well-being. Here, the authors focus on the impact of the programme on health and well-being and reflect on gardening as an embodied practice and the garden as a space that promotes humanisation and self-worth, community and a connection to nature. Chapter 8, *The 'Dead Zone' in the Stories of People in Prison* by Alan Farrier (University of Central Lancashire), derives from a qualitative evaluation on the impact of a prisons-based horticulture and environmental programme concerning the health and well-being of participants selected from four English prisons. The primary research approach used was the biographic-narrative interpretive method (BNIM). This chapter explores some of the strengths and challenges with regards to conducting BNIM interviews with people in prison in order to build individual case studies. One such case study, with a participant serving a life sentence, is used to illustrate the challenges and benefits of understanding the stories of people in prison, including notions such as rehabilitation of the participant when the criminal act for which they are serving their sentence is consciously avoided in the telling of their story.

Mental health issues consistently emerge as a significant factor in shaping experiences of prison (James and Glaze 2006). Within this context, Chap. 9 by Dr David Woods and Dr Gavin Breslin (Ulster University), *Evaluation and Reflections from the Use of Implementation Science to Accommodate a Community Mental Health Awareness Programme to a Prison*, takes an explicitly reflective approach. This chapter provides an overview of health issues in relation to mental well-being and men in prison, alongside the role of sport in promoting mental health and well-being in custodial settings. These topics formed the backdrop for the implementation and evaluation of the State of Mind Sport community programme aimed at raising awareness of mental health and tackling stigma. The chapter continues with a detailed reflexive account of key ethical and methodological considerations of conducting the research within the prison environment in line with the principles of implementation science. The chapter concludes with practical guidance on planning and conducting health research in prisons, based on the reflexive learnings detailed.

Chapter 10, *Oral Health as a Door to Promoting Psychosocial Functioning for People in Custody: Lessons Learnt from the Development of the Mouth Matters Intervention* by Prof Ruth Freeman (Dundee University), provides insights into a vital but often overlooked area of health—oral health. In 2005 the Scottish Executive called for the need for oral health improvement for 'adults most in need such as prisoners'. This led to the oral health intervention called 'Mouth Matters' to be used across the Scottish prison estate. The aim of this chapter is to report on the development of Mouth Matters and its progression to a peer health coaching intervention. The chapter uses the development work to illustrate the links between oral health and psychosocial functioning within an often challenging prison setting. It shows the importance of adopting an alternative approach to intervention development that includes an interactive framework and uses a co-design and co-production philosophy to ensure that the psychosocial functioning for people in custody may start at the door of oral health.

Chapter 11 has a unique focus—*Health Arts and Justice* by Dr Alison Frater (Royal Holloway University of London) offers a critique of the transforming value of the arts on the health and life chances of people in prison. Against a background of health inequalities and evidence of the damaging impact of incarceration, the arts seem able to provide motivation for individual growth and development with a range of beneficial effects. At a population level, evaluations from across the prison system covering all art forms raise the possibility of a public health strategy that could inform a changed paradigm for rehabilitation. Drawing on both her extensive experience of working in the health in justice and arts in criminal justice sectors and her interviews with prison governors and people with lived experience of incarceration, the author presents a critical and compelling summary of the prison regime. Problems of measurement are discussed, and proposals made for a new interdisciplinary, evaluative framework which draws on theories of participation and inclusion used by arts practitioners working in prisons and other criminal justice settings.

The final three chapters of the book are explicitly gendered in focus, considering the gendered experiences of prison health by pregnant women and men in custody. Chapter 12 is *Pregnancy in Prison* by Dr Laura Abbot (University of Hertfordshire). It is thought that approximately 400–600 women at various stages of pregnancy are incarcerated each year and in the region of 100 babies are born to women in prison every year. Pregnant women may have complex physical and mental health needs which require expert, individualised care. Dr Abbot's qualitative research looked at the experience of being a pregnant woman in the English prison system, through interviews with pregnant women, staff and by undertaking extensive time observing prison life. Analysis revealed themes relating to stigma, survival and resilience. Some of the research participants went to some lengths to navigate the masculine system of prison in order to access food and exercise by being a "role model prisoner" and finding strategies of resistance. The author concluded that women have to navigate the prison system in order to access resources such as the right kinds of nutrition and ways to avoid stress. They may find strategies of resistance and resilience in order to survive and for some women, being in prison helps to facilitate change. Some women reported finding that being in prison was the thing that enforced this resistance, tenacity and capacity for change, if a woman gains the right kind of support. The chapter concentrates on some of the findings of the current research, specifically: equivalence of health care; nutritional well-being; basic provisions (or lack of); changes in identity, and compassion and support for pregnant women in prison. The chapter describes how prison can be a safe haven for some women experiencing their pregnancy in prison, which not only highlights the desperate situations many incarcerated women have experienced prior to their imprisonment, but also introduces the concept of pregnancy itself being a unique 'turning point' in desistance and health.

In Chapter 13, by Dr Matt Maycock, Prof Cindy Gray, Prof Kate Hunt (Scottish Prison Service, University of Glasgow and University of Stirling)—*Masculinity, Doing Health, Performances of Masculinity Within the Fit for Life Programme Delivered in Two Scottish Prisons*—the authors argue that masculinities can be aligned with positive health behaviours, not exclusively the health practices which are damaging to health.

Although the fluid, performed nature of gender is well established, constructions of masculinity have commonly been linked to practices that are 'toxic' to health, particularly in relation to 'hyper-masculine' ideals. In this concluding chapter the authors consider how masculinities were performed over the course of pilot deliveries of a health promotion programme in a largely male environment, two Scottish prisons holding adult men. In exploring performances of hegemonic and inclusive masculinities, the authors aim to advance theories of masculinities through moving from a binary, at times oppositional, orientation to a more nuanced reading of masculinity within a specific gendered context. Additionally, they highlight aspects of change in the performance of prison masculinities within the context of the delivery of the Fit for LIFE programme, such as in the men's weight management programme—Football Fans in Training (FFIT)—which inspired it. This illustrates the potential for health promotion interventions to provide new opportunities for performances of masculinity that positively contribute to health in prison.

The final chapter in the book (Chap. 14), by Jamie Grundy (Inside Out Support Wales) and Professor Rosie Meek (Royal Holloway University of London), is titled *More Than Just a Game: The Impact of a Prison Football Team on Physical and Social Well-Being in a Welsh Prison*. This again focuses on the potential for sport and similarly to Chap. 13, football to improve the health of those in prison. This chapter celebrates the importance of football at HMP Prescoed as a meaningful and engaging activity, highlighting its contribution in improving the physical and social well-being of the prisoner participants. The location of the pitch away from the main prison camp, which gives a taste of life post-release away from a prison background was found to be the most significant aspect of its success and reflected an underlying culture of trust presented by the conditions in an 'open' prison, of which football presented a literal extension towards. Participation in football was used as a way for prisoners serving a long sentence (and therefore more used to 'closed' conditions) to adapt to a different regime in HMP Prescoed. Football was being used twofold in this respect: to help prisoners adapt to the conditions of an 'open' prison and to prepare prisoners for release into the community. Participants who engaged in such activities received additional, 'informal' behaviour management sessions. Playing in the league games required participants to adhere to three sets of rules: prison rules that all other prisoners were subject to, as well as additional rules set by the Physical Education Officers linked to etiquette, including time management and tasks associated with the smooth running of the team, and lastly they also had to stick to the laws of the game of football. Fundamental to the project's perceived success was the ability of the first author to embed himself within the team over the whole period of the season, as a crucial process of ethnographical research.

References

Anonymous. (2013). *Health and social care services for older male adults in prison: The identification of current service provision and piloting of an assessment and care planning model.* UK: National Institute for Health Research.

Arboleda-Flórez, J. (2005). The ethics of biomedical research on prisoners. *Current Opinion in Psychiatry, 18*, 514–517.

Baidawi, S., Turner, S., Trotter, C., Browning, C., Collier, P., O'connor, D., & Sheehan, R. (2011). Older prisoners – A challenge for Australian corrections. *Trends and Issues in Crime and Criminal Justice, 423*, 1–11.

Binswanger, I. A., Stern, M. F., Deyo, R. A., Heagerty, P. J., Cheadle, A., Elmore, J. G., & Koepsell, T. D. (2007). Release from prison — A high risk of death for former inmates. *New England Journal of Medicine, 356*, 157–165.

Binswanger, I. A., Blatchford, P. J., Mueller, S. R., & Stern, M. F. (2013). Mortality after prison release: Opioid overdose and other causes of death, risk factors, and time trends from 1999 to 2009. *Annals of Internal Medicine, 159*, 592–600.

Brewer-Smyth, K. (2008). Ethical, regulatory, and investigator considerations in prison research. *Advances in Nursing Science, 31*, 119–127.

Bridgwood, A., & Malbon, G. (1995). Survey of the Physical Health of Prisoners 1994: A Survey of Sentenced Male Prisoners in England and Wales, Carried Out by the Social Survey Division of OPCS on Behalf of the Prison Service Directorate. HM Stationery Office.

Brosens, D., De Donder, L., Dury, S., & Verté, D. (2015). Building a research partnership in a prison context: From collaboration to co-construction. *Sociological Research Online, 20*, 79–93.

Cinar, A. B., Jones, C., Richards, D., Fernandes, F., White, P., & Freeman, R. (2017). PeP-SCOT a health coaching intervention for people in prisons: The development of the intervention protocol. *Community Dent Health, 34*, 97–101.
Crighton, D. A. (2006). Methodological issues in psychological research in prisons. *Psychological Research in Prisons*, 138–147.
Drake, D. H., Earle, R., & Sloan, J. (2015). *Palgrave handbook of prison ethnography*. Basingstoke: Palgrave Macmillan.
Earle, R. (2016). *Convict criminology: Inside and out*. London: Policy Press.
Eldridge, G. D., Johnson, M. E., Brems, C., & Corey, S. L. (2011). Ethical challenges in conducting psychiatric or mental health research in correctional settings. *AJOB Primary Research, 2*, 42–51.
Elger, B. S., Ritter, C., & Stöver, H. (2017). *Emerging issues in prison health*. Dordrecht: Springer.
Farrell, M., & Marsden, J. (2008). Acute risk of drug-related death among newly released prisoners in England and Wales. *Addiction, 103*, 251–255.
Feest, J., & Paul, B. (2020). *Does abolitionism have a future? Definitionsmacht, Renitenz und Abolitionismus: Texte rund um das Strafvollzugsarchiv*. Wiesbaden: Springer Fachmedien Wiesbaden.
Fine, M., & Torre, M. E. (2006). Intimate details: Participatory action research in prison. *Action Research, 4*, 253–269.
Freudenberg, N. (2007). *Health research behind bars: A brief guide to research in jails and prisons* (Public health behind bars). Springer.
Ginn, S. (2012). Elderly prisoners. *BMJ, 345*, e6263.
Gostin, L. O. (2007). Biomedical research involving prisoners: Ethical values and legal regulation. *JAMA, 297*, 737–740.
Graham, L., Fischbacher, C. M., Stockton, D., Fraser, A., Fleming, M., & Greig, K. (2015). Understanding extreme mortality among prisoners: A national cohort study in Scotland using data linkage. *The European Journal of Public Health, 25*, 879–885.
Hammersley, R. (1990). *Heroin use and crime: A comparison of heroin users and non-users in and out of prison*. Edinburgh: Scottish Office.
Hatton, D. C., & Fisher, A. A. (2011). Using participatory methods to examine policy and women prisoners' health. *Policy, Politics, & Nursing Practice, 12*, 119–125.
Hek, G. (2006). Unlocking potential: Challenges for primary health care researchers in the prison setting. *Primary Health Care Research & Development, 7*, 91–94.

Herbert, K., Plugge, E., Foster, C., & Doll, H. (2012). Prevalence of risk factors for non-communicable diseases in prison populations worldwide: A systematic review. *The Lancet, 379*, 1975–1982.

HMIP. (1996). *Patient or prisoner? A new strategy for health care in prisons*. London: Home Office.

Holligan, C. (2016). An absent presence: Visitor narratives of journeys and support for prisoners during imprisonment. *The Howard Journal of Crime and Justice, 55*, 94–110.

Hornblum, A. M. (1997). They were cheap and available: Prisoners as research subjects in twentieth century America. *BMJ: British Medical Journal, 315*, 1437–1441.

Houchin, R. (2005). *Social exclusion and imprisonment in Scotland*. Glasgow: Glasgow Caledonian University.

James, D. J., & Glaze, L. E. (2006). *Mental health problems of prison and jail inmates*. Washington, DC : U.S. Dept. of Justice, Office of Justice Programs, Bureau of Justice Statistics.

Lazzarini, Z., & Altice, F. L. (2000). A review of the legal and ethical issues for the conduct of HIV-related research in prisons. *AIDS & Public Policy Journal, 15*, 105–135.

Liebling, A. (1999). Doing research in prison: Breaking the silence? *Theoretical Criminology, 3*, 147–173.

Malloch, M. S. (1999). Drug use, prison, and the social construction of femininity. *Women's Studies International Forum, 22*, 349–358.

Marshall, T., Simpson, S., & Stevens, A. (2001). Use of health services by prison inmates: comparisons with the community. *Journal of Epidemiology & Community Health, 55*(5), 364–365.

Mcleod, K. E., Butler, A., Young, J. T., Southalan, L., Borschmann, R., Sturup-Toft, S., Dirkzwager, A., Dolan, K., Acheampong, L. K., & Topp, S. M. (2020). Global prison health care governance and health equity: A critical lack of evidence. *American Journal of Public Health*, e1–e6.

Meek, R. (2014). *Sport in prison: Exploring the role of physical activity in correctional settings*. London: Routledge.

Millie, A., Jacobson, J., & Hough, M. (2003). Understanding the growth in the prison population in England and Wales. *Criminal Justice, 3*, 369–387.

Morris, T., & Morris, P. (1963). *Pentonville: A sociological study of an English prison*. London: Routledge.

Moser, D. J., Arndt, S., Kanz, J. E., Benjamin, M. L., Bayless, J. D., Reese, R. L., Paulsen, J. S., & Flaum, M. A. (2004). Coercion and informed consent in research involving prisoners. *Comprehensive Psychiatry, 45*, 1–9.

Overholser, J. C. (1987). Ethical issues in prison research: A risk/benefit analysis. *Behavioral Sciences & the Law, 5*, 187–202.

Paanila, J., Hakola, P., & Tiihonen, J. (1999). Mortality among habitually violent offenders. *Forensic Science International, 100*, 187–191.

Paton, J., Jenkins, R., WHO Collaborating Centre for Research and Training in Mental Health, King's College London, & University of London Institute of Psychiatry. (2002). *Mental health primary care in prison: A guide to mental ill health in adults and adolescents in prison and young offender institutions.* London: Royal Society of Medicine Press.

Phillips, J., Gelsthorpe, L., & Padfield, N. (2017). Non-custodial deaths: Missing, ignored or unimportant? *Criminology & Criminal Justice*. https://doi.org/10.1177/1748895817745939.

Pope, A., Vanchieri, C., & Gostin, L. O. (2007). *Ethical considerations for research involving prisoners*. National Academies Press.

Pratt, D. (2016). *The prevention of suicide in prison: Cognitive behavioural approaches* (Advances in mental health research series). Abingdon, Oxon; New York, NY: Routledge.

Ramluggun, P., Lindsay, B., & Pfeil, M. (2010). Research in prison: A researcher-practitioner's view. *Nurse Researcher, 17*.

Read, M., & Mccrae, N. (2016). Preventing suicide in lesbian, gay, bisexual, and transgender prisoners: A critique of U.K. policy. *Journal of Forensic Nursing, 12*, 13–18.

Roberts, L., & Indermaur, D. (2003). Signed consent forms in criminological research: Protection for researchers and ethics committees but a threat to research participants? *Psychiatry, Psychology and Law, 10*, 289–299.

Ross, M. W. (2013). *Health and health promotion in prisons*. Abingdon, Oxon; New York, NY: Routledge.

Ross, J. I., & Richards, S. C. (2003). *Convict criminology*. Belmont, CA; London: Thomson/Wadsworth.

Scott, D. (2014). Prison research: Appreciative or critical inquiry? David Scott argues about 'value commitment'and 'taking sides' in fieldwork. *Criminal Justice Matters, 95*, 30–31.

Senior, J., & Shaw, J. (2007). *Prison healthcare* (Handbook on prisons) (pp. 377–398). Cullompton: Willan Publishing.

Shaw, D. M., Wangmo, T., & Elger, B. S. (2014). *Conducting ethics research in prison: Why, who, and what?* Springer.

Silva, D. S., Matheson, F. I., & Lavery, J. V. (2017). Ethics of health research with prisoners in Canada. *BMC Medical Ethics, 18*, 31.

Sim, J. (1990). *Medical power in prisons*. Milton Keynes: Open University Press.
Simpson, P. L., Guthrie, J., & Butler, T. (2017). Prison health service directors' views on research priorities and organizational issues in conducting research in prison: Outcomes of a national deliberative roundtable. *International Journal of Prisoner Health, 13*, 113–123.
Sloan, J., & Wright, S. (2015). *Going in green: Reflections on the challenges of 'getting in, getting on, and getting out' for doctoral prisons researchers* (The Palgrave handbook of prison ethnography). Springer.
Social Inclusion Unit. (2002). *Reducing re-offending by ex-prisoners*. London: Office of the Deputy Prime Minister.
Spittal, M. J., Forsyth, S., Pirkis, J., Alati, R., & Kinner, S. A. (2014). Suicide in adults released from prison in Queensland, Australia: A cohort study. *Journal of Epidemiology and Community Health, 68*, 993–998.
Sturge, G. (2019). UK prison population statistics. Briefing Paper, House of Commons Library.
Verger, P., Rotily, M., Prudhomme, J., & Bird, S. (2003). High mortality rates among inmates during the year following their discharge from a French prison. *Journal of Forensic Sciences, 48*, 614–616.
Waldram, J. B. (1998). Anthropology in prison: Negotiating consent and accountability with a "captured" population. *Human Organization*, 238–244.
Walsh, L. (2005). Developing prison health care through reflective practice. *Transforming Nursing Through Reflective Practice, 65*.
Ward, J., & Bailey, D. (2012). Consent, confidentiality and the ethics of PAR in the context of prison research. *Ethics in Social Research*, 149–169.
Ward, T., & Willis, G. (2010). Ethical issues in forensic and correctional research. *Aggression and Violent Behavior, 15*, 399–409.
Weijer, C., Grimshaw, J. M., Taljaard, M., Binik, A., Boruch, R., Brehaut, J. C., Donner, A., Eccles, M. P., Gallo, A., & Mcrae, A. D. (2011). Ethical issues posed by cluster randomized trials in health research. *Trials, 12*, 100.
Williams, B., & Abraldes, R. (2007). *Growing older: Challenges of prison and reentry for the aging population* (Public health behind bars). Springer.
World Health Organisation (2007). Health in prisons: A WHO guide to the essentials in prison health. WHO Regional Office Europe.
World Health Organisation. (2009). Health Literacy: Improving Health, Health Systems, and Health Policy Around the World: Workshop Summary.
Zlodre, J., & Fazel, S. (2012). All-cause and external mortality in released prisoners: Systematic review and meta-analysis. *American Journal of Public Health, 102*, e67–e75.

2

Participatory Research in Prison: Rationale, Process and Challenges

James Woodall

This chapter reinforces the principle that research can be about working with and alongside, not 'on', people and communities. Despite widespread support for this from those working in health research (Green et al. 2019), there has been reluctance for the translation of these ideas into prison contexts—this, it could be surmised, is for several reasons, including: security concerns and a predominance historically for more quantitative approaches in prison health research. This chapter seeks to outline what participatory research means in prison and moreover to exemplify this using contemporary examples. The added value of participatory methods within prison research will be discussed before the challenges, and ways in which they can be managed, are outlined.

The meaning of participatory research varies, as noted by Mantoura and Potvin (2013), but it is most often defined in relational terms describing the interaction between those conducting research and those whose lives are the focus of the research (Wright et al. 2010). The power

J. Woodall (✉)
Leeds Beckett University, Leeds, UK
e-mail: J.Woodall@leedsbeckett.ac.uk

© The Author(s) 2021

M. Maycock et al. (eds.), *Issues and Innovations in Prison Health Research*, Palgrave Studies in Prisons and Penology, https://doi.org/10.1007/978-3-030-46401-1_2

imbalance between researcher and researched is usually inescapable (Cross and Warwick-Booth 2016) and is perhaps exemplified by experimental research designs which are often predicated on the researchers having complete control of all aspects of the design, implementation and dissemination of the study. Participatory approaches to research, in contrast, operate in a more egalitarian way, with a greater commitment to the inclusion of individuals and communities in the research process:

> *It requires an authentic partnership in which power and empowerment are shared by all participants.* (Ramsden et al. 2015, p. 50)

There is clearly a spectrum of participation in research processes, ranging from simply informing and consulting individuals and communities on research processes or findings derived from a study, through to full control of all aspects of the design, research budget, data collection and dissemination. Brosens (2018), in relation to the prison context, has suggested five levels of participation of prisoners in activities such as research, these are: informing, consulting, involving, collaborating and empowering. Clearly, the latter levels of participating see greater power and control by prisoners over research processes—examples of this, however, are limited. Most research seeking the participation of prisoners tend to operate at the informing and consulting levels, perhaps through 'patient and public involvement' activities (Brett et al. 2014). 'Listening exercises', for example, have been deployed in prison contexts to gather a 'sense check' on research findings but stop short at engaging in a more participatory way. South et al. (2014a) used listening exercises in three prisons with serving prisoners to gain practical understanding of their systematic review findings examining the effectiveness of peer interventions in prisons. These exercises served to juxtapose common themes in the research literature with real-life experiences of serving prisoners in the male and female estate.

Justifying Participatory Research in Prison

This chapter does not seek to suggest that participatory research should always be adopted for all health studies in prison—such a position would be naïve and unhelpful and downplay the value of research designs, such as randomised control trials, where prisoner influence on the research project is likely to be minimal. Nevertheless, historically, it is clear that research in prison has been antithetical to participative methods and values and, in some cases, have been abusive, unethical and without the full informed consent of prisoners or a clear explanation of the risks and benefits of involvement (Johnson et al. 2018). Thankfully, the prison health research community and its practices have moved considerably and there is little doubt that such unethical and coercive processes are of the past. However, some commentators have suggested an ethical overprotection of people in prison which may prevent valid and potentially impactful research being undertaken due to significant over-caution about the relative risk of research versus its benefits (Byrne 2005).

There has been a tendency, however, for prison research to largely remain 'one-dimensional', drawing on methods and designs that have an absence of participation—such as surveys or qualitative studies with predetermined questioning and lines of inquiry. This seems unsatisfactory given the huge range of health and social challenges faced by the prison population (as outlined in the introduction to this book)—much of which we have poor understanding. Johnson et al. (2018), for instance, reiterates this, suggesting that the scope and amount of health-related research is considerably underwhelming when the extent of the health challenges faced by prisoners is considered. They suggest that the absence of participation of prisoners in the research process has exacerbated health inequalities and disparities. Indeed, one of the primary justifications for adopting participatory research processes to understanding health and healthcare is that prisoners often provide a conceptualisation of health that is out-with professional judgements and therefore adds greater nuance and understanding which can aid intervention design (O'Gorman et al. 2012). More broadly, the value of lay views in understanding health and social context cannot be underplayed (Green et al. 2019).

A peer research project conducted in a Canadian women's prison, for example, exemplified how the academic research team reconfigured their reductionist medical model of health in prison, with its focus on research of diseases such as HIV, cancer, addiction, hepatitis C, after working with the female peer researchers whose views of health were far larger and more complex (Elwood Martin et al. 2009). Robertson (2006) suggests that lay perceptions have been influential in supporting a cultural shift away from a bio-medical perspective towards a more holistic and integrated understanding of health and well-being. This kind of shift is of importance given that prison health has traditionally been associated with medical treatment and the bio-medical paradigm more generally (Sim 1990). Indeed, previous research has raised questions about the definitions of health which are currently deployed in the prison environment (Smith 2002). Participatory research in prison, therefore, can shift the agenda and move 'expertise' away from those who are traditionally seen as having health expertise in prisons, such as nurses and primary care professionals (Woodall 2010), towards those who subscribe to a social model of health and its determinants—for example those working in housing and accommodation for prisoners (Elwood Martin et al. 2012). As Fine and Torre (2006, p. 261) have noted: "insiders know more, know better and in more depth how an organization, community and indeed a prison operates."

The rationale for participatory approaches also pertains to the quality and utility of research in prisons. Through the participatory planning and research process, health programmes can become more relevant to those they serve where involvement has taken place (O'Gorman et al. 2012). A commentary by Eakin et al. (1996) outlines how power is a salient issue for health research, with the inclusivity and participation of individuals and the community in health research processes as important. Indeed, this philosophy of research with, not on, communities has been suggested to have contributed to the generation of new data, more sensitive and knowledgeable stakeholders, increased advocacy and more meaningful, sustainable policy change (Green et al. 2019). Critics have questioned whether data quality or research rigour is compromised if 'professional researchers' relinquish control to 'lay' individuals and communities (Woodall et al. 2018). However, participatory approaches often increase the quality and richness of data and the ultimate utility of it to affect practice and policy (Woodall et al. 2018); there is no evidence to suggest that rigour is lost as a consequence.

Perhaps most saliently, prisoners' participation in research can be empowering and emancipatory producing positive, even transformative outcomes (Elwood Martin et al. 2009). Such goals resonate with a rehabilitative and supportive ideology of incarceration and imprisonment. Peer research processes, as an example, have been shown to be empowering for those involved and can provide opportunities for confidence building, raising self-esteem as well as acquiring skills that can be transferred to other contexts (like applying for employment, etc.) (Woodall et al. 2018). Elwood Martin et al.'s (2009) and Ramsden et al.'s (2015) studies utilising the assets of trained peer researchers in a female prison reported the outcomes of participation for prisoners as follows:

- Optimism
- Changed perspective
- Advocacy skills
- Technical skills (e.g. writing, transcribing, analysis of data)
- Effective communication
- Confidence
- Self-respect and self-esteem

The impact that can potentially occur as a result of participation in research activities is therefore beneficial not only for individuals, but also more broadly contributing to a more positive organisational ethos and the potential for reduced re-offending. Future research would benefit from exploring these outcomes and potential impacts.

The Process of Participatory Research in Prison

The participation and involvement of prisoners in the broader aspect of prison life are themes that have recently moved up political agendas in Europe (Brosens 2018). Nonetheless, there is limited published guidance providing practical approaches to including prisoners in research activities (either for researchers or policy makers). While not exhaustive, some of the processes and guiding principles used when establishing or facilitating participative methods in prison are provided.

Organisational Access and Support

Negotiating and gaining access to any organisation to conduct research is a key consideration in the early parts of any study, regardless of whether there is a participatory component or not. Piacentini (2007, p. 154) describes "penetrating the penal periphery", as a notoriously multi-layered, convoluted and time-consuming process, where often academic researchers are viewed with an element of mistrust and suspicion by prison authorities as well as prisoners themselves. This suspicion is arguably compounded when participatory forms of research are proposed, as prison authorities are likely to be unaware about what these processes consist of or are clear on the implications for the institution. In some prisons this may not be the case, especially where there is strong democratic inclusion of prisoners in parts of institutional life, such as being involved in strategic decision-making forums or groups with prison staff and management (Edgar et al. 2011). However, Johnson et al. (2018), in their study using participatory action research, reported very poor understanding of what participatory research entailed by prison officials. This does mean that researchers wishing to establish participatory approaches in prison must be clear on the purpose of the study and why the approach has benefits institutionally. Indeed, the importance of broader managerial support within the prison for participatory processes is, of course, paramount. The importance of identifying 'key gatekeepers' in the prison at various levels (i.e. strategic and operational) is critical for the success of establishing the participation of prisoners in these activities (South et al. 2016). So, although physically accessing the prison allows the research to get under way (following ethical approval by university and prison committees in most instances), the process of acquiring social acceptability and trust is fundamental if any meaningful work is to be undertaken. Reuss (2000, p. 33) notes:

Not only has the actual physical difficulty of gaining entry to a prison to be considered i.e. facing the 'gate' each morning, removing items from pockets, removing shoes, outer clothing etc., but there is also the difficulty of building up sufficient trust to form the positive research relationships.

Woodall et al. (2015b) has provided a conceptual model to describe critical relationships necessary at various levels within the prison in order for activities involving prisoners to occur. Clearly, at a micro level, effective relationships are required between those prisoners engaging in participatory research activities, prisoners participating in the research and the academic research team. Secondly, the importance of positive relationships between prisoners engaging in participatory research activities and prison staff (uniformed and non-uniformed) is critical. Prison staff can facilitate the smooth running of research by assisting with unlocking and escorting of prisoners and, more generally, by managing the logistics within wing/residential environments. Thirdly, institutional 'buy-in' and support from the establishment's Governor is a major factor. Establishments with progressive senior management teams are considered an essential ingredient for participatory research processes to become established and to flourish. Finally, where relationships can be established with key organisations, like the Prison Officers Association (POA) and the NHS, the potential for the research to prosper is increasingly more likely.

Shared Research Values

Values related to democracy, inclusion and participation must be shared by all of those involved in participatory research processes in prison if participatory studies are to be successful. Without this recognition and shared value base, it is likely that participation will erode, at best, to elements of tokenism (Brosens 2018). Bolder values related to 'empowering' prisoners through participatory research processes is also a key value and indeed, as already alluded to, a desirable outcome of participatory research. Whilst empowering prisoners has never been an accepted pursuit in prison systems, even regarded as "morally questionable and politically dangerous" (The Aldridge Foundation and Johnson 2008, p. 2), there is a growing recognition that prisons should be "supportive and empowering" (de Viggiani et al. 2005, p. 918). Such values pose challenges for prison authorities and indeed for those wishing to implement participatory approaches in prison (such challenges are outlined later in the chapter). The 'power over' individuals in prison can be particularly damaging to health and potentially contributes to a loss of control and disempowerment (Woodall et al. 2013). Within the prison context, this is difficult to evade as prisons must keep the public protected through control and order within the prison walls. Nonetheless, 'power over' must be proportional and kept to an absolute minimum in line with safe prison conditions upheld by respected and proportionate prison rules, if participatory approaches are to be effective. This raises broader questions pertaining to whether participatory approaches are better suited in lower security, rather than maximum-security, establishments.

Ethical Practice

Prisoners are a vulnerable sub-section of the population and it is clear that extreme sensitivities are required when conducting research with this particular group (Smith and Wincup 2002; Liamputtong and Ezzy 2005). Vulnerable populations have been described by Peternelj-Taylor (2005) as those who are impoverished, disenfranchised, or those who are subject to discrimination, intolerance, subordination and stigma. From a research perspective, this provides theoretical and practical considerations that may impinge on an individual's ability to participate in research activities and provide consent to do so (Peternelj-Taylor 2005). Prisoners pose a number of unique challenges for researchers, as not only may they lack the freedom to make choices in comparison to individuals in the general community, but also because of other issues such as low literacy levels or mental health issues (Freudenberg 2007). Notwithstanding the myriad of ethical issues that can arise during participatory research activities, some salient ethical issues are briefly outlined.

The first relates to involving prisoners as co-researchers, as they should participate voluntarily and free from any coercion. The failure to provide culturally sensitive and accessible study information to participants in prison settings is unethical and can result in individuals agreeing to contribute to participatory research studies without being fully aware of its implications. This may mean that prisoners may become 'sucked into' research without actually understanding why they are participating (Smith and Wincup 2000). Prisoners are, in general, a powerless group where often decisions about their institutional routine are made on their behalf (Martin 2000). This can leave prisoners feeling unable to refuse participation or 'walk away' from research activities due to the fear that there will be possible reprisals (Wincup 1999; Buckland and Wincup 2004; Moser et al. 2004; Waldram 2007). On the other hand, prisoners may perceive that the research is of direct benefit to themselves, perhaps understanding that their participation will result in gaining early release or impact favourably on decisions for parole (Buckland and Wincup 2004). On this point, extra care needs to be taken when considering the process of informed consent, as prisoners are traditionally a group who are likely to contribute to research activities. This has been largely attributed to prisoners' desire to occupy their time within the institution and to alleviate boredom (Moser et al. 2004; Quraishi 2008). These types of influences are unavoidable in the prison setting, but could conceivably alter individuals' motivation for participation.

The broader issue of payments and incentives for prisoners involved in participatory research activities is a thorny and complex issue (South et al. 2014b). Such decisions require careful consideration in collaboration with various stakeholders within the prison.

Time

Given the unique obstacles and barriers found in prisons, researchers must be prepared to expend additional time and effort to fully engage prisoners as co-researchers (Johnson et al. 2018). Indeed, to adequately support, train and work alongside individuals and communities in participatory processes is highly time consuming. The literature is consistent in representing participatory research processes as lengthy and resource-intensive process, which can take far longer than traditional research methods (Blumenthal 2011). This is further compounded by working in a setting and context, such as a prison, whereby delays and extensions to research studies is commonplace—often outside of the researchers' control. Recognising that this is the situation is fundamental to collaborative planning processes and does pose serious challenges in relation to the retention and recruitment of those prisoners participating in the research activities.

Boundaries and Reflexivity

One key professional practice issue is understanding boundaries that you have as a researcher involved in the participatory process. In short, never promise something you cannot deliver and always be realistic about what you can achieve. Engaging in reflexive practice is therefore critical in understanding the research processes and recognising your own limitations as a researcher. More broadly, Stanley and Wise (1993), have suggested that researchers must understand the role they play in the research process. The concept of reflexivity, defined by Ali et al. (2004, p. 25) as the "capacity to reflect on our role in generating research knowledge", is, therefore, crucial. Previous prison researchers have noted the importance of their own biography when conducting research with prisoners. Smith (2009) alluded to her gender as being important to gaining women prisoners' trust, especially when taking openly about sensitive issues. In this study, Smith argued that male researchers may not have been able to build sufficient rapport and would be unable to understand the female experience fully (Smith 2009). In her doctoral research, Smith also found that being female was beneficial in encounters with women prisoners, many of whom had been victims of violence and abuse (Smith and Wincup 2000). In a similar way, Quraishi (2008) noted the methodological implications of being a Muslim undertaking research with peers. Such reflexive thoughts and journaling can be a useful strategy for everyone involved in the research process, illuminating and making transparent issues that may influence the collaborative research endeavour.

Understanding and Recognising Risk

Prisons are unique and exciting social environments to conduct participatory research. However, safety, security and surveillance govern all activities, which can often mean that planned research activities can be postponed or cancelled without prior warning. It is necessary to keep the research in perspective, and whilst the importance and overall execution of the study is of central concern to the researcher, in reality, the research is not a principal concern or priority to the establishment. As a researcher and those prisoners collaborating on the research, following some basic rules will mitigate and minimise risk:

- The security of the prison must never be compromised.
- Although physical assaults on non-uniformed visitors to prison are rare (Martin 2000), participatory research approaches can pose risk both in terms of the physical safety of the researchers and the potential for verbal assault. To this extent, always be prepared to attend security training, inductions and tours before working in the prison to become familiar with protocols.
- Always take time to understand the 'procedures' of the prison you are working in and appreciate that these may change from prison to prison.
- Fit in with the regime, do not expect it to fit around you and your work. If in doubt ask a member of prison staff.
- Always inform a member of staff of what you are doing and how long you intend to be.
- Always be aware of your professional boundaries.
- Never accept gifts from prisoners and never bring anything into the prison for prisoners. Never pass on any messages from a prisoner.
- Be aware of what you can and cannot take into the prison before arriving.

The Challenge of Participatory Approaches in Prison

There are many challenges when adopting participatory research approaches in prison. Prisons are amongst the most difficult institutions in which to find ways of ensuring full collaborative participation (Drake 2014). Indeed, where prisoner involvement has emerged it is often sporadic and uneven and not consistent across the prison estate (Solomon 2004; Solomon and Edgar 2004). While literature reporting on participatory research processes in isolated prison settings suggests that the approach is transferable across the prison estate (Elwood Martin et al. 2009), there are difficulties in translation. While there are certain overlaps and commonalities between prisons, strategies and approaches to prisoner involvement need to reflect the institutional profile and be realistic in terms of the outcomes to be achieved (Woodall et al. 2015b). Poland et al. (2009), for example, have warned practitioners and academics to be conscious of the diversity that lies behind the apparent homogeneity of settings. There is little evidence or understanding as to whether participatory research approaches are better suited to certain prison establishments based on the security level of the institution. Intuitively, however, it seems reasonable to assume that establishing participatory research activities may be more challenging in higher-security establishments, but these contexts may foster greater potential to empower prisoners as individuals have relatively less autonomy and agency due to the nature of their crimes. It is hoped that researchers and those engaged in participatory approaches in prison provide reflections and share learning so that understanding is increased.

A further challenge potentially lies in staff views and attitudes. Woodall et al. (2015a) reported how some staff found the notion of allowing prisoners greater levels of freedom in the prison difficult to comprehend and the antithesis of prison values and principles. Some prison staff could find the power shift produced by allowing prisoners more autonomy in conducting research, for example, problematic. Such concerns are not unwarranted—a systematic review which examined peer interventions in prison (where some prisoners are afforded greater power and authority) found eleven studies describing either perceived risks or actual instances where prisoners in peer roles had abused their position of trust, with distribution of contraband, such as tobacco or mobile telephones, as the primary concern (South et al. 2016). That said, some participatory research studies in prison have shown the prison context and the issues and challenges this presents are not insurmountable—Ramsden et al. (2015), as an illustration, showed how researchers and senior peer researchers in prison were able to work together to complete an on-line literature review.

Finally, some have suggested that participatory research activities "speaks to an outside world" (Fine and Torre 2006, p. 264) where such approaches are more commonplace than within prison communities where greater power and control are not encouraged. This generates a further critical question, which is, whether the participation of prisoners in research activities exacerbates inequalities through only engaging with a small sub-section of the prison population—perhaps the better educated, articulate and motivated? Some studies, for example, have shown how recently arrived prisoners, foreign-language-speaking prisoners and 'criminally irresponsible offenders' were less involved at all levels of participatory activities (Brosens 2018). In a study looking at prisoners moving into participatory roles within the prison, security factors were a major determinant of eligibility, with the exclusion of prisoners perceived to be at risk of security breaches, such as distribution of contraband. Other selection criteria included: providing a voluntary drugs test; having knowledge of the system and 'jail craft'; basic literacy skills; and the period of time the prisoner was likely to be staying within the institution (South et al. 2016). All of these factors provide challenges in relation to the recruitment and retention of prisoners in participatory research activities and requires careful planning and thought to enable the approach to benefit prisoners fairly and equitably.

Conclusions

This chapter has sought to provide an overview of participatory approaches to health research in prison. While there are significant challenges in operationalising participatory methods in this context, the potential benefits for individuals and prison organisations seems highly worthwhile. We can think of people in prison in two discrete ways—as 'citizens in prison' or as prisoners (Svensson 1996). A contemporary prison system, embracing rehabilitative values, should embrace the former rather than the latter and equip individuals with greater responsibility and the necessary skills to reintegrate successfully back into society. When executed effectively, involving prisoners in research processes can provide this opportunity.

By embracing a participatory philosophy in health research in prison, there is a greater likelihood of having a better understanding of health experiences in prison. Through this understanding, health interventions and programmes can be designed that have the potential to be effective in addressing the poor health of the majority of the prison population. This laudable aim is not only beneficial to prisoners and their families, but also to society more generally.

References

Ali, S., Campbell, K., Branley, D., & James, R. (2004). Politics, identities and research. In C. Seale (Ed.), *Researching society and culture* (2nd ed.). London: Sage.

Blumenthal, D. S. (2011). Is community-based participatory research possible? *American Journal of Preventive Medicine, 40*, 386–389.

Brett, J., Staniszewska, S., Mockford, C., Herron-Marx, S., Hughes, J., Tysall, C., & Suleman, R. (2014). Mapping the impact of patient and public involvement on health and social care research: A systematic review. *Health Expectations, 17*, 637–650.

Brosens, D. (2018). Prisoners' participation and involvement in prison life: Examining the possibilities and boundaries. *European Journal of Criminology*, 1–20.

Buckland, G., & Wincup, E. (2004). Researching crime and criminal justice. In J. Muncie & D. Wilson (Eds.), *Student handbook of criminal justice and criminology*. London: Cavendish Publishing.

Byrne, M. W. (2005). Conducting research as a visiting scientist in a women's prison. *Journal of Professional Nursing, 21*, 223–230.

Cross, R., & Warwick-Booth, L. (2016). Using storyboards in participatory research. *Nurse Researcher, 23*, 8–12.

de Viggiani, N., Orme, J., Powell, J., & Salmon, D. (2005). New arrangements for prison health care provide an opportunity and a challenge for primary care trusts. *British Medical Journal, 330*, 918.

Drake, D. H. (2014). Researching prisoner experiences with prison officers: An action research-inspired approach. *Action Research, 12*, 94–109.

Eakin, J., Robertson, A., Poland, B., Coburn, D., & Edwards, R. (1996). Towards a critical social science perspective on health promotion research. *Health Promotion International, 11*, 157–165.

Edgar, K., Jacobson, J., & Biggar, K. (2011). *Time well spent: A practical guide to active citizenship and volunteering in prison*. London: Prison Reform Trust.

Elwood Martin, R., Murphy, K., Hanson, D., Hemingway, C., Ramsden, V., Buxton, J., Granger-Brown, A., Condello, L. L., Buchanan, M., Espinoza-Magana, N., Edworthy, G., & Hislop, T. G. (2009). The development of participatory health research among incarcerated women in a Canadian prison. *International Journal of Prisoner Health, 5*, 95–107.

Elwood Martin, R., Hanson, D., Hemingway, C., Ramsden, V., Buxton, J., Granger-Brown, A., Condello, L.-L., Macaulay, A., Janssen, P., & Gregory Hislop, T. (2012). Homelessness as viewed by incarcerated women: Participatory research. *International Journal of Prisoner Health, 8*, 108 116.

Fine, M., & Torre, M. E. (2006). Intimate details: Participatory action research in prison. *Action Research, 4*, 253–269.

Freudenberg, N. (2007). Health research behind bars: A brief guide to research in jails and prisons. In R. B. Greifinger, J. Bick, & J. Goldenson (Eds.), *Public health behind bars. From prisons to communities*. New York: Springer.

Green, J., Cross, R., Woodall, J., & Tones, K. (2019). *Health promotion. Planning and strategies*. London: Sage.

Johnson, M. E., Brems, C., Mills, M. E., & Eldridge, G. D. (2018). Involving incarcerated individuals in the research process: Perspectives of key stakeholders. *Action Research, 16*, 43–64.

Liamputtong, P., & Ezzy, D. (2005). *Qualitative research methods*. Oxford: Oxford University Press.

Mantoura, P., & Potvin, L. (2013). A realist–constructionist perspective on participatory research in health promotion. *Health Promotion International, 28*, 61–72.
Martin, C. (2000). Doing research in a prison setting. In V. Jupp, P. Davies, & P. Francis (Eds.), *Doing criminological research*. London: Sage.
Moser, D. J., Arndt, S., Kanz, J. E., Benjamin, M. L., Bayless, J. D., Reese, R. L., Paulsen, J. S., & Flaum, M. A. (2004). Coercion and informed consent in research involving prisoners. *Comprehensive Psychiatry, 45*, 1–9.
O'Gorman, C. M., Martin, M. S., Oliffe, J. L., Leggo, C., Korchinski, M., & Elwood Martin, R. (2012). Community voices in program development: The wisdom of individuals with incarceration experience. *Canadian Journal of Public Health, 103*, e379–e383.
Peternelj-Taylor, C. (2005). Conceptualizing nursing research with offenders: Another look at vulnerability. *International Journal of Law and Psychiatry, 28*, 348–359.
Piacentini, L. (2007). Researching Russian prisons: A consideration of new and established methodologies in prison research. In Y. Jewkes (Ed.), *Handbook on prisons*. Cullompton: Willan Publishing.
Poland, B., Krupa, G., & McCall, D. (2009). Settings for health promotion: An analytic framework to guide intervention design and implementation. *Health Promotion Practice, 10*, 505–516.
Quraishi, M. (2008). Researching Muslim prisoners. *International Journal of Social Research Methodology, 11*, 453–467.
Ramsden, V., Martin, R., McMillan, J., Granger-Brown, A., & Tole, B. (2015). Participatory health research within a prison setting: A qualitative analysis of 'Paragraphs of passion'. *Global Health Promotion, 22*, 48–55.
Reuss, A. (2000). The researcher's tale. In D. Wilson & A. Reuss (Eds.), *Prison(er) education*. Winchester: Waterside Press.
Robertson, S. (2006). 'Not living life in too much of an excess': Lay men understanding health and well-being. *Health, 10*, 175–189.
Sim, J. (1990). *Medical power in prisons*. Milton Keynes: Open University Press.
Smith, C. (2002). Punishment and pleasure: Women, food and the imprisoned body. *Sociological Review, 50*, 197–211.
Smith, C. (2009). A period in custody: Menstruation and the imprisoned body. *Internet Journal of Criminology*, 1–22.
Smith, C., & Wincup, E. (2000). Breaking in: Researching criminal justice institutions for women. In R. D. King & E. Wincup (Eds.), *Doing research on crime and justice*. Oxford: Oxford University Press.

Smith, C., & Wincup, E. (2002). Reflections on fieldwork in criminal justice institutions. In T. Welland & L. Pugsley (Eds.), *Ethical dilemmas in qualitative research*. Aldershot: Ashgate.

Solomon, E. (2004). Criminals or citizens? Prisoner councils and rehabilitation. *Criminal Justice Matters, 56*, 24–25.

Solomon, E., & Edgar, K. (2004). *Having their say: The work of prisoner councils*. London: Prison Reform Trust.

South, J., Bagnall, A., Hulme, C., Woodall, J., Longo, R., Dixey, R., et al. (2014a). *A systematic review of the effectiveness and cost-effectiveness of peer-based interventions to maintain and improve offender health in prison settings*. Report for the National Institute for Health Research (NIHR) Health Services and Delivery Research (NIHR HS&DR) programme Project: 10/2002/13.

South, J., Purcell, M. E., Branney, P., Gamsu, M., & White, J. (2014b). Rewarding altruism: Addressing the issue of payments for volunteers in public health initiatives. *Social Science & Medicine, 104*, 80–87.

South, J., Woodall, J., Kinsella, K., & Bagnall, A.-M. (2016). A qualitative synthesis of the positive and negative impacts related to delivery of peer based health interventions in prison settings. *BMC Health Services Research, 16*, 1–8.

Stanley, L., & Wise, S. (1993). *Breaking out again: Feminist ontology and epistemology*. London: Routledge.

Svensson, S. (1996). Imprisonment – A matter of letting people live or stay alive? Some reasoning from a Swedish point of view. *Journal of Correctional Education, 47*, 69–72.

The Aldridge Foundation, & Johnson, M. (2008). *The user voice of the criminal justice system*. London: The Aldridge Foundation.

Waldram, J. B. (2007). Everybody has a story: Listening to imprisoned sexual offenders. *Qualitative Health Research, 17*, 963–970.

Wincup, E. (1999). Researching women awaiting trial: Dilemmas of feminist ethnography. In F. Brookman, L. Noaks, & E. Wincup (Eds.), *Qualitative research in criminology*. Aldershot: Ashgate.

Woodall, J. (2010). Exploring concepts of health with male prisoners in three category-C English prisons. *International Journal of Health Promotion and Education, 48*, 115–122.

Woodall, J., Dixey, R., & South, J. (2013). Control and choice in English prisons: Developing health-promoting prisons. *Health Promotion International, 29*, 474–482.

Woodall, J., South, J., Dixey, R., de Viggiani, N., & Penson, W. (2015a). Expert views of peer-based interventions for prisoner health. *International Journal of Prisoner Health, 11*, 87–97.
Woodall, J., South, J., Dixey, R., de Viggiani, N., & Penson, W. (2015b). Factors that determine the effectiveness of peer interventions in prisons in England and Wales. *Prison Service Journal, 219*, 30–37.
Woodall, J., Warwick-Booth, L., South, J., & Cross, R. (2018). What makes health promotion distinct? *Scandinavian Journal of Public Health, 46*, 118–122.
Wright, M. T., Roche, B., von Unger, H., Block, M., & Gardner, B. (2010). A call for an international collaboration on participatory research for health. *Health Promotion International, 25*, 115–122.

3

Promoting Health Literacy with Young Adult Men in an English Prison

Anita Mehay, Rosie Meek, and Jane Ogden

Introduction

This chapter outlines a health literacy framework and approach with which to explore the prison as a place for supporting positive changes in health and wellbeing. Health literacy describes the 'cognitive and social skills which determine the motivation and ability of individuals to gain access to, understand and use information in ways which promote and

A. Mehay (✉)
University College London, London, UK
e-mail: a.mehay@ucl.ac.uk

R. Meek
Department of Law and Criminology, Royal Holloway University of London, Surrey, UK
e-mail: r.meek@rhul.ac.uk

J. Ogden
University of Surrey, Guildford, UK
e-mail: J.Ogden@surrey.ac.uk

© The Author(s) 2021

M. Maycock et al. (eds.), *Issues and Innovations in Prison Health Research*, Palgrave Studies in Prisons and Penology, https://doi.org/10.1007/978-3-030-46401-1_3

maintain good health' (Nutbeam 1998, p. 10). Globally, many people experience limitations in their health literacy where one large European study of 8000 people found that almost 1 in 2 people (47%) experience limited health literacy, which was associated with lower rates of physical activity, increased body mass index and alcohol consumption (Sørensen et al. 2015). Financial deprivation, low social status, low education or old age are all associated with limited health literacy, suggesting the presence of a social gradient (Sørensen et al. 2015). Health literacy is now established as a determinant of health and one which is modifiable, thereby holding potential to reduce health inequalities (Batterham et al. 2016). Indeed, systematic reviews of health literacy research suggest that health literacy interventions are associated with improvements in clinical outcomes and healthcare utilisation (Bailey et al. 2014; Berkman et al. 2011; Taggart et al. 2012). Eliminating health literacy barriers is posited as the 'essential ingredient' in the effort to increase health equity and reduce health inequalities.

Over the past few decades, health literacy work has occurred in diverse settings; from settings where people are overwhelmed by an abundance of choice to settings where people have limited education and few options. Few studies, however, have focused on prisons as context for supporting health literacy. The relevance is clear; the prison population is made up of those from the most marginalised, socially disadvantaged, socially excluded sections of society with multiple and complex needs (Senior and Shaw 2007). Young adult men (aged 18–21 years) in prison are a particularly high-need group within the prison population with increased vulnerabilities relating to histories of social exclusions, violence, bereavement, abuse, neglect and time spent in local authority care (Bradley 2009; Harris 2015; House of Commons Justice Committee 2016). These young people have been excluded from some of the valuable life experiences and learning opportunities such as formal education, positive peer learning and navigating health systems which are important to support transition into healthy adulthoods. Clearly though, there is a value in (re)-engaging with young adults who end up in prison to support healthy lives and a generation-level reduction of health inequalities.

There is now a clear evidence-based mandate for supporting the health and social needs of people in prison (WHO 2007). Whilst the policy is laudable, translating these intentions into practice in diverse jurisdictions is challenging. The paradox is that whilst prisoners enter custodial settings with a range of complex health needs, prisons also expose them to further risks to their health. Politically, we have seen an increasing number of people receiving custodial sentences in England and Wales over the past 10 years with the prison population exceeding 83,000 (Ministry of Justice 2019). The large number of people in prison has resulted in increased demands on the prison service which have been further compounded by constraints in resources and staffing, leading to serious calls around prison safety standards and the ability to fully provide rehabilitative support (Independent Monitoring Boards 2019). Structurally, prisoners face barriers to accessing and engaging with prison-based and community-based health services (Herbert et al. 2012), as well as limited exposure to a variety of healthy food, physical activity and fresh air, green and blue spaces (Jewkes et al. 2019). Psychologically, living in close proximity with others places prisoners under considerable pressures relating to the loss of freedom and isolation from friends and family (de Viggiani 2007). Prisons have complex social hierarchies based on power relations, where bullying and violence are common and have a negative impact on health and wellbeing (de Viggiani 2003; HM Chief Inspector of Prisons 2018; Jewkes 2005).

Although the prison landscape appears bleak, there are, reassuringly, examples of prison staff, third sector organisations and researchers seeking to support and advocate for those in prison. The chapter draws upon findings from a doctoral research project to outline a health literacy framework and approach to working with young adults in prison. The chapter provides insights into the lived experience of imprisonment and ways to strengthen young men's knowledge and skills in navigating the prison as a place for managing their health and wellbeing.

Literacy, Education and Health

Health literacy is an evolving field which brings together both the health and literacy fields with the idea that both are critical resources for everyday living. Education and literacy are established as significant determinants of health (Marmot et al. 2012), where difficulties in applying basic literacy skills to health-related materials has been associated with poorer satisfaction with healthcare (Altin and Stock 2015), decreased rates of healthy behaviours (von Wagner et al. 2009), and poorer general health (Dewalt et al. 2004; Institute of Medicine 2004). The field of health literacy has evolved further from basic literacy to include higher-order cognitive and social skills required for good health, which are now recognised as one of the central life skills needed in healthy societies (WHO 2009). The prototypical model of health literacy distinguishes between three levels:

1. Functional health literacy: refers to the ability to apply basic literacy skills to health-related materials, such as reading the label on a medication bottle. This most resembles 'medical'-focused health literacy and is described as the most basic level of health literacy but an important one since limitations can be a major barrier to educating patients (Nutbeam 2008).
2. Interactive health literacy: focuses on the development of more advanced cognitive skills and the ability to operate in a social environment. This level often relates to improved self-confidence and motivation since individuals with high levels of interactive literacy skills will negotiate options with their doctors, will actively seek out self-help strategies and support from their peers.
3. Critical health literacy: builds on functional and interactive levels of health literacy and describes the critical appraisal skills required to evaluate health issues, determine the challenges and advantages of issues and deciding on the benefits and problems of health strategies.

Here, health literacy is viewed as a continuous interplay between the three levels which places equal value on all forms of the concept rather than reflecting a linear progression from one to the next; therefore high levels of functional health literacy is no guarantee that an individual will demonstrate interactive and critical literacy skills nor is a high level of functional health literacy required to develop interactive and critical health literacy skills (Chinn 2011; Ishikawa and Yano 2011; Smith et al. 2013).

Empowerment is a central tenant of health literacy where '...by improving people's access to health information and their capacity to use it effectively, health literacy is critical to empowerment' (WHO 2009, p. 357). Promoting health literacy has been closely aligned with psychological empowerment, including feelings of self-confidence and self-efficacy to seek information and support (Mogford et al. 2010; Sykes et al. 2013). However, health literacy in itself does not automatically lead to empowerment (or vice versa); having adequate skills in understanding health (health literacy) yet lacking the power and the motivation to take control (empowerment) can result in a lack of action. Conversely, programs aimed at psychological empowerment alone can also often assume a high level of knowledge or expertise in individuals (Crondahl and Karlsson 2016; Porr et al. 2006; Schulz and Nakamoto 2013). The challenge is therefore developing health literacy interventions which can promote empowerment, whilst aligning with healthcare systems and social context demands. Notably, targeted, culturally appropriate interventions that examine the challenges in peoples' lives and promote empowerment tend to have a positive impact on participant knowledge, attitudes and behaviours (Logan et al. 2015). For many, the value of health literacy is situated in promoting critical levels of health literacy which promote higher-order critical appraisal skills and empowerment.

Living Our Best, Healthy Lives: Critical Health Literacy

Critical health literacy refers to the critical appraisal skills required to evaluate health issues and for many, promoting critical health literacy focuses on raising individual's understanding of the social determinants of health combined with the skills to take action at both the individual and community level (Nutbeam 2000). Whilst psychological empowerment is fundamental to gaining increased control over health, it is limited as it does not directly or fully consider the wider environmental influences on health nor lead to an increase in actual power or resources. Since population health inequities are rooted in structural and social determinants, education that focuses exclusively on individual-level risk factors is unlikely to eliminate inequities across social or economic groups because it fails to address their upstream causes. The idea here is that individuals who understand the determinants of their health and have the skills to take action are more likely to take action to address health priorities and meet their respective needs (Nutbeam 2000). Therefore, health literacy is an educational tool that can be used to "inform, enlighten and empower individuals and communities" (Sparks 2009, p. 201) and is an essential ingredient in co-production approaches (Palumbo and Manna 2018).

Within this framework, rather than becoming passive recipients of information, learners are empowered through reflections and co-producing knowledge that is based on their social and cultural experiences. Methods such as dialogical and social learning, brainstorming and problem-posing tend to be popular approaches to promoting critical health literacy as they not only increase participation but raise awareness and personal reflections over one's life. For example, Estacio (2013) highlights the value of adopting a critical health literacy framework in a community-based project with a small indigenous community in the Philippines. Participants were engaged in critical reflection to gain a better understanding of how health is conceptualised within their environment and its implications for practice, power relations and subjective experiences. Through this dialogue, participations reflected on the frustrations of just developing literacy skills, which the author postulates only 'scratches the surface of the problem' and actually contributes to the dominant discourses that those with lower literacy were inferior and pose a burden on society, which potentially disempowered communities further (Estacio 2013). By refocusing efforts towards understanding the needs and solutions within communities rather than easing the burden off the healthcare system, the researcher was able to co-develop health literacy programs in line with their needs.

Within a Western context, the 'Bigger Picture' in the USA also presents a series of health literacy projects with young people (Rogers et al. 2014). The project aims to engage youth in the social and environmental factors around type 2 diabetes to move the diabetes dialogue away from individual behaviour alone through developing a 'fresh, engaging, and relevant campaign' (p. 156) which targets young people most effected by diabetes. They use a collaborative, 'learners-as-interpreters' (p. 149) approach, in which health information was interpreted and retold as prevention messages for participants' own communities (Handley et al. 2009). Several workshops were conducted with young adults where they were encouraged to develop their own narratives and poems which are then transformed into a public service campaign.[1] Through a series of evaluation surveys with key stakeholders, the researchers concluded that the campaign effectively reached young people most at risk of diabetes, particularly those from minority groups where using 'youth-generated spoken-word' (p. 157) created a more authentic, personalised and relevant message to engage young people around the social determinants of diabetes. They advocate for greater use of participation and the learners-as-contributors approach to develop a more comprehensive and empowering model of health literacy.

The field of health literacy presents an innovative opportunity to develop and frame prison health within this lens of self-management, health equity and reducing health disparities. Within prisons, programs to promote health literacy have not been directly or fully examined to our knowledge. There have however been notable developments in supporting access, understanding and use of health information through peer-based approaches in the UK (Edgar et al. 2011) as well as internationally (Wright et al. 2013). A systematic review of peer-based approaches for prison health demonstrated the positive influence of peer education and support (Bagnall et al. 2015). Although the use of peers represent a positive development for prison health, much of the focus has been towards utilising peers as avenues to deliver healthcare and taking on consultative roles, rather than directly embodying some of the participatory elements described in critical health literacy. Peer support models have also been seen as a public health intervention in search of a theory with one realist synthesis indicating that organisations, researchers and health professionals that implement peer-based models tend adopt an authoritarian design rather than drawing on peers experiential knowledge to deliver culturally tailored support. Conversely, peer-based models taking on more

[1] see www.thebiggerpicture.org.

co-design approaches allow for development of relationships and connections and investigations into the root causes and potential solutions to poor health and wellbeing (Harris et al. 2015).

The work presented in this chapter was part of a doctoral research project exploring health literacy within a single English prison for young adults. A programme of research was undertaken, involving a series of studies to understand the barriers to health literacy in prison and the potential opportunities to promote and strengthen skills to manage health and wellbeing. Some of this work has been published (or in press) as individual studies (see Mehay et al. 2019; Mehay and Meek 2016) where this chapter provides an overview of the whole programme of research and provides reflections on some of the findings and implications for prison health.

Prison as a Setting for Health Research

The doctoral research programme was conducted in a single prison site for young adult offenders which had a capacity for around 650 at the current certified accommodation, and was at 82% capacity at the time of the research. The prison held a sentenced population meaning there was little 'churn' through the prison from remand prisoners who tend to be held for shorter periods. Recent independent inspections had reported than rates of violence were deemed too high with a high use of force, adjudications and segregation. Furthermore, inspections also report a lack of opportunities for young men to engage in purposeful activities with most activities centred around prison maintenance such as cleaning, orderly work and laundry. Health promotion was deemed to be underdeveloped and that although there was health literature on display, much of it was deemed too complex for those with literacy difficulties. As such, one recent inspection recommended that the views of prisoners should be investigated, which prompted the prison to expedite plans to develop participatory and peer-based models of health and welcomed support from a doctoral researcher.

Prisoners are a vulnerable group and there are very specific ethical issues to be considered (King and Wincup 2008). Notably, the extent to which prisoners can provide consent has been highly contested (Freudenberg 2007; Klockars 1974). Prisoners are rarely afforded any options or choices within a prison context so may feel little choice as to whether to take part in the research when requested. Furthermore, prisoners are traditionally inclined to contribute to research activities largely due to their desire to occupy their time within the institution, to alleviate boredom and to spend time talking to someone viewed as outside of the core prison staff (Moser et al. 2004). Although it can be difficult to evade this type of influence, this research took extra care when presenting study information to ensure that the young men were fully informed of the facts and consequences of taking part. They were particularly encouraged to discuss any concerns around the boundaries of confidentiality and the potential implications of the disclosure. Indeed, research and ethics approval to conduct this research was obtained from a University and the National Offender Management Service (NOMS) (now Her Majesty's Prison and Probation Service).

Prison as a Health Literate Context: Barriers and Assets

Health literacy is an asset to be developed where progressive levels of knowledge and critical skills supports greater autonomy and empowerment in health in the context of everyday life. However, prisons are examples of settings which embody deprivations and disempowerment with values, rules and rituals that enable prisoners to be observed and restricted (de Viggiani 2007); these are at odds with any notion that prisoners can be encouraged to take charge of their health (Smith 2000). Imprisonment, however, is not a uniform experience (Liebling 2004) and a number of studies demonstrate that prisoners do not simply submit and become passive within the restrictive context (Baer 2005; Bosworth and Carrabine 2001; Crewe 2007; Dirsuweit 1999; Rowe 2015; Sibley and Van Hoven 2009). Therefore, in understanding health literacy in the prison context, it is important to consider the actual experience of imprisonment and the everyday realities of prison life. The first phase of this programme of research therefore involved examining the barriers to health literacy as well as the opportunities within the prison context.

An initial phase of research utilised different methodologies, taking the approach of first conducting semi-structured interviews with 37 young adult men to explore the barriers to health literacy. We then adapted (with a group of young men) an established measure of health literacy (see the Health Literacy Survey for Europe [HLS-EU] Sørensen et al. 2015) to administer in the prison context. The measure consisted of 47 statements relating to various skills and opportunities within three distinct domains of health literacy (as a patient within prison healthcare, in preventing disease and illness, and as a citizen for health promotion). Items included statements such as 'understanding what the doctor or nurse says to you', 'understanding why you need vaccinations' and 'joining a sport or exercise club' where respondents are asked to select the level of ease/difficulty for each. Collectively, the items provide an overall score of health literacy, as well as individual sub-scores for each of the three domains. The survey was administered through individual, assisted interviews across a representation sample of the prison population (n = 104, around a third of the prison population). Additional semi-structured interviews were conducted with another 35 young adult prisoners who scored as managing well in the prison to examine the potential skills and opportunities related to health literacy in prison. The findings from this phase of research are outlined.

Barriers to Health Literacy

Findings from the health literacy survey for prisons reveal that large proportions of the young adult prison population experienced limitations in health literacy (see Fig. 3.1). Overall, 72% (n = 75) of young men scored within a range indicating limited health literacy and 28% (n = 29) as adequate health literacy. These limitations were seen across all three dimensions of health literacy, with limitations in health promotion (n = 80, 77%), disease prevention (n = 76, 73%) and healthcare contexts (n = 61, 59%).

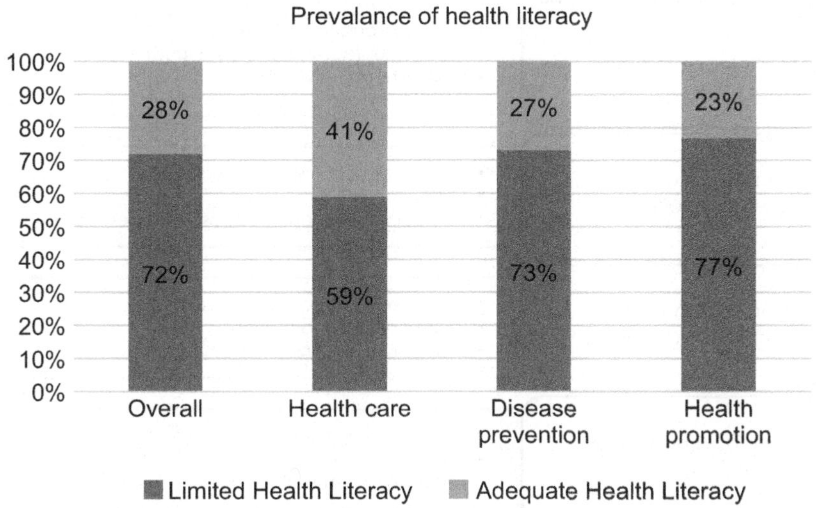

Fig. 3.1 Prevalence of health literacy in the prison

Qualitative interviews reveal details which might explain some of the reasons for the limitations, with significant challenges identified in individual's knowledge and beliefs of health, experience with prison healthcare, maintaining status in the social world and recognising structural restrictions (see Fig. 3.2).

All the young men highlighted the *social world of prison* as a barrier to managing their health and wellbeing. The social world of prison was described as a precarious place where young men had to actively avoid violence and bullying as well as gain status for one's protection. The precariousness and threat of violence was ever present for the young men, and those who experienced attacks were left both physically and emotionally traumatised. Some young men described how conflicts from outside the prison followed them into the prison where they had to be vigilant to potential dangers for their own safety. Javon (participant 17) described his affiliation with gangs as adding another layer of complexity to the prison experience where he has to both survive the usual pressures within the prison's social world whilst being aware of his additional risks associated with his gang status. He says:

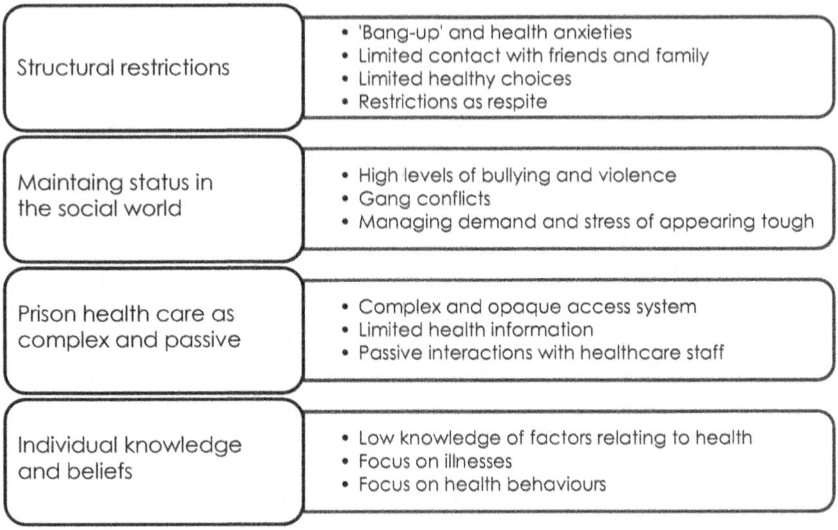

Fig. 3.2 Barriers to health literacy in the prison

> …you just don't want to be weak in here. I got a lot of issues like gang dramas. So I get strong really for my own safety. I don't look for drama but I am ready for it if it comes to me… it's called 'staying on point'. You can never be relaxed or let your guard down. You're always anxious. (Participant 17)

Young men's ability to manage their health therefore partly depended upon their ability to maintain their status where surviving involved appearing tough, aggressive and hyper-confident to avoid being seen as weak.

Structural restrictions also limited the ability to self-manage and build health literacy skills. Activities such as managing stress, keeping themselves and their environment hygienic and clean, adopting a healthy diet and taking part in physical activities were all severely impeded by the prison regime and decisions made for them. As Ray (participant 21) states:

> …to me right now, it [my health] doesn't matter while I am here. It's about what they want me to eat. I don't have a say. I would like to manage myself

> more with fruit and fitness choice but it's up to them. They choose what you do... and it's made my health worse in here. (Participant 21)

These restrictions meant coping mechanisms tended to focus on unhealthy behaviours such as smoking. Furthermore, 'bang-up' was a time where anxieties around health were often heightened, where ordinarily young and healthy men were fearful of serious illness and sometimes even death. Harry (participant 4) reflected on one situation and his heightened anxiety;

> ...I had a lump under my arm and I was scared because at night you have nothing to think about. I asked the nurse and he gave me paracetamol. I can't ask my mum because she is not here but I thought it was cancer. (Participant 4)

Young men often referred to feeling infantilised and subjected to greater levels of restrictions since they perceived these restrictions were imposed on them due to their age. Most had experienced part of their sentence in an adult prison prior to arriving at the YOI where they were able to compare the regimes. Adult prisons were overwhelmingly favoured as they offered the young men with greater opportunities to make decisions for themselves. Ricardo (participant 23) expressed his frustration and explained;

> ...in adult jails, you're given more responsibilities and you're given more opportunities...On my wing it was really good. We even had a kitchen area where we could use a microwave and stuff and make our own food. We used to cook together and hang out there. It was proper homely. We all ended up looking out for each other there and the adults looked after the younger ones and kept some of us in check too. And they didn't tolerate bullying at all. It was like a community and we helped each other and it was a good place to be. (Participant 23)

However, for a small number of young men, the prison restrictions offered a time for respite and reflections. The restrictions of prison life provided a break from some unhealthy behaviours, such as drug use and smoking. For young men like Gavin (participant 27), prison was viewed as having a partly positive impact on health:

> ...it's good really as being in prison has helped me—it's cleansing my body. (Participant 27)

In this sense, prison provided restrictions which were beneficial and gave the young men's bodies some respite from unhealthy behaviours. However, restrictions were largely viewed as negatively impacting on health while in custody, while also failing to equip individuals to pursue healthy lives on release. Few young men described long-term abstinence in their drug use and smoking, where both were still relatively available to them and were often used to cope with the stress and boredom in prison.

Most of the young men interviewed held *individual knowledge and beliefs about health* which would likely pose challenges in developing health literacy. Many young men noted that being healthy was tied in with not being ill and unwell, with few viewing health through the lens of self-management, empowerment or something which was linked to their wider social and contextual world. For instance:

> *...being unhealthy—that's about being ill and unwell. So maybe being healthy is the opposite, so not having problems or illnesses.* (Participant 30)

The focus on illness and being unwell held implications for young men in how they went about managing their health and wellbeing, with a high level of reliance on formal healthcare information and services in prison. However, *prison healthcare was seen as complex and passive* where young men reflected their frustrations with health information efforts which were seen as tokenistic and a box-ticking exercise. For instance, young men spoke about the presence of health information posters on the corridors between wings, which were spaces where young men were not allowed to enter freely, meaning posters were only seen when being escorted within the prison with little opportunity to stop and actually consider the information. Young men also highlighted the difficulties of being expected to navigate what was described as complex and opaque prison healthcare processes. Here, the prison healthcare application system involved completing a short form and posting it in a box on the prison wing. The box is checked daily where a nurse (or healthcare assistant) aims to see the young person within 24 hours of receiving the form where health concerns are assessed and treatment provided or triaged to another member of healthcare staff if required. This system was viewed as archaic and seen as an overly lengthy and inefficient process with anxieties around paper forms going missing. Responses to requests were also deemed too slow, particularly since many young men required support from healthcare for a current episode of ill health. For example, Emmanuel (participant 9) reflected his frustration in that:

> ...you put in a sick app and they see you 24 hours later but if you are in excruciating pain then you have to still wait. (Participant 9)

These frustrations were further compounded when seeing health professionals entering the wings where they reside and being unable to ask for immediate advice and support. The young men felt that they were subjected to a double-punishment, were they were unable to self-manage their health conditions so were reliant on prison healthcare services, but were subject to what they deemed as inefficient and slow healthcare responses. Once contact was made with a member of healthcare staff, interactions were described as passive, lacking person-centred care or compassion; healthcare was something which was done *to* them, rather than *with* them. Fred (participant 12), for example, described a recent encounter with a primary care health professional who dealt with his health issue efficiently but Fred was left not fully understanding his health condition:

> ...it's like he's done the working out but doesn't show you how he did it—just the end result. (Participant 12)

Many like Fred described similar experiences with healthcare staff, where interactions lacked a collaborative approach with health needs managed with no explanations to the young men. The experiences reported by the participants suggested that greater consultation and explanations would in turn provide them with a greater sense of control over their health as well as the tools to prevent future problems. Furthermore, some young men expressed the imposing role of healthcare which prioritised their own agendas whilst failing to meet their individual needs. This was particularly pertinent for young men who valued their physical appearance as signs of good health where they stated that they wanted healthcare to be able to provide protein shakes or skin creams for their health. Harinder (participant 31) reflects on an occasion where his own health needs were not prioritised by the prison healthcare. He explains in detail the experience of being viciously attacked in prison by a group of other prisoners. The attack left him with visible scars on his face from the use of makeshift blades. The visibility of the scars were of great distress to Harinder as this served of a visible reminder of the attack which had affected his confidence. He explains his encounter with healthcare;

> …I went to healthcare as I wanted some cream and oils for my scars. They just came and were worried about my asthma. But the scar thing really bothered me. I hate myself when I look in the mirror. (Participant 31)

For Harinder and others, healthcare had failed to provide a person-centred care and this was a missed opportunity to provide him with reassurance and support.

The findings from the wider prison survey and qualitative interviews confirm that health literacy should be considered as a dynamic construct which concerns the interaction of individual, social and structural factors. Developing health literacy in prison would likely require a shift in individual knowledge and beliefs to focus on considering managing and maintaining good health, rather than just preventing illness. Efforts would also require consideration to developing the skills to operate in the precarious social environment and in interactions with prison healthcare services (interactive health literacy) and strengthening critical appraisal skills to evaluate challenges and advantages in this context (critical health literacy). This clearly requires healthcare and prison services to adapt to support more health literate environments for young men to take control of their health. Although the findings present a bleak picture of life in prison, there were nuggets of insights where young men demonstrated knowledge, skills and self-efficacy and resilience in managing and maintaining health within the prison context. This inspired the next stage of research to consider what health literacy skills and opportunities were present within these barriers.

Health Literacy Skills and Opportunities

Much of the findings relating to the barriers to health literacy are fairly established within the literature exploring the challenge in promoting health in prison. What is less well known are the ways which young men adopt to respond to the challenges in managing their health and wellbeing and mitigating some of the negative health effects of imprisonment. Young men who scored below a threshold on a scale for anxiety and depression were invited to take part in a semi-structured interview. The interviews were designed to elicit tangible and specific details relating to how the young men might be managing their health and wellbeing as an indication of their health literacy. The findings reveal that young men stitch together an intricate and complex set of tactics to alter and retexture the prison space to mitigate some of the risks to their health and wellbeing (Mehay et al. 2019). These included *controlling time* through meticulous scheduling of routines, including prison activities, TV watching, listening to music and sleeping. Young men also described *reclaiming their young adulthood* through reconstructing and reframing the prison experience through re-enacting what they may ordinarily be doing on the outside as a tactic to reassure themselves that they were not missing out key experiences. Jeffrey (participant 19) describes this where he and his cell mate re-enact situations from the outside world to reclaim a sense of normality as young adults. He explains that:

> ...every Friday and Saturday we play the radio and we try and imagine we are out like raving and we stay up late like we are out partying, like we would have been on the outside... you feel so free and you feel you can be yourself. (Participant 19)

For Jeffrey, tuning into the outside world in this sense enabled him to retain normality and reclaim young adulthood. Young men also described the need to *balance food* in choosing 'healthy' options with 'good' comfort food, which held memories and a connection to the outside world (e.g. a treat given by a parent). Prison was overwhelmingly described as a place of control and restrictions, where young men struggled to find opportunities for both managing ill health and engaging in healthy lifestyles. However, our participants described being vigilant to opportunities which would help them manage their health and wellbeing within the rules and regulations of the prison regime, what we called the *cracks in the grid*. These cracks included re-appropriating items (e.g. making weights for physical training, playing games to pass time) as well as learning jail remedies from everyday items. For example, Neil states:

> I've now learnt jail remedies to deal with my health issues. Like I put squash in a kettle and you got Lemsip. If you drink lots and lots of orange juice it works out your system, flushes everything out and good for your stomach… I've learn how to do so much in here! (Participant 34)

Young men also described ways to *construct* spaces *for comfort* through accessing religious spaces (even if not subscribing to the religion) and creating a homely cell environment through investing in items for comfort (e.g. new pillows).

The findings confirm that prisons are largely regarded as unhealthy places rather than health promoting. However, the findings go beyond an analysis of how prison can compromise health to understanding the ways prisoners attempt to mitigate these risks within an unhealthy place.

Strengthening Health Literacy: A Group-Based Model

The insights gained from the initial phase of research suggest that health literacy efforts require change at an individual, social and structural level to enable young men to develop and strengthen health literacy to support them into healthy adulthood whilst in prison and beyond. Clearly, health literacy efforts require healthcare and prison services to adapt to support more health literate environments for young men to take control of their health. The second phase of the research, however, sought to build on the insights through (co-)developing an intervention which would be relevant, authentic and personalised for young men in prison to support them to manage within these spaces. This section describes the development and delivery of the workshop and provides some reflections for future developments.

Participants in the Workshops

A group of nine young men were identified as suitable participants to take part in the workshops as they were enrolled in a marketing and design course run by the prison education department. The first author initially gained approval from the head of education and the teacher of the course to approach the group. The objective of running a workshop was presented to the learners. The young men were given the opportunity to ask questions and consider both individually and collectively if they wanted to take part in the workshop. All the young men in the group agreed.

Structure and Delivery

The workshop sessions were developed under supervision and as part of practitioner training of the first author as a Health Psychologist. The workshop sought to cover key topics, including definitions of health, reading and understanding health information, communicating with health professionals and friends and family about health information. The workshop took a social and discussion-based approach to learning where the young men's experiential knowledge and personal reflections were encouraged. During the workshop sessions, young men applied their reflections and learnings to co-design a leaflet, which served as both an artefact of their own learning and a tangible output to disseminate within the wider prison (see Fig. 3.3 for individual session structure).

Session 1: What is health?

- Objectives: introduction to the workshop and health Literacy
- Activities: group discussions on what being healthy means to you

Session 2: Keeping healthy in prison

- Objectives: Consideration of the prison environment as a place for health promotion
- Activities: work in small groups around a typical day in prison - discuss barriers and facilitators for health (including previous study findings)
- Leaflet development: identify opportunities, behaviours and focus for health leaflet

Session 3: Reading health information critically

- Objectives: where to get health information and importance of language and communication
- Activities: bring and discuss health information literature from the prison
- Leaflet development: translating opportunities and behaviours for health promotion for the leaflet

Session 4: Communicating effectively for health

- Objectives: understanding the effect of negative versus positive messages in health promotion
- Activities: bring and discuss visual images relating to health and illness
- Leaflet development: constructing language and visual image for leaflet

Session 5: Health advocates and action

- Objectives: disseminate evidence on social and peer models for health
- Activities: outline a job description for a peer-health worker in prison
- Leaflet development: finalising leaflet design and content

Fig. 3.3 Session structure of the health literacy workshops

The workshops were designed to be delivered in small groups of up to 10 young men and consisted of five sessions, held on a regular afternoon of the week. The five-session, weekly structure was established to account for the churn within prison estates where there is potentially limited time with cohorts of prisoners. As such, we anticipated the workshops would be feasible and effective in reaching a stable cohort of prisoners with low attrition in the workshops. Each workshop was designed to last approximately two hours from 2pm to 4pm in accordance with the prison regime.

Reflections on the Workshop

The aim of the workshops were to increase health knowledge and strengthen health literacy. Here, the focus was on developing critical dialogue relating to the context of young adults' lives and their health needs to raise self-efficacy and health literacy. Young men were able to work together as a group to collate and amass critical knowledge around health literacy in prison and develop a leaflet based on this for the benefit of the others. The co-developed leaflet was an artefact to demonstrate their learnings and create something they could reflect and take pride in. In the final workshop session, participants were also asked to reflect on their development during the workshop where participants stated that they had gained further knowledge about health and were confident in speaking with others about health. The leaflet was also subsequently distributed within the wider prison with an evaluation suggesting that such a co-developed leaflet was acceptable and useful in encouraging positive behaviours in prison. Furthermore, participants were keen to progress onto further training as peer-health workers, representing their motivation and intentions to engage in broader collective action for health promotion: see Mehay and Meek (2016) which details developments towards establishing these peer-health worker roles at the prison.

'Proper Storm': Benefits and Challenges in Strengthening Health Literacy

One of the workshop participants described the whole progress of building health literacy through the workshops and developing the leaflet as 'proper storm', a colloquial term used by young men to describe something positive and exciting. 'Proper storm' is a useful metaphor to consider the benefits and challenges in strengthening health literacy in prison; the findings demonstrate the potential for utilising a health literacy framework for guiding efforts ('proper') yet there are significant tensions that present ('storm'). Health literacy is defined as the 'cognitive and social skills which determine the motivation and ability of individuals to gain access to, understand and use information in ways which promote and maintain good health' (WHO 2009) yet the initial phase of the research programme highlighted numerous barriers to health literacy, including individual knowledge and beliefs of health, experience with prison healthcare, maintaining their status in the social world and recognising structural restrictions. However, despite these barriers, some young men were able to adopt a range of health tactics to reclaim some control over their physical, mental and emotional needs. These included a combination of utilising the resources and opportunities within their surroundings as well as accessing internal psychological resources. These insights were used to develop the second phase of the research programme, a group-based model for strengthening health literacy.

In considering the findings across the research programme, a number of key themes emerged. Young men in prison have unique developmental and health needs, where strengthening health literacy is a core component in supporting their *transition to adulthood*. The findings reveal that young men frequently associate gaining these critical skills for health as part of the transition to adulthood. The young men were aware that imprisonment meant that they were missing out on vital stages of development which marked their transition to adulthood; this included celebrating key birthdays (e.g. 18th, 21st), developing relationships, taking on parental roles and gaining employment and careers plans. The young men were keen to utilise the time spent at the prison to gain skills and knowledge to continue some of their personal development into adulthood, where gaining the skills and knowledge for health (health literacy) was part of becoming an adult. The workshops demonstrate that young men were keen to be supported and guided in understanding the broader factors associated with health and participate in decision making to benefit not just themselves but the broader prison population. Opportunities to take part in meaningful activities, particularly those that were civic and could benefit the wider prison, were lacking and thus severely limited the chance for young men to develop and demonstrate their skills towards health-literate adulthood. Future work should encourage these approaches and work *with* young men in these ways.

Young men frequently described their unique health needs as young adults and the transition to adulthood, where in doing so, they also described the contradictions of the prison regime which was characterised by an 'authoritarian paternalism'. Here, young men described how prisons for young adults were meant to be different to adult prisons in that they were supposed to provide a greater level of safety to both protect them from themselves (since they were not mature adults yet) as well as support their unique needs and transitional stage towards adulthood. However, all young men reflected that the prison approach was actually more damaging to their health compared with adult prisons and did not provide any kind of safeguarding or support. Most young men described long periods of being locked away with many spending up to 23 hours a day at weekends locked in their cell with little access to meaningful activities. Although these experiences are characteristic of many adult prison contexts, the young adults reflected that the restrictions were placed under a kind of 'guise' of safeguarding, that this was for their own good. They referred to being labelled as unreliable and untruthful therefore requiring guidance and protection from themselves and other young adults which differed from the approach within adult prisons. Therefore the prison took on an additional, paternalistic function, one which served to protect them through reducing their exposure to risks. However, this role was authoritative and punishing in nature. Prisons for young adults were therefore viewed as particularly restrictive and further reducing opportunities to develop health literacy.

Fundamental to health literacy is empowerment and the findings also highlight the *paradox of empowerment* within prison contexts. Indeed, promoting health literacy is closely aligned with psychological empowerment, including feelings of self-confidence and self-efficacy to seek information and support (Mogford et al. 2010; Sykes et al. 2013) as well as collective empowerment to promote the development of skills and capabilities to enable people to exert more control over the wider determinants of health. These notions are at odds with some of the coercive and authoritarian approaches of the prison. The young men reflect on the juxtaposition in being expected to take charge of aspects of their lives in prison, yet experiencing significant barriers in doing so. The young men report the tactics in which they may gain some agentic power but these are within the confines set by the prison regime and authorities, and possibly, their tactics reflect more on the structures that they seek to circumvent in their efforts to 'survive'. Healthcare frequently was seen as imposing what was deemed as unrealistic goals which lacked relevance and consideration of the challenges within the prison context. In this sense, healthcare did not seem to have fully embraced some of the developments in health literacy programmes within community settings, and had further aligned themselves to the more dominant culture of the prison. Therefore, health promotion efforts in prison need to not just situate themselves within the actual experiences and priorities of those in prison but need to consider wider structural reforms needed to 'loosen' the grid of control.

Conclusion

Although the primary aim of incarceration is not health improvement, prisons provide an opportunity for health services to access a hard-to-reach and underserved population (Bridgwood and Malbon 1995; Marshall et al. 2001). This chapter outlines a health literacy framework and approach to explore the prison as a place for managing health and wellbeing. Health literacy describes the 'cognitive and social skills which determine the motivation and ability of individuals to gain access to, understand and use information in ways which promote and maintain good health' (WHO 2009). This programme of research provides some insights into developing a framework for prison health through applying understandings from the field of health literacy. This model of health literacy supports a holistic model that recognises that health is more than just the absence of disease and would herald a move towards developing more integrated and social frameworks for prison health with greater understanding of what is required. The chapter outlines what could be achieved; however, this clearly requires healthcare and prison services to adapt to support more health-literate environments for young men to take control of their health. This includes stripping away barriers to health literacy, including simplifying access to prison healthcare and supporting staff in communicating more effectively with young men, and ensuring greater choices and opportunities. Despite the challenges in achieving this, the opportunities to address the health needs of a marginalised and vulnerable young adult population is immense and requires greater commitment at a practice and policy level.

References

Altin, S. V., & Stock, S. (2015). Impact of health literacy, accessibility and coordination of care on patient's satisfaction with primary care in Germany. *BMC Family Practice, 16*, 148. https://doi.org/10.1186/s12875-015-0372-0.

Baer, L. D. (2005). Visual imprints on the prison landscape: A study on the decorations in prison cells. *Tijdschrift voor Economische en Sociale Geografie, 96*, 209–217.

Bagnall, A.-M., South, J., Hulme, C., Woodall, J., Vinall-Collier, K., Raine, G., Kinsella, K., Dixey, R., Harris, L., & Wright, N. M. (2015). A systematic review of the effectiveness and cost-effectiveness of peer education and peer support in prisons. *BMC Public Health, 15*, 290. https://doi.org/10.1186/s12889-015-1584-x

Bailey, S. C., O'Conor, R., Bojarski, E. A., Mullen, R., Patzer, R. E., Vicencio, D., et al. (2014). Literacy disparities in patient access and health-related use of Internet and mobile technologies. *Health Expectations*, n/a–n/a. https://doi.org/10.1111/hex.12294.

Batterham, R. W., Hawkins, M., Collins, P. A., Buchbinder, R., & Osborne, R. H. (2016). Health literacy: Applying current concepts to improve health services and reduce health inequalities. *Public Health, 132*, 3–12. https://doi.org/10.1016/j.puhe.2016.01.001.

Berkman, N.D., Sheridan, S.L., Donahue, K.E., Halpern, D.J., Viera, A., Crotty, K., et al., 2011. Health literacy interventions and outcomes: An updated systematic review.

Bosworth, M., & Carrabine, E. (2001). Reassessing resistance race, gender and sexuality in prison. *Punishment and Society, 3*, 501–515. https://doi.org/10.1177/14624740122228393.

Bradley, K. (2009). *The Bradley Report. Lord Bradley's review of people with mental health problems or learning disabilities in the criminal justice system.* Department of Health, London.

Bridgwood, A., & Malbon, G. (1995). *Survey of the physical health of prisoners 1994: A survey of sentenced male prisoners in England and wales*. London: Stationery Office Books.

Chinn, D. (2011). Critical health literacy: A review and critical analysis. *Social Science & Medicine, 73*, 60–67.

Crewe, B. (2007). Power, adaptation and resistance in a late-modern men's prison. *British Journal of Criminology, 47*, 256–275.

Crondahl, K., & Karlsson, L. E. (2016). The nexus between health literacy and empowerment. *SAGE Open, 6*. https://doi.org/10.1177/2158244016646410.

DeWalt, D. A., Berkman, N. D., Sheridan, S., Lohr, K. N., & Pignone, M. P. (2004). Literacy and health outcomes: a systematic review of the literature. *Journal of General Internal Medicine, 19*(12), 1228–1239. https://doi.org/10.1111/j.1525-1497.2004.40153.x

de Viggiani, N. (2003). *(Un)healthy prison masculinities: Theorising men's health in prison*.

de Viggiani, N. (2007). Unhealthy prisons: Exploring structural determinants of prison health. *Sociology of Health & Illness, 29*, 115–135. https://doi.org/10.1111/j.1467-9566.2007.00474.x.

Dirsuweit, T. (1999). Carceral spaces in South Africa: A case study of institutional power, sexuality and transgression in a women's prison. *Geoforum, 30*, 71–83.

Edgar, K., Jacobson, J., & Biggar, K. (2011). *Time well spent: A practical guide to active citizenship and volunteering in prison*. London: Prison Reform Trust.

Estacio, E. V. (2013). Health literacy and community empowerment: It is more than just reading, writing and counting. *Journal of Health Psychology, 18*, 1056–1068. https://doi.org/10.1177/1359105312470126.

Freudenberg, N. (2007). Health research behind bars: A brief guide to research in jails and prisons. In R. B. G. Md (Ed.), *Public health behind bars* (pp. 415–433). New York: Springer.

Handley, M. A., Santos, M. G., & McClelland, J. (2009). Reports from the field: Engaging learners as interpreters for developing health messages – Designing the "Familias Sin Plomo" English as a Second Language curriculum project. *Global Health Promotion, 16*, 53–58. https://doi.org/10.1177/1757975909339773.

Harris. (2015). *The Harris review – Changing prisons, saving lives report of the independent review into self-inflicted deaths in custody of 18–24 year olds*.

Harris, J., Springett, J., Croot, L., Booth, A., Campbell, F., Thompson, J., et al. (2015). *Can community-based peer support promote health literacy and reduce inequalities? A realist review.*

Herbert, K., Plugge, E., Foster, C., & Doll, H. (2012). Prevalence of risk factors for non-communicable diseases in prison populations worldwide: A systematic review. *Lancet, 379*, 1975–1982. https://doi.org/10.1016/S0140-6736(12)60319-5.

HM Chief Inspector of Prisons. (2018). *HM Chief Inspector of Prisons for England and Wales Annual Report 2017–18.* HM Inspectorate of Prisons.

House of Commons Justice Committee. (2016). *The treatment of young adults in the criminal justice system (No. Seventh Report of Session 2016–17).* House of Commons.

Independent Monitoring Boards. (2019). *IMB National Annual Report 2017/18.*

Ishikawa, H., & Yano, E. (2011). The relationship of patient participation and diabetes outcomes for patients with high vs. low health literacy. *Patient Education and Counseling, 84*, 393–397.

Institute of Medicine. (2004). *Health Literacy: A Prescription to End Confusion.* Washington: National Academies Press.

Jewkes, Y. (2005). Men behind bars "doing" masculinity as an adaptation to imprisonment. *Men and Masculinities, 8*, 44–63. https://doi.org/10.1177/1097184X03257452.

Jewkes, Y., Moran, D., & Turner, J. (2019). Just add water: Prisons, therapeutic landscapes and healthy blue space. *Criminology and Criminal Justice.* https://doi.org/10.1177/1748895819828800.

King, R., & Wincup, E. (2008). *Doing research on crime and justice.* Oxford University Press.

Klockars, C. B. (1974). Professional researchers and prisoner subjects: Some ethical problems and practical solutions. *Prison Journal, 54*, 34–42. https://doi.org/10.1177/003288557405400204.

Liebling, A., 2004. Prisons and their moral performance: A study of values, quality, and prison life.

Logan, R. A., Wong, W. F., Villaire, M., Gem, D., Parnell, T. A., Willis, E., & Paasche-Orlow, M. K. (2015). *Health literacy: A necessary element for achieving health equity.* National Academy of Medicine.

Marmot, M., Allen, J., Bell, R., Bloomer, E., & Goldblatt, P. (2012). WHO European review of social determinants of health and the health divide. *The Lancet, 380*, 1011–1029. https://doi.org/10.1016/S0140-6736(12)61228-8.

Marshall, T., Simpson, S., & Stevens, A. (2001). Use of health services by prison inmates: Comparisons with the community. *Journal of Epidemiology and Community Health, 55*, 364–365. https://doi.org/10.1136/jech.55.5.364.

Mehay, A., & Meek, R. (2016). The development of a peer-based approach for promoting prisoner health in an English male young offender institution. In *The voluntary sector in prisons: Encouraging institutional and personal change, Palgrave studies in prisons and penology*. Palgrave Macmillan.

Mehay, A., Meek, R., & Ogden, J. (2019). "I try and make my cell a positive place": Tactics for mitigating risks to health and wellbeing in a young offender institution. *Health & Place, 57*, 54–60. https://doi.org/10.1016/j.healthplace.2019.03.012.

Ministry of Justice. (2019). *Population Bulletin: Weekly*, 1 November 2019.

Mogford, E., Gould, L., & Devoght, A. (2010). Teaching critical health literacy as a means to action on the social determinants of health. *Health Promotion International*. https://doi.org/10.1093/heapro/daq049.

Moser, D. J., Arndt, S., Kanz, J. E., Benjamin, M. L., Bayless, J. D., Reese, R. L., et al. (2004). Coercion and informed consent in research involving prisoners. *Comprehensive Psychiatry, 45*, 1–9. https://doi.org/10.1016/j.comppsych.2003.09.009.

Nutbeam, D. (1998). Health promotion glossary. *Health Promotion International*, 349–364.

Nutbeam, D. (2000). Health literacy as a public health goal: A challenge for contemporary health education and communication strategies into the 21st century. *Health Promotion International, 15*, 259–267. https://doi.org/10.1093/heapro/15.3.259.

Nutbeam, D. (2008). The evolving concept of health literacy. *Social Science & Medicine, 1982*(67), 2072–2078. https://doi.org/10.1016/j.socscimed.2008.09.050.

Palumbo, R., & Manna, R. (2018). What if things go wrong in co-producing health services? Exploring the implementation problems of health care co-production. *Policy and Society, 37*, 368–385. https://doi.org/10.1080/14494035.2018.1411872.

Porr, C., Drummond, J., & Richter, S. (2006). Health literacy as an empowerment tool for low-income mothers. *Family & Community Health, 29*, 328–335.

Rogers, E. A., Fine, S., Handley, M. A., Davis, H., Kass, J., & Schillinger, D. (2014). Development and early implementation of the bigger picture, a youth-targeted public health literacy campaign to prevent type 2 diabetes.

Journal of Health Communication, 19(Suppl 2), 144–160. https://doi.org/10.1080/10810730.2014.940476.
Rowe, A. (2015). 'Tactics', agency and power in women's prisons. *British Journal of Criminology*. https://doi.org/10.1093/bjc/azv058.
Schulz, P. J., & Nakamoto, K. (2013). Health literacy and patient empowerment in health communication: The importance of separating conjoined twins. *Patient Education and Counseling, 90*, 4–11. https://doi.org/10.1016/j.pec.2012.09.006.
Senior, J., & Shaw, J. (2007). Prison Healthcare. In Y. Jewkes (Ed.), *Handbook on Prisons* (pp. 377–398). London: Routledge.
Sibley, D., & Van Hoven, B. (2009). The contamination of personal space: Boundary construction in a prison environment. *Area, 41*, 198–206.
Smith, C. (2000). 'Healthy prisons': A contradiction in terms? *The Howard Journal of Criminal Justice, 39*, 339–353. https://doi.org/10.1111/1468-2311.00174.
Smith, S. K., Nutbeam, D., & McCaffery, K. J. (2013). Insights into the concept and measurement of health literacy from a study of shared decision-making in a low literacy population. *Journal of Health Psychology, 18*, 1011–1022. https://doi.org/10.1177/1359105312468192.
Sørensen, K., Pelikan, J. M., Röthlin, F., Ganahl, K., Slonska, Z., Doyle, G., et al. (2015). Health literacy in Europe: Comparative results of the European health literacy survey (HLS-EU). *European Journal of Public Health*. https://doi.org/10.1093/eurpub/ckv043.
Sparks, M. (2009). Acting on the social determinants of health: Health promotion needs to get more political. *Health Promotion International, 24*, 199–202. https://doi.org/10.1093/heapro/dap027.
Sykes, S., Wills, J., Rowlands, G., & Popple, K. (2013). Understanding critical health literacy: A concept analysis. *BMC Public Health, 13*, 150. https://doi.org/10.1186/1471-2458-13-150.
Taggart, J., Williams, A., Dennis, S., Newall, A., Shortus, T., Zwar, N., et al. (2012). A systematic review of interventions in primary care to improve health literacy for chronic disease behavioral risk factors. *BMC Family Practice, 13*, 49. https://doi.org/10.1186/1471-2296-13-49.
von Wagner, C., Steptoe, A., Wolf, M. S., & Wardle, J. (2009). Health literacy and health actions: A review and a framework from health psychology. *Health Education & Behavior, 36*, 860–877. https://doi.org/10.1177/1090198108322819.

WHO. (2007). *Health in prisons: A WHO guide to the essentials in prison health*. WHO Regional Office Europe.

WHO. (2009). *7th global conference on health promotion* [WHO document]. WHO. Retrieved May 1, 2015, from http://www.who.int/healthpromotion/conferences/7gchp/en/.

Wright, N., Bleakley, A., Butt, C., Chadwick, O., Mahmood, K., Patel, K., & Salhi, A. (2013). Peer health promotion in prisons: A systematic review. *International Journal of Prisoner Health*. https://doi.org/10.1108/17449201111256899.

4

Challenges and Practicalities in Adopting Grounded Theory Methodology When Conducting Prison Research

Nasrul Ismail

Introduction

Despite its widespread use as a qualitative methodology in various social science fields over the last five decades (Glaser and Strauss 1967), grounded theory remains under-utilised in prison research. Juxtaposed by a systematic and flexible framework for collecting and analysing data (Charmaz 2006), one of its distinctive characteristics is its inductive approach, which can build intellectual theory. Grounded theory remains a challenging research methodology for researchers. In parallel, qualitative research on prisons has, to date, tended to focus on the lived experiences of the prisoners, or "studying down" the phenomena (Morris 2015). What remains scarce, however, is "studying up", especially the examination of the interactions between actors and institutions, as well as sectoral cultures, in particular when they undergo structural reorganisation.

N. Ismail (✉)
University of the West of England, Bristol, UK
e-mail: Nasrul.Ismail@uwe.ac.uk

© The Author(s) 2021

M. Maycock et al. (eds.), *Issues and Innovations in Prison Health Research*, Palgrave Studies in Prisons and Penology, https://doi.org/10.1007/978-3-030-46401-1_4

Using perspectives from 87 research participants, this chapter seeks to articulate the challenges and practicalities of adopting grounded theory methodology, based on my sole investigation of the impact of macroeconomic austerity on prison health governance in England. It will seek to examine why configuring the appropriate grounded theory typology from the outset will result in a suitable epistemology, ontology and subjective orientation for this research. This methodological justification will be an appropriate guide for the investigation into the foundation of reality and the extent to which the researchers play a proactive role in their research design.

The discussion will subsequently illustrate how the concurrent data collection and analysis phases in grounded theory are both logistically and intellectually intensive. This is an area of discussion which deserves further scholarly attention. From overseeing the synchronous data collection and analysis stages to managing uncertainty and "ghosting" by potential participants, increased clarity regarding these challenges can democratise the use of grounded theory amongst qualitative researchers. The chapter will conclude by highlighting the balance between embracing the fluidity of the methodology and demonstrating sufficient rigour to legitimise the trustworthiness of the research. To warrant the wider utility of these challenges, this chapter articulates good research management skills that can be acquired when adopting grounded theory, whilst inviting the readers to reflect on the lessons learnt for consideration with their own field.

The Research Study

My research project, funded by the Economic and Social Research Council (ESRC), investigates the impact of macroeconomic austerity on prison health governance in England. The entitlement of prisoners towards healthcare and decent living provisions was first recognised by the United Nations Standard Minimum Rules for the Treatment of Prisoners 1957 (the so-called "Nelson Mandela Rules"). Ever since, supportive international legal and policy frameworks, from the United Nations Rules for the Treatment of Women Prisoners and Non-custodial

Measures for Women Offenders 2011 ("The Bangkok Rules") to the most recent, the United Nations' Sustainable Development Goals 2030, have bounded the national prison health framework in the United Kingdom in recognising the capacity of prisons in addressing the health of prisoners, and alongside them, prison staff.

The efficacy of these frameworks, however, has been threatened since May 2010 by the implementation of fiscal austerity. Rooted in the neo-liberal ideology, the state advanced public sector spending reductions as a means of securing deficit reductions in the short-term and maintaining confidence in the country's financial stability in the long-term (Gamble 2015). The state reduced funding for Her Majesty's Prison and Probation Service by 22%, from £3.47 billion in 2010/2011 to £2.71 billion in 2016/2017 (The Institute for Government 2019). The number of front-line prison officers in English and Welsh prisons dropped by around 30% between 2014 and 2017 (European Committee for the Prevention of Torture and Inhuman or Degrading Treatment or Punishment 2017; The Institute for Government 2019). Despite the recent nationwide prison officers' recruitment, figures remain below pre-austerity figures, which is further tempered by constant retention issues (The Institute for Government 2019). The number of prisoners, on the other hand, has remained consistently high at 179 per 100,000, as opposed to the global rate of imprisonment of 144 per 100,000 population (Coyle et al. 2016; House of Commons Library 2019).

Grounded theory positions itself as a suitable methodology for new, emerging phenomena (Charmaz 2006). This methodology is apposite for my investigation because the extant research illustrates the way in which prison health institutions and actors contemplated, mobilised and evaluated the impact of austerity on macro-, meso- and micro-layers of prison health governance in England is notably absent. The preliminary findings of this research, published elsewhere, demonstrated the link between the declining level of resources and the obstruction to prisoners' access to healthcare, the degradation of their living conditions, impediment of their purposeful activities and subjected them to an increasing level of violence (Ismail 2019a, b).

A 13-month research fieldwork was undertaken, intermittently, between January 2018 and September 2019 with 87 prison health professionals, operating in international, national and local governance. At the first fieldwork stage, 29 policymakers from key organisations pertinent to international prison work, such as the United Nations, the World Health Organization and the Council of Europe, in conjunction with other non-governmental organisations such as Amnesty International and the Association for the Prevention of Torture, were invited to provide accounts on the research topic. This preceded the second wave of fieldwork, where 27 national policymakers from governmental (e.g. HM Prison and Probation Service, NHS England and Public Health England) and non-governmental organisations participated in this research. These organisations reflect the broad composition of the prison health landscape in England. Reflecting ground-level experiences, 22 prison governors and officers across 17 prison sites took part in this research. These individuals were from high, medium and low security, as well as resettlement, prisons, from a mixture of public and private sector institutions. In addition, nine representatives from voluntary and private sector organisations which support and deliver prison health agenda across prisons were invited to take part in this research. Overall, the discussions sought to contextualise the findings within the broader debate regarding prison rehabilitation and the ways in which the politics of austerity is shaped at the various levels of prison health governance.

This research has two unique qualities in being a large-scale qualitative research study which is interdisciplinary in nature. It purports to be one of the largest qualitative studies in prison health, with 87 participants from the international, national and local level of governance. Similarly, its interdisciplinarity mandates sophisticated investigations from several disciplinary lenses. Inspired by Denzin and Lincoln (1994, pp. 4–5), researchers should attempt to arbitrate competing and overlapping perspectives to produce bricolage, which is "… a complex, dense, reflexive, collage like creation that represents the researcher's images, understandings, and interpretations of the world or phenomenon under analysis". Viewing the phenomena from the varying standpoints of Public Health, Criminology, Sociology, Economics, Law, Policy and Politics has enabled me to theorise the sense of austerity on prison health from different dimensions in an attempt to generate novel insights.

First Challenge: Aligning Methodology with Philosophical Viewpoints

Embracing grounded theory methodology requires an alignment between the choice of grounded theory typology and the appropriate philosophical viewpoints. Each grounded theory typology is underpinned with a different ontological underpinning of reality (Denzin and Lincoln 2000) and epistemological understanding of a social phenomenon (Lipscomb 2008). Awareness of these typologies is vital in guiding the researchers' paradigm and in influencing the investigation process. My research, specifically, adopts a constructivist grounded theory approach (Charmaz 2006). Considering these epistemological, ontological and subjectivity factors, this choice was fully cognisant, and is underscored with research imperatives and practicalities.

Opting for the right grounded theory typology dictates the level of engagement and preoccupation of the researchers with the participants. From an epistemological standpoint, constructivism asserts that knowledge and meaning about the world are constructed by participants as they engage with the subject (Appleton and King 2002). The relativism of multiple social realities is recognised (Charmaz 2006) wherein informants' experiences, along with the context within which these experiences take place, play a key role in theorising the impact of austerity on prison health governance. Meaning was negotiated and comprehended through my interactions with them during my full immersion in the research process.

Unlike the classical grounded theory approach that dictates a distant, positivistic relationship between the researcher and the participants (Glaser 1978), a constructivist stance encourages a study "with the participants". This provides them with a safe space to engage with the topic, humanises the interactions and avoids tokenistic engagement processes. Through their responses to my first question—"In what way did this study appeal to you?"—informants articulated how the research provided them with a reflective space in critically examining the impact of austerity on the prison health governance that they experienced on a daily basis since 2010.

> Your questions articulate some of the issues that we have all been skirting around. We know that there have been austerity measures and reductions in budget. We know that there have been challenges in prison … We have all been kind of talking about it in a roundabout way, whereas you've gone straight to the question. I think that's just a useful discussion to have. (Participant 20, Public health specialist at an international health organisation)

> … As an academic, [you have] more freedom than we have … so [your research] can add value beyond what we could do within our [regulatory] remits. We comment on the effectiveness and efficiency of delivering services, but [we are] prevented from commenting on the merits of policy objectives … (Participant 49, Investigator for a national regulatory organisation)

> … Your [research] seemed to be quite hard hitting about austerity. It is quite blunt. We are on the receiving end of lots of cuts and pressures because the prison population is rising. It is always good to have people challenging us to look at how we do things … (Participant 61, Governor of a resettlement prison)

These interactions signify a symbiotic relationship between myself and the research participants. Through prolonged one-to-one engagement with each participant, my interaction was heuristic, in which discourses are used to unpack the phenomenon of austerity and how it regulates the parameter of the overall governance of prison health in England.

Simultaneously, rather than positing the view that truth can only be discovered through a posteriori knowledge, the ontological perspective of the constructivist grounded theory acknowledges the existence of multiple realities. Realities, as constructed by the participants, are shaped by intersections of political, cultural and social norms. When the interviewees were asked as to how the increasing level of prison instability has yet to result in substantial funding improvement, they pointed out the fact that those in power were impervious to the mounting evidence.

> I tried to advise [a former Minister] … I had a totally dismissive, rude, cold response. I had been stunned in silence for a while by how uninterested in

> evidence [this Minister was] … I turned to stone like the basilisk in *Harry Potter* and felt really intimidated … I was trying to be polite and helpful and the unspoken message from the cold, disdainful individual, was "bugger off" (Participant 15, Former cabinet office advisor)

> You have the political approach to the world. Then you have the truth … I don't think those things are ever going to align. It is not politically savvy to be telling anybody the truth, frankly. (Participant 36, Head of Health and Justice of a National Health Organisation)

These themes demonstrate the extent to which prison actors framed reality, based on their observations which reflected the reality of austerity over nearly a decade. These observations were riddled with implicit and explicit political values, such as inaction and denial towards the consequences of austerity. By examining variegated responses at every layer of prison health governance, this cross-cutting theme illustrates how power, inequalities, and oppression differentially affect not only prisons but also prison staff.

Next, the different typology of grounded theory dictates the spectrum from the objective to subjective role of the researcher throughout the research. A constructivist grounded theory approach acknowledges the subjective role of the researcher in the process of both co-creating and analysing the research data (Charmaz 2000). This is reinforced via two ways: (1) my professional experiences as a health commissioner prior to entering academia and (2) the prior knowledge of the field generated via an initial literature review exercise.

Constructivist grounded theory celebrates my experiences of the prison health field prior to entering academia. It incorporates me as part of the heuristic journey rather than enforcing *tabula rasa* (i.e. remote observation) and passive theorisation of the social phenomena examined (Birks and Mills 2011). Given that researchers play an active role in unfolding the story and constructing the theory (Charmaz 2006), my background as a former community and prison health commissioner for nearly a decade has safeguarded me against superficial examination of the phenomenon. I am able to draw upon my first-hand witnessing of the phenomenon in multiple prison institutions. As argued by Kools et al.

(1996), it is rare for researchers to abandon their subject or methodological knowledge in order to understand a complex social norm. As such, reality is socially constructed and so cannot be viewed as independent from those who have co-constructed it (Creswell 2007). To guard against the undue imposition of my personal background experiences onto the participants' experiences, I opted for self-reflexivity throughout the process. Writing a reflective journal and taking general field notes provided an audit trail that provided clear documentation relating to the views and various decision points concerning changes to methods throughout the study (Seale 1999; Creswell and Miller 2000). Regular debriefings with the research supervisory team and research collaborators assisted the sense-checking process.

Additionally, I opted for self-disclosure of my background to the participants. At the beginning of each interview, I explained my background and how I came to be investigating this area of work. The disclosure of my insider status, according to Bosworth et al. (2005), was useful in building rapport, balancing the power between myself and the participants, and for gaining their respect and kudos. The research participants did not consider possessing knowledge, experiences and interests in the prison health field unusual. In fact, such an intimate level of familiarity helped instil their confidence in me whilst simultaneously reinforcing my credibility through my knowledge and experiences in the field of prison health.

In its embracing of practicality, constructivist grounded theory encourages the researcher to become acquainted with the extant literature, the aim of which is to augment knowledge prior to entering the field. Conducting a literature review using grounded theory is an area where there is recurrent epistemic struggle. Classical grounded theorists objected to engaging with existing literature prior to commencing data collection (Glaser and Holton 2004). Glaser and Strauss (1967, p. 37) even went as far as arguing that researchers should "literally ignore the literature of theory and fact on the area under study". This stance, however, does not reflect the contemporary reality which researchers are conducting their studies in. Researchers like myself do not exist in a vacuum, meaning that the context surrounding individual perceptiveness and framework thinking cannot be side-lined. My background knowledge reinforces my knowledge, credibility and authority of the ensuing arguments, following Dey's assertion that "... there is a difference between an open mind and an empty head" (1993, p. 65).

Equally, I was also mindful that the extant literature should not limit theorisation. Recognising the criticism that preconceived ideas can impede participants' accounts, efforts were taken to remain open and creative toward concepts that were missing from the initial literature review (Henwood and Pidgeon 2003; Charmaz 2006). This became clear to me following discussions with the participants concerning the recent announcement by the Chancellor of Exchequer that austerity was finally coming to an end (HM Treasury 2019). This theme was not covered in the initial literature review, where this announcement was depicted as mere rhetoric.

> It is a political sound bite ... the increase in NHS funding is still below increase in the level of demand for the NHS (Participant 35, Regional Head of Health and Justice Commissioning of a National Health Organisation)

> ... If austerity is coming to an end, why have we got an increased level of food banks and an increased level of people accessing it? The two do not marry up ... People living on the streets. Homelessness. You only have to walk through any city centre. I have never seen so many people begging living on the streets. So, if austerity is coming to an end why are these people still living on the streets? Why is not there more jobs for the youngsters? (Participant 63, prison officer)

In hearing these unexpected data, I avoided being resistant towards data that do not support certain theories. Doing so guarded myself from acting in a self-fulfilling prophetic manner (Thornberg and Dunne 2019). At the same time, it also demonstrated empathy and sensitivity towards the participants' disclosure.

Finally, in keeping with the theme of practicality, research gatekeepers often impose the requirement of undertaking a prior literature review. When obtaining the funding for my research, I was required to demonstrate how my research was in line with the Economic and Social Research

Council (ESRC) priority research areas whilst simultaneously positioning my research proposal as being original and authentic. Beyond understanding the fundamentals of relevant works and identifying significant findings and connections between the research and earlier studies, research collaborators also needed to be convinced of "what is in it for them" and to know how the outputs from this research could support their strategic and operational desires. Undertaking a literature review meant that I was able to articulate the potential academic originality, theoretical advancement and conceptual contributions to these gatekeepers. This was an advantage in that I was aware of the suitable grounded theory paradigm that would suit the inquiry path.

In summary, this section advocates embracing appropriate grounded theory methodology in dictating epistemological, ontological and subjectivity perspectives of the research. Embracing constructivism enabled me to immerse myself within the phenomena, to co-construct the reality of austerity that is laden with prevailing political, sectoral and institutional norms with the research participants, and encouraged me to play an active role throughout the data collection and analysis process. Furthermore, it is a typology that is imbued with practicality, thereby allowing me to use my prior knowledge of the field to my advantage, which I gained through professional and academic settings.

Second Challenge: Intellectual and Logistical Demands

Whilst intellectually stimulating, grounded theory methodology demands both logistical and intellectual labour. This section provides insights into the challenges that are prevalent during the data collection and analysis stage. Considering the interdisciplinarity and scale of investigations into the governance strata of prison health in England, the sample size was, inevitably, large. Figure 4.1 below demonstrates the number of participants who were contacted and participated during the three phases of this research, alongside the attrition rate. Out of 246 potential participants approached, 87 (35%) agreed to take part. In order to minimise the

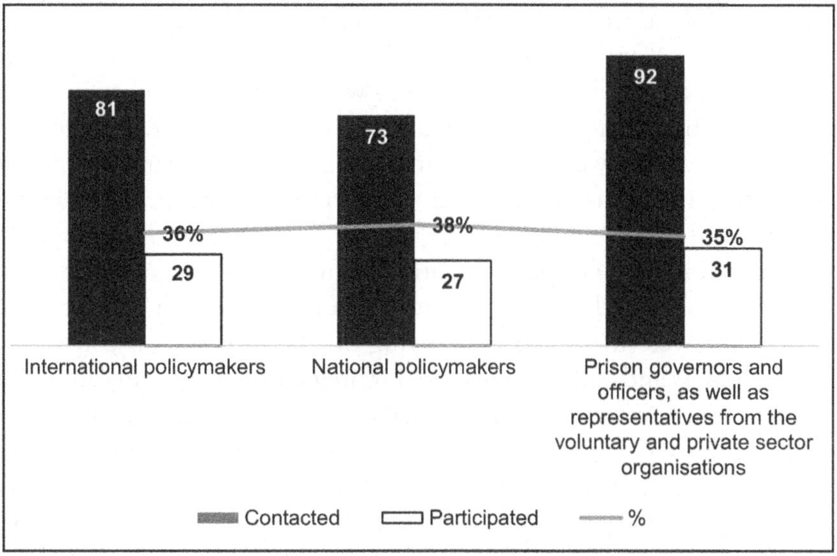

Fig. 4.1 Number of participants who were contacted and participated in the research

uncertainty around non-participation, I had to draw upon a large group of potential participants.

There were three phases to the recruitment of professionals: purposive, theoretical and snowball. In so doing, I sought "… individuals where the processes of being studied are most likely to occur" (Denzin and Lincoln 1994, p. 202). This stage was preceded by theoretical sampling, a stage which required considerable intellectual labour in that I had to be alert to the emerging nuances in the data, which obliged me to think creatively as to how I could obtain the views of those who might either support or challenge my tentative findings. Theoretical sampling was implemented when, following a preliminary data analysis, certain data categories became saturated and participants introduced new concepts (Milliken and Northcott 2003). Similarly, this strategy was adopted to explore new concepts which were not introduced through the initial literature review. For instance, there was the emerging issue of how closed, medium-sized prisons were perceived to be more heavily impacted by austerity in comparison to high-security or open prisons. Furthermore, the discovery that

Brexit (a euphemism of Britain leaving the European Union) was a cause of distraction from discussions about austerity with the government prompted me to seek participants who would provide a more in-depth account of this phenomenon. Pursuing these emerging avenues required me to multitask between undertaking data analysis and pursuing potential participants who could either support or challenge the emerging account.

Finally, snowball sampling, as utilised during the participant recruitment process, placed demands on my resourcefulness and social capital. Participants were identified by drawing on the professional contacts of the researchers and collaborators, predominantly to avoid cold canvassing (Patton 2002). At times, research collaborators introduced me directly to the potential participants. Moreover, at the end of each interview, the participants were speculatively asked: "Who else should I talk to about this research?" This allowed me to penetrate the participants' network (MacDougall and Fudge 2001). In order to get this support, I tried to create a good impression with my participants during the data collection process. Equally, I was mindful of my demeanour and how I came across with the collaborators, i.e. whether I could be trusted with their network and represent their views. Overall, relying on the network of collaborators and participants indubitably made the logistical process more manageable.

Additionally, I had to overcome the logistical barrier of "ghosting" by potential participants. This occurred when those who were approached did not reply, even when I approached them repeatedly. This complicated the data collection and analysis process. For each research phase, participants who did not respond to the initial invitation were chased every two weeks until the completion date of the interview wave was reached. A maximum of seven chase emails were sent to each potential participant. In my research, the ghosting issue was especially prevalent among regulatory and voluntary sector organisations. Debriefing sessions were held with research collaborators, who provided valuable insights into the ghosting act. Reasons given included the potential perception of my work as competing against their workstreams and institutional agendas, concern that speaking out would put their funding position in jeopardy, institutional secrecy and competing priorities and resources. To mitigate these issues, good research management skills were adopted. These included: being resilient and facing challenges as and when they surfaced, exploring alternatives and maintaining a balance between persistence and perseverance whilst being polite and courteous throughout the engagement.

Overall, the data collection phase of grounded theory methodology can be both logistical and intellectually demanding. It requires researchers to be both resilient and perseverant. Uncertainty and rejection from potential participants has to be anticipated, whilst the interplay between data collection and analysis can challenge the researchers to think creatively as to obtaining additional views which may either confirm or disconfirm the findings. Moreover, to gain deeper access to the collaborators' and participants' networks, it was crucial to create a lasting positive impression to these gatekeepers. Finally, to overcome the act of "ghosting" by the potential participants, being persistent whilst remaining polite and courteous, as well as exploring suitable alternatives, was vital. Being aware and sensitive towards these fieldwork challenges can ensure that the researchers minimise the risks and can prevent the research from being stifled by external factors, and thereby take control of their research trajectory.

Third Challenge: Being Flexible Whilst Demonstrating Rigour

The final challenge in adopting grounded theory methodology is the ability to strike a balance between embracing the messiness of the process and demonstrating sufficient rigour. Some academics caution that the fluidity and incoherence inherent within grounded theory do not necessarily provide a guaranteed level of certainty in scrutinising data. On the one hand, Skodol-Wilson and Ambler-Hutchinson (1996) describe how researchers are prone to methodological slurring, whereby they take advantage of the flexibility to either combine grounded theory versions or to adopt methods outside of the methodology altogether. On the other hand, Pulla (2016) posits that grounded theory offers scant guidance, and therefore cautions novice researchers from adopting it. To regulate against the perceived flexibility of the grounded theory analytical process, I resorted to operationalising constant comparative methods as well as devising a new concept of the fourth data order as part of the coding phase, and deploying a data saturation strategy.

Constant Comparative Method

Using a constant comparative method enabled me to identify patterns and compare tacit meanings amongst the codes. Bowen (2008, p. 139) indicates that "the constant comparative method serves to test concepts and themes with a view to producing a theory grounded in the data". Aided by NVivo 12 software, this method denotes the going back and forth between different levels of data abstraction. At each phase, data were inspected thoroughly. Following this, relationships between the emerging categories was identified. At the same time, using the constant comparison method enabled me to remain flexible during the data analysis process, especially when encountering data that did not fit the theory. Charmaz (2008, p. 168) encourages researchers to "learn to tolerate ambiguity [and] become receptive to creating emergent categories and strategies". I made sense of the inconsistencies in the data by situating them into the bigger context of the research as I searched to discover the most plausible reason which fitted my theory.

Fourth Data Order

From the outset, condensing the data from 87 interviews and devising cross-cutting theories across all samples appeared to be an insurmountable task. I was conscious that the large sample size might prove too vast to fully realise any theories which could provide a thorough coverage of the key issues under study. Following open, focused and axial coding stages with different participant groups, I introduced a new analysis stage. I coined this "The Fourth Order", and during this phase all axial categories from different interview phases underwent a further deductive and synthesis process in order to form a central research thesis. Devising this central thesis involved refining the tacit meaning to ensure that the categories explicate all properties and are faithful towards their axial essence, which funnels towards a central thesis. The central thesis is subsequently realised when all major themes from the interviews with international and national policymakers, as well as those who work on the ground, are covered by these categories.

Data Saturation

When approaching the analysis endpoint, I adopted a data saturation strategy—a hallmark of grounded theory—which reflected the fact that no new themes appeared in the interviews. The concerns of some academics towards data saturation stems from the perception that this point could never be achieved in real research. Marshall (1996, p. 523), for example, was concerned that "… an iterative, cyclical approach to sampling, data collection, analysis and interpretation makes predicting sample size in advance difficult". To date, guidance on how to achieve data saturation has been vague. Kvale (2007, p. 43) advised that researchers should interview "… as many subjects as necessary to find out what you need to know", whilst others went as far as suggesting the "magic number" of the sample size, for instance, a variation between 20 and 30 participants (Polit and Beck 2012; Creswell 2013).

In my research, saturation occurred at 29 interviews with the international participants, 27 interviews with the national participants, and 31 interviews with the institutional participants. This data saturation was achieved by continuing to code through the entire data set, returning to what seemed to be the most divergent stories within the sample. In so doing, I searched for deviant cases where the theory did not fit, and also looked at contextual and intrapersonal influences that the model did not address (Charmaz 2006). To achieve this, I drew upon the following five-dimension taxonomy (Morse et al. 2009; Aldiabat and Le Navenec 2018):

- The scope of the investigation: The scope of my research cuts across many disciplines, alongside the experiences of participants who occupy institutions, sectors and geographical areas. This dictated that I should spend more time interviewing and making sense of the theories which emerged from the fieldwork. The gathering of data must continue until saturation occurred in the data analysis.

- Heterogeneity of the sampling strategy: The heterogeneous sample—predicated by the interdisciplinarity of the research—means that data saturation cannot be achieved by a small number of interviews. In this regard, 87 participants helped foster data saturation to reflect the experiences of the interviewees at all layers of prison health governance.
- Theoretical sampling: Theoretical sampling helped achieve data saturation by connecting the categories together to form an emergent theory (Glaser and Strauss 1967). It directed me to inspect the data and, subsequently, focus further data collection on the emerging theories from the initial interviews. Using this strategy was beneficial for determining the sampling size. The constant comparative method and theoretical sampling were used to investigate the data to ensure that "there was no stone left unturned" (Morse et al. 2009).
- Triangulation of sample: Aldiabat and Le Navenec (2018) suggested that triangulation should be applied to the sample selection. Applying this premise, data saturation was achieved via snowballing sampling. At the end of the interview, I asked for recommendations for additional potential participants for the research. At this juncture, I devised a new concept called "participant saturation" which refers to the fact that researchers have been given recommendations of some names, and that those names were already approached for interviews. Discussions with each participant, as well as research collaborators tended to confirm that all key stakeholders had been approached for interviews, and that the majority had agreed to participate in this research. Once such a saturation has been achieved, it is futile to interview additional stakeholders for the research.
- Experience of the researcher: Given that the researcher is the instrument for data collection, researchers need to use subjectivity and intuition so as to determine data saturation. My previous research experience helped me to judge whether data saturation had been achieved. Regular discussions with supervisors and research collabora-

tors also helped the sense-checking of the thesis' data analysis section in order to demonstrate data saturation.

Whilst the non-overt procedures of grounded theory afford researchers some room to manoeuvre, it is possible to guard against the fluidity of the methodology by using measures such as constant comparison, fourth data order, and data saturation. Although these tools should not be used with mathematical precision, analytical tools during and post analysis are at the researchers' disposal to ensure that the process remains systematic, rigorous, transparent and reflexive.

Conclusion

In operationalising my research into the impact of economic austerity with 87 prison health governance actors in England, this chapter has critically examined the challenges and practicalities in embracing grounded theory methodology in large-scale, interdisciplinary prison health research. Firstly, it underscores the importance of embracing the appropriate grounded theory typology that will orientate the epistemological, ontological and subjectivity orientations of the research. Secondly, encompassing constructivism in my research has permitted me to be pro-active in the data collection and analysis process whilst simultaneously being able to use my professional background and prior knowledge to gain credibility and enhance my access within the field. Conducting grounded theory research also compounded my ability to tolerate the ambiguity which is presented by the contemporaneous data collection and analysis processes, as well as dealing with rejection and ghosting by potential research participants.

Finally, grounded theory researchers must be able to endure cognitive dissonance and the overtly incoherent process presented by the back-and-forth nature of the data analysis phase. Whilst avoiding a rigidly structured framework, in a world that is driven by credibility, rigour and transparency, the principles of constant comparison, the newly devised fourth data order and data saturation frameworks are valuable research compasses for thesis production and peer-reviewed publications and, in time, for Research Excellence Framework (REF) submissions.

Despite its idiosyncrasies, grounded theory reinforces and develops researchers' soft skills. Being resilient, persistent, persevere, patient, consensus-focused, conciliatory, creative and reflective throughout the life course of the project will ensure that challenges do not halt the fieldwork project. The theories, behaviour, experiences and context emerging from this research are modifiable and transferable across social science disciplines beyond the field of prison research, and go further than the spatial and temporal frontier. Grounded theory can be perceived as a seemingly challenging methodology. It is, however, underutilised, and its intuitiveness should appeal to the interests of qualitative prison researchers, especially those who are interested in examining the dynamics between actors, institutions and sectoral cultures in the prison sector.

References

Aldiabat, K. M., & Le Navenec, C. (2018). Data saturation: The mysterious step in grounded theory method. *The Qualitative Report, 23*(1), 245–261.

Appleton, J. V., & King, L. (2002). Journeying from the philosophical contemplation of constructivism to the methodological pragmatics of health services research. *Journal of Advanced Nursing, 40*, 641–648.

Birks, M., & Mills, J. (2011). *Grounded theory: A practical guide*. Los Angeles: SAGE.

Bosworth, M., Campbell, D., Demby, B., et al. (2005). Doing prison research: Views from inside. *Qualitative Inquiry, 11*(2), 249–264.

Bowen, G. A. (2008). Naturalistic inquiry and the saturation concept: A research note. *Qualitative Research, 8*(1), 137–152.

Charmaz, K. (2000). Grounded theory: Objectivist and constructivist methods. In N. K. Denzin & Y. S. Lincoln (Eds.), *Handbook of qualitative research* (2nd ed., pp. 509–535). Los Angeles: SAGE.

Charmaz, C. (2006). *Constructing grounded theory: A practical guide through qualitative analysis*. London: SAGE.

Charmaz, K. (2008). Constructionism and the grounded theory method. In J. A. Holstein & J. F. Gubrium (Eds.), *Handbook of constructionist research* (pp. 397–412). New York: Guilford Press.

Coyle, A., Fair, H., Jacobson, J., et al. (2016). *Imprisonment worldwide: The current situation and an alternative future*. Bristol: Policy Press.

Creswell, J. (2007). *Qualitative inquiry and research design: Choosing among five approaches*. London: SAGE.

Creswell, J. (2013). *Qualitative Inquiry and Research Design: Choosing among Five Approaches*. Los Angeles: SAGE.

Creswell, J. W., & Miller, D. L. (2000). Determining validity in qualitative inquiry. *Theory Into Practice, 39*, 124–130.

Denzin, N. K., & Lincoln, Y. S. (1994). *Handbook of qualitative research*. London: SAGE.

Denzin, N. K., & Lincoln, Y. S. (2000). *Handbook of qualitative research*. Los Angeles: SAGE.

Dey, I. (1993). *Qualitative data analysis: A user-friendly guide for social scientists*. London: Routledge.

European Committee for the Prevention of Torture and Inhuman or Degrading Treatment or Punishment. (2017). *Report to the government of the United Kingdom on the visit to the United Kingdom carried out by the European Committee for the prevention of torture and inhuman or degrading treatment or punishment from 30 March to 12 April 2016*. Retrieved December 1 2019, from https://rm.coe.int/168070a773.

Gamble, A. (2015). Austerity as statecraft. *Parliamentary Affairs, 68*(1), 42–57. https://doi.org/10.1093/pa/gsu016.

Glaser, B. (1978). *Theoretical sensitivity: Advances in the methodology of grounded theory*. Los Angeles: SAGE.

Glaser, B., & Holton, J. (2004). *Remodelling grounded theory*. Forum Qualitative Sozialforschung/Forum: Qualitative Social Research. Retrieved December 1, 2019, from http://www.qualitative-research.net/index.php/fqs/article/view/607.

Glaser, B. G., & Strauss, A. L. (1967). *The discovery of grounded theory: Strategies for qualitative research*. Chicago: Aldine Publishing.

Henwood, K., & Pidgeon, N. (2003). Grounded theory in psychological research. In P. M. Camic, J. E. Rhodes, & L. Yardley (Eds.), *Qualitative research in psychology: Expanding perspectives in methodology and design* (pp. 131–155). Washington, DC: American Psychological Association.

HM Treasury. (2019). *Spending round 2019: Chancellor Sajid Javid's speech*. Retrieved December 1, 2019, from https://www.gov.uk/government/speeches/spending-round-2019-sajid-javids-speech.

House of Commons Library. (2019). *Briefing paper number CBP-04334, 23 July 2019: UK prison population statistics*. Retrieved December 1, 2019, from http://researchbriefings.files.parliament.uk/documents/SN04334/SN04334.pdf.

Ismail, N. (2019a). Contextualising the pervasive impact of macroeconomic austerity on prison health in England: A qualitative study among international policymakers. *BMC Public Health, 1043*. https://doi.org/10.1186/s12889-019-7396-7.

Ismail, N. (2019b). Rolling back the prison estate: The pervasive impact of macroeconomic austerity on prisoner health in England. *Journal of Public Health (Oxford)*, fdz058. https://doi.org/10.1093/pubmed/fdz058.

Kools, S., McCarthy, M., Durham, R., et al. (1996). Dimensional analysis: Broadening the conception of grounded theory. *Qualitative Health Research, 6*(3), 312–330.

Kvale, S. (2007). *Doing Interviews*. London: Sage.

Lipscomb, M. (2008). Mixed method nursing studies: A critical realist critique. *Nursing Philosophy, 9*, 32–45.

MacDougall, C., & Fudge, E. (2001). Planning and recruiting the sample for focus groups and in-depth interviews. *Qualitative Health Research, 11*(1), 117–126.

Marshall, M. N. (1996). Sampling for qualitative research. *Family Practice, 13*, 522–525.

Milliken, P. J., & Northcott, H. C. (2003). Redefining parental identity: Caregiving and schizophrenia. *Qualitative Health Research, 13*(1), 100–113.

Morris, A. (2015). *The scholar denied: W.E.B. Du Bois and the birth of modern sociology*. Los Angeles: University of California Press.

Morse, J. M., Stern, P. N., Corbin, J., et al. (2009). *Developing grounded theory: The second generation*. Los Angeles: Left Coast Press.

Patton, M. Q. (2002). *Qualitative research and evaluation methods* (3rd ed.). Los Angeles: SAGE.

Polit, D. F., & Beck, C. T. (2012). *Nursing research: Principles and methods*. Philadelphia: Lippincott Williams & Wilkins.

Pulla, V. (2016). An introduction to the grounded theory approach in social research. *International Journal of Social Work and Human Services Practice, 4*(4), 75–81.

Seale, C. (1999). Quality in qualitative research. *Qualitative Inquiry, 5*, 465–478.

Skodol-Wilson, H., & Ambler-Hutchinson, S. (1996). Methodological mistakes in grounded theory. *Nursing Research, 45*(2), 122–124.

The Institute for Government. (2019). *Performance tracker 2019: Prisons*. Retrieved December 1, 2019, from https://www.instituteforgovernment.org.uk/publication/performance-tracker-2019/prisons.

Thornberg, R., & Dunne, C. (2019). Literature review in grounded theory. In A. Bryant & K. Charmaz (Eds.), *The SAGE handbook of current developments in grounded theory* (pp. 206–221). London: SAGE.

5

The Research Experience from an Insider Perspective

David Honeywell

Introduction

As a former prisoner interviewing other former prisoners, I already had strong links with my participants because of our shared lived experiences and it soon became clear that as a consequence of my insider experience they were willing to be more open with me than a researcher with limited experience of the custodial environment. Several admitted that had I not been a former prisoner they would not have even taken part in the study and some told me they felt they could be more open because they knew I would understand where they were coming from. In terms of gathering rich data, this was invaluable, but it also meant that revealing some of their deepest, most traumatic personal experiences would begin to affect my own emotions. From the outset I began to realise how much I had underestimated the affects face-to-face interviews could have on me.

D. Honeywell (✉)
The University of Manchester, Manchester, UK
e-mail: David.honeywell@manchester.ac.uk

© The Author(s) 2021

M. Maycock et al. (eds.), *Issues and Innovations in Prison Health Research*, Palgrave Studies in Prisons and Penology, https://doi.org/10.1007/978-3-030-46401-1_5

Because their lives were so similar to my own, each story opened up old wounds for both the participants and me, but there is a need for researchers to be open about the impact their research has on their own sense of selves. Jewkes (2011) writes that many researchers have kept such personal feelings hidden for many years through fear of their findings being seen as somehow invalid. However, as someone who has always been very open with my innermost feelings I find no shame or feelings of restriction about being completely open about the impact my research had on my own sense of self. Nor do I conform to the expectations within some academic schools of thought that personal narrative is somehow not scientific enough. Lois Presser (2009) developed the concept of narrative criminology with her article *The Narratives of Offenders*, which has since received international attention and is now central to the Nordic Research Network (see Presser and Sandberg 2015).

This is in part because I feel my own life experiences as an ex-prisoner/offender and others with the same lived experiences offers an invaluable insight, but also because throughout my PhD I was continually frustrated by the constraints on personal narrative born from traditional sociological positivist expectations. This resonates with the anthropological narrative such as that of Amy Pollard in her article, 'Field of Screams' (2009) in which she draws from her own experiences as an anthropology PhD student. She interviews 16 anthropology PhD students who report the emotional impact of their study during and after their PhD studies. Anecdotal evidence also suggests that individuals continue to experience emotional turmoil long after the fieldwork and PhD has been completed. Therefore, the tensions and emotions that are felt within a research study are long lasting, but for the researcher who shares the same traumatic, social and cultural lived experiences as their participants, these emotions can become overbearing and penetrate deep into the psyche to the extent of evoking trauma as the researcher is forced to relive their past experiences (Honeywell 2018).

Because of this lack of acknowledgement towards the researchers own positionality, I was unprepared following my interviews where I struggled for many weeks afterwards, unable to analyse the transcripts, and though this may have been a traumatic time for us all, sharing our experiences with one another had been an important process. Dan McAdams (1993,

2006), who uses biographical research method in psychology, argues that sometimes the tragic narrative is as important as the positive narrative. More recently, Nugent and Schinkel (2016) has highlighted the importance of understanding the more painful experience of desistance and it is from this premise that I write this chapter as, despite the negativity of the narrative in this chapter, I learned a great deal from them. And although I had not prepared myself for what would become a very traumatic period of soul searching and emotional struggle during the research process, it was a period of enlightenment. In hindsight it seems obvious that if a researcher conducts a qualitative study with individuals who have shared lived experiences, they will encounter difficult emotions, but I was not prepared for the intensity of these emotions and the impact they would have on my own sense of self. But my own story in this chapter is implicit as my aim in this chapter is to give you a glimpse into the lives of some of the people I interviewed, including the challenges they faced and the traumas they recounted, and although I do not refer to my own painful experiences specifically, they are always present within every word of each narrative. Therefore, in a way readers will be able to gauge an understanding about the impact these interviews had on my own sense of self through reading the participant's narratives.

Method

The study of ex-prisoner's transformations through education to which I refer to in the introduction is derived from my PhD study for which I interviewed 13 male and 11 female participants. Some of the participants were undergraduates, postgraduates, lecturers and/or researchers. They were initially contacted through prisoner charities and organisations such as The Prisoners Education Trust, The Howard League of Penal Reform, Clinks, The Lord Longford Trust and The Convict Criminology Organisation. Each of these have their own databases of members which can give a rich source of participants that represent the sample population and is a very effective way of generating a sample frame—particularly for 'hard to reach' populations such ex-prisoners (Faugier and Sargeant 1997). Using these organisations enabled a sample frame to be generated because the criteria of the intended sample is not identified through official statistics or administration records, for example the prison population or those on probation. In addition, I used a snowball sampling approach because as Browne (2005) explains: 'Snowball sampling is often used because the population under investigation is "hidden" either due to low numbers of potential participants or the sensitivity of the topic' (p. 47).

I conducted 24 face-to-face, semi-structured interviews which allowed free-flowing conversations. My approach was from a symbolic interactionist position whereby individuals behaviours can be described through language and symbols. Within desistance theory Giordano et al. (2002) use this approach drawing on a cognitive theory to gain a real insight into the complex factors of identity transformation. The overall approach to data collection was driven by a desire to hear the lived experiences of other ex-prisoners who had followed the same pathway I did. Therefore, my emphasis was on listening to the stories that the participants were telling me. The use of narrative interviews and discussion groups ensured that people had the opportunity to be heard but care was needed because of the vulnerability of some of the participants.

In terms of the methodologies for this study, the ontology relates to how the participants exist in the world (both inside and outside of prison) and how this is analysed through their narratives and speech. The interpretative approach was the most appropriate epistemological approach because of the emphasis on theories of the self and the participants own interpretative process throughout their journeys. The 'insider' researcher positionality I occupied in this research provided me with a strong basis whereby experience informs theoretical approaches towards the understanding of human interactions and personal experience. The views and interpretations of the insider is inevitably affected by the experiences, knowledge and understanding derived from years of living with, and among, criminals and inmates (Jones et al. 2009). This is an important point because an ex-prisoner's insight of imprisonment, stigma, labelling, the desistance process and the transformation of self is developed through experience and therefore 'there's a risk of their perceptions being unintentionally biased' (Cullen 2003, cited in Jones et al. 2009). It was essential to be mindful of the possibility of bias through continual self-reflection and understanding of its potential pitfalls. Yet while these challenges exist, the methodology and methods adopted for this study were the most suitable approach, given my specific positionality in relation to the study.

My Positionality

My desire to conduct this study stemmed from my own position as a former prisoner turned academic. During my early transformative years, I fully understood that moving away from crime was not an issue but changing my lifestyle and identity was essential. I had many unanswered questions such as why after spending five years at university and gaining two degrees, I was still stigmatised and rejected by potential employers. I felt that I must be the only person in existence who was in this position until I discovered the Convict Criminology Organisation, which consists of ex-prisoners turned academics. Their achievements gave me a renewed inspiration which had been damaged through the obstacles I encountered. I also learned through my study that my participants had encountered the same frustrations.

> ***Carla***: *Even though I've not had another conviction for years—I've done a master's, I've done a under-graduate degree—but still they will focus on that (criminal conviction) at your (job) interview.*

Carla was born a generation earlier than me and yet was still experiencing what I had 20 years earlier. On reflection, as a convict criminologist, I now know that my own lived experiences influenced the focus of this study. But as Crooks (2001) explains, her insider position was an advantage because it gave her insight into what questions she needed to ask. Most importantly, how to ask them and how to probe leads as far as the participants were able to take them. Also, contrary to Liem and Richardson's (2014) claim that there are limitations on the validity of data in studies that rely on ex-prisoner's accounts, the ability for ex-prisoners to develop and maintain social relationships is an advantage when ex-prisoners study ex-prisoners (Crooks 2001; see also Farrall 2005). Liam & Richardson were not being critical but rather explaining:

> … studies that have emphasised transformation narratives rely upon qualitative data and take for granted what respondents say about their desistance as being an accurate representation of what has happened, or as something that they hope will happen (see also Cid and Marti 2012; Stevens 2012). This is not to say, as Farrall and Bowling (1999) pointed out, that respondents are actively lying, but rather that they may attempt to make sense of their lives with rationality and intent during the interview. Desistance can only truly be determined retrospectively, after significant crime-free periods. (Bottoms et al. 2004) (as cited in Liem and Richardson 2014, pp. 696–697)

This process of exploration is not passive but reciprocal in that both researcher and participant are transformed (Honeywell 2018). My insider researcher position gives further insight into generating research themes and interpreting the lived realities of ex-prisoners; though I was aware that my positionality may bias some of the research and therefore it was necessary for me to maintain objectivity as much as I could (and as far as this is possible). This was mainly because my study was towards a PhD which required an objective approach where I was expected to demonstrate a third-person narrative rather than a first-person narrative. But there is a strong argument for a process of immersing oneself in a study whereby the researcher shares their lived experience with their participants, and as Crooks (2001) had, I was able to maintain objectivity through continual reflection. This was done by steering the interviews towards the scheduled topics, if I felt the conversation was diverting too much while at the same time I was aware that it was essential to allow a free flow of conversation to continue. The participant's speech and narratives are at the heart of this approach and throughout the interviews, it was clear that participants were in the process of re-negotiating their sense of selves and identities. In his prison ethnography study, Davies (2015) disclosed his ex-prisoner status from the outset which enabled him and his interviewees to formulate a mutual trust and rapport. He argues that had he not done so, his study may have been less productive and taken much longer:

> I argue that my ideas, meanings and understandings were greatly facilitated by utilising my personal history of being an ex-prisoner, which enabled me to build up a rapport with the individual respondents through reciprocal information sharing of personal experiences. (Davies 2015, p. 463)

I too found that using my personal history built a rapport that enabled a sharing of reciprocal information. Some of my participants were already aware of my past which, as mentioned earlier, led to their decision to take part in the study. And as mentioned above, the rapport that developed between me and the participants became an essential tool for analysis because of how they used our rapport to negotiate their identities. However, it was difficult to write myself into the narrative which became confusing because of where to position myself, either in the first person or the third person.

The Painful Narrative

As stated previously in the introduction, analysing the painful narrative is as essential as analysing the positive narrative within desistance, furthering an understanding of the psychosocial transitions. The participants had to overcome continual barriers and obstacles that may have and do prevent others from continuing with their goals but it was through the more difficult experiences that they developed an unwavering resilience. From the start of their desistance journeys, some have overcome the pains of imprisonment (Sykes 1958) through a desire to change and develop new identities and resilience. With this in mind, it could therefore be argued that for some (although painful), experiencing anxieties and anguish was as important for their transformation of self as their positive experiences because these painful experiences led to catalysts for change (McAdams 2006), while for others they merely added to their already existing feelings of anguish and anxiety.

Judy, 41, a white, middle-class, heterosexual female had spent time remanded in custody, had served a three-month prison sentence and spent time on probation for shop lifting. Here she draws on painful memories to explain how she has transformed her 'self.' Judy's narrative was very emotional and somewhat melancholic as she continued to talk about her life experiences. However, it became clear that drawing on both her traumatic as well as positive experiences was essential in demonstrating how both had been important towards her transformation of self:

> **Judy**: There was one occasion when a woman walked up to me, and I was sat at a bus stop miserable and the woman walked up to me and said are you homeless. I said yes and she pulled a tenner out of her purse and gave it to me. So, there's things like that—but overall a very shit experience.
> **DH**: I can tell that because you're getting quite teary eyed.
> **Judy**: Yes ... I got a job in a homeless charity in London and I've been here ever since.

Judy is very emotional when she recalls her encounter with a member of the public who handed her a ten-pound note. This gesture of kindness would impact on Judy's sense of self so much that she is able to recall it many years later but not just as something that impacted on her emotionally, also as something that strengthened her resilience which she later extended through her work with vulnerable homeless people. Resilience is not inherent but rather involves behaviours, thoughts and actions that can be learned and developed in anyone but strengthened through social bonds and the support from others (McNeill 2016). Reliving their pasts through the interview process was a painful process for the participants because they do visit painful narratives while explaining their journeys. Yet their narratives suggest how important they view their painful experiences as well as their positive experiences, which further presents a diversity of crises as discussed previously. The idea that painful experiences are a useful life lesson in relation to the desistance theory is found within Maruna's (2001) redemptive script, whereby individuals see themselves as 'wounded healers' (p. 102). For example, Judy's employment is relevant to her own painful experiences of being homeless and though her narrative is linked to 'giving back' (Maruna 2001), it focusses on the more tragic times in her life. Judy recalled quite emotionally an encounter when she was homeless and a stranger's kind gesture that has stayed with her ever since. She still finds her life experiences difficult to talk about but clearly feels the need to relive her pain as much as her happier times, which are balanced with accepting or even embracing the pains we suffer (McAdams 2006). Judy's narrative of painful experiences provides us with some insight into how she develops resilience through her determination to leave her environment and prove to others her academic capabilities:

> **Judy**: I went to see someone in the [prison] education wing there and asked her about colleges because I had the idea in my head that I had to get out of Blackpool. Nothing was going to change unless I got out of Blackpool. She gave me some information about them, but then I got out, carried on as before (homeless and using drugs).

Here Judy recalls how the prison environment gave her a sense of stability and structure, which offers an additional insight into how release from prison can create isolation for desisters within society. She was keen to start a course of education but was then released from prison after which she regressed to her previous existence, living on the streets and using drugs. However, she had the opportunity to transform her life through education again when she was returned to prison and regained the structure that she felt had supported her when she was previously in prison. Nugent and Schinkel's (2016) pains of desistance study can explain what is actually happening to Judy's sense of self through their use of the term 'displacement'. In other words, as Judy begins to make a new life for herself and leave her associates and family behind in Blackpool, she feels isolated once leaving prison. This is one of the more distinctive pains of desistance whereby despite the need to leave negative things in one's life behind, it still leaves a feeling of emptiness. Nugent and Schinkel argue that their participant's 'new-found introversion' caused by alienating oneself also meant that they did not recognize themselves, and that they had lost their sense of self and personal identity (p. 572). For almost all, there was a sense of displacement, a sense that they were living a life with which they were unfamiliar. This helps to explain what is happening to Judy's sense of self where through her attempts to improve her life chances she leaves her old life behind, but in doing so also becomes displaced and loses her sense of self.

This also happened to Dylan but from a completely unexpected source. Dylan, 27, was a white, working class, heterosexual male who served prison time for drug dealing and violence. He came from a family who were involved in criminality and had a difficult start at university after disclosing his past during a seminar. Therefore, he had already had a difficult start in life which had been influenced by his family's criminal lifestyle, but it was a lifestyle he was accustomed to; however, he tried to escape it by going to university. He had a difficult start at university when he was ostracised by his fellow students after he disclosed his past during a seminar, but did eventually graduate with a degree in criminology and has continued to postgraduate study. He draws heavily on his pains of desistance when he recounts the moment his fellow students began to disassociate from him:

> **Dylan**: I declared I was an ex-offender. Leading up to this I was constantly spoken to by the rest of the course. Invited for cups of coffee. Then as soon as I declared that I was an ex-offender, I was instantly pushed to one side by the rest of the course. It must have got out to the seminar and on the rest of the course. I stopped getting asked to go for cups of coffee. I stopped getting messages on Facebook from my fellow students and also, I was in lectures and they had obviously been 'Googling' my former crimes and laughing about it behind my back, whilst I was in lectures. I felt like that kid in school again. It really affected my confidence. The lecturers here have been absolutely brilliant. So, so supportive. I ended getting really depressed about it and had to repeat the first year. I just didn't say. I didn't want to make a fuss. Well I did say something actually, but I told them to get it off my chest. I've learnt now that it's good to talk about things isn't it, rather than bottle it up.

Being shunned and outcast by his former friends was the last thing Dylan had expected, and talking about his experiences at university, he recounts the impact these negative experiences had on his sense of self. Dylan was in a difficult predicament when he was excluded by his peers which forced him to make the decision to re-take his first year at university, yet through this anxiety and anguish and a strengthening of resilience, he still managed to achieve his degree.

Dylan is clearly passionate about his roots, and in an attempt to defend his 'own people' it backfired. His sense of self and personal identity was lost through this disconnection with others, creating a sense of displacement and isolation (Nugent and Schinkel 2016). Sociologically, Dylan was labelled (Becker 1963) and stigmatised (Goffman 1963) and shamed (Braithwaite 1989) by his peers due his criminal past and therefore excluded from his circle of so-called friends. The impact this had on Dylan's sense of self resulted in him having to repeat his first year of study—already a period of instability, vulnerability and transition.

Dylan's experiences are paralleled in Karen Graham's (2014) study of male prisoner's past school experiences which revealed their feelings of isolation after being excluded—memories that resonated with their experiences of imprisonment. This was described by Dylan earlier when after being ostracised by his peers he said: 'I felt like that kid at school again'. Graham's sample reported that as a result of being excluded from school, their friendships were tested because they were treated as being undeserving and therefore alienated from their peers:

> What is common to the narratives is that the men were recognised as naughty kids, bad kids, kids with behavioural problems (and so on) at an early age, and these definitions seemed to be widely accepted by the majority of teaching staff, peers and the men themselves. These definitions or labels continued on from primary to secondary school, securing them reputations of tough or problem kids. (Graham 2014, p. 830)

Being isolated impacted on Dylan's sense of self during his time at university as he becomes socially outcast by his peers and as with Judy, he also felt displaced. An essential process of Dylan's desistance and self-transformation was that he had become reintegrated within the university culture (as Judy had) but would now have to start again from the beginning, this time with more caution about disclosing his past, silenced within an environment which encourages sharing challenging information. As McAdams (2006) argues, sustained desistance improves when ex-offenders develop social links with people in different social hierarchies because it enables them to access wider social resources. Getting jobs, taking up new hobbies and being exposed to new experiences assist desisters in 'moving on' and building a new life, rather than merely existing, as in remaining in a stage of liminality (Healy 2010; Laub and Sampson 2003; Weaver 2013). But although Dylan had developed social links at university they were then severed; however, rather than returning to criminal activity he continued with his education. Dylan's account highlights the possible vulnerabilities when divulging certain information and links back to an underexplored area within biographical research of people with convictions and over-disclosing. It also demonstrates Dylan's resilience and ability to overcome this painful period of his life. Dylan and Judy's experiences were quite typical of the sample in my PhD study because they have all managed to overcome obstacles and achieve their educational goals although psychologically they are all at very different stages of their lives as some feel more positive than others and some are more haunted by their pasts than others.

But perhaps over-disclosing is a necessary part of the desisters' reconstruction of identities, whereby they use this narrative to make sense of the discord within their lives. For example, Sykes and Matza's (1957) neutralisation theory can be translated to narratives of ex-offenders who over-disclose their pasts as a way of re-negotiating of identities (i.e. trying to make sense of the world and re-biographing) (Maruna 2001). The process of over-disclosing one's criminal past is absent within narrative criminology and the desistance literature, yet could be useful in analysing how individuals use narrative to make justifications having paid their debt to society. To put this into perspective, in terms of the transformative process, the idea of over-disclosing ones past offending to others begins with a narrative that can be associated with Sykes and Matza's (1957) 'techniques of neutralisation', where individuals dissociate themselves from their past offending, followed by reconstructive narrative (Maruna 2001).

For example, Chloe came out of prison 'completely broken' she says. While trying to mend her life her re-biographing (Maruna 2001) included using narrative to try and make sense of who she was and where she belonged. At the time of writing, Chloe, 38, worked for a prison reform charity and has gained degrees in health studies and social science and social research. She felt as though she used to over-disclose her past to others, which also suggests a 'looking glass self' (Cooley 1902) concept where she feels it was important how others viewed her.

> **Chloe**: … I just felt like, I'd tell everybody because, I felt like everybody knew, like it was stamped on me and I would literally tell people [upset] probably inappropriately, over disclosing.

Chloe's expression 'like it was stamped on me' is an interesting reference to how she felt she was labelled to the extent that others instinctively were aware of her past, and it corresponds with Becker's (1963) labelling theory, but to what extent were her feelings real? She may have felt this way but in reality, no one could actually know about her past by merely looking at her. Similarly, Stacey covers up the scars on her arms as it is a reminder of her past where she self-harmed during her early traumatic years, but also, she does not want others knowing about her past or making assumptions about her. Stacey, 26, was a white, middle-class, heterosexual female and one of the youngest of the sample. She had the longest criminal record than the others with over 100 convictions which included mainly violence and criminal damage. In terms of desistance, Stacey's journey was unusual by the fact that she had desisted by her early twenties, when criminal activities tend to be at their peak.

The difference here of course is that while Chloe feels that her past from within is somehow transparent and visible to others, Stacey's scars are outwardly visible. Yet despite Chloe feeling self-conscious about what others may be thinking about her, she continued to over-disclose her past convictions. When Chole applied for a two-year college place, again she felt the need to over-disclose her past:

> **Chloe**: … Again, I probably over explained my situation, I don't anymore. I don't actually think it's anyone's business anymore; I don't do it in this job; I don't go to meetings and say, 'oh yes I'm ex-prisoner blah de blah'. It's not that I hide it from people. It's not like I'm ashamed. I just think that everybody's different. Like some people, they do that, and that's fine. I don't think that's a wrong thing. It's just something that I've learnt from my own experiences of doing that … that actually now I do this job now because I really enjoy it.

Chloe has now completely transformed her life and rejects her past, which Laub and Sampson (2003) refer to as 'knifing off' the past, and in terms of identities Maruna (2001) refers to as 'casting off' former identities. Chloe has found that her ex-offender identity has no bearing on her ability to progress her life. For some, it is important to cling to it while for others, such as Chloe, it is something that they can disassociate themselves from.

Experiences of Education

The participant's experiences of education in relation to their self-transformations were varied. For example, some of those who had suffered domestic and sexual abuse as children felt that education added to their painful memories, which was one of the most alarming findings of this study. This linked directly to their suffering both in childhood and adulthood, whereby knowledge gave them an insight into their own suffering. Some of the participants who were victims of abuse and domestic violence did not realise what they were subjected to was wrong, until they developed further insight through education. Although education can be liberating, it can also be a negative, painful experience for some. For example, sociologically speaking, education can give insights in to the injustices they experienced and suffered. Interestingly, this resonates significantly with Frederick Douglass's (1851) classic works as a freed slave who claimed education gave him insight into all the injustices of the world.

Len, 48, was an English, white, working-class, heterosexual male who served a life sentence for murder and continues to deal with the psychological problems that led to his offence. Len has had many internal issues to deal with and even felt education was more of a curse as it opened his eyes to the cruel world he once inhabited. Education, however, still gives him a goal to succeed and he continues his education, which he feels has given him structure.

Len was the only life sentence prisoner in the sample and came from an abusive, dysfunctional family life dominated by his patriarchal father, where he was abused and beaten. Being a victim of domestic violence and bullying would have had a detrimental effect on his initial experiences of studying sociology. Len found that education not only opened his eyes to the world around him, but he became confused and more sensitised to his childhood traumas as he gained more insight and a realisation that he had been a victim of abuse:

DH: Have you found learning therapeutic?

Len: No, the more I've learned, the more confused I've become [...]. Sociology is the subject that really screwed my head up, because all the life that I had accepted up to that point, hit me as being totally wrong. You know being beaten up by your dad—leather belt buckle and his steel toe cap boots, was all wrong. Up to that point it wasn't. I wanted to be like my dad. I wanted to be a friend of my dad [...].

From a psychosocial perspective, education has caused Len more psychological trauma which affected his relationship with his father, although he has explained that he does not blame his parents for his own wrongdoings. Similarly, Jimmy found education to be both enlightening and at the same time a painful experience, claiming that education opens one's eyes to all the injustices in the world through gaining greater knowledge. He argues that the prison system assumes prisoners are 'basically thick or stupid' but actually being a criminal (and surviving prison) takes a lot of skill. He feels the education they provide (in prison or in society?) is 'patronising':

Jimmy: Bear in mind as well what education brings you. It brings enlightenment. You can see out of the box ... when you become educated. In your dumb ignorance you just plod along in your own wee world. You do your own little thing. But when you became enlightened to the ways of the world and how things actually work and you see the corruption, you see the wrong doings by people of standing, people of note.

At times it is suggested that it is best to remain ignorant to what is happening in the world around us and that while education has opened doors and opportunities, it has also given them insight into an unfolding, unpleasant existence.

Chloe said she had a confidence crisis during her second year at university because of not having dealt with personal issues:

> **Chloe**: I think I was thinking, I don't know why I am doing this [studying at university]. It's hard to get a balance between doing it because of your own experience. I just felt like I needed to get away from it. I don't think I had processed enough of my own stuff and perhaps it was still too close.
>
> **DH**: Too raw?
>
> **Chloe**: Yes and that kind of explains the over disclosing things like that. I think it's really challenging and I think a lot of people, whether they have personal issues, experience with substance misuse or going to prison, not everyone is cut out to do that. Anyway, I got away from it. I didn't really focus on anything like that in my Master's—that was the last thing I did.

Chloe is referring to the cognitive transformation (Giordano et al. 2002) stages that are an essential process for change, but the pains of education was an unexpected finding within this study because of its hypothesising that education could only produce positive experiences which were a major contribution towards the desistance process. Len was disowned by other family members in later life for highlighting his abuse, but until he began studying sociology he was unaware that his early life was even dysfunctional. At 48, he still breaks down and is deeply ashamed for taking another person's life for which he received a sentence known as 'Her Majesty's Pleasure' (HMP) at the age of 15. This confirms that his childhood was a significant factor towards his offending, as predicted by others from a very young age:

> **Len**: I had my hand around a student's neck and he was turning purple, and it was predicted that one day I would take somebody's life. [...]. Very few instances I actually initiated aggression. It was an outpouring if you like. ... And yeah, eventually, I did take someone's life.

Len talks about how a person's upbringing is often used as the main focus when examining prisoner's identities and can see how some of his fellow inmates have also come from very 'damaged backgrounds':

Len: … it's not just because they come from dysfunctional backgrounds, it's they've come from damaged backgrounds. It's one of my sad reflections of my upbringing. I don't say that's why I committed this offence, I wish I could identify specifically why I did what I did, but it contributed to the mind set of what led me to it. I wasn't blaming my dad, I wasn't blaming my mum. I was the one that did it, but it (upbringing) contributes to it.

Len's narrative tries to make a distinction between 'dysfunctional' and 'damaged' which suggests 'damaged' is something much deeper than dysfunctional. Despite this he does not identify that his upbringing was a direct cause of his later offending. There were some problems within his upbringing that affected his sense of self and attributed to his behaviour, for example he admitted that he had anger issues and outbursts, but he does not specifically blame his parents. We can see within Len's narrative a thought process of trying to understand himself and make sense of what led him to commit murder.

Therefore, there were varying levels of pain for each of the participants when revisiting painful narratives. Some of their experiences were more recent than others and all had different levels of psychosocial traumas. Also, for some, reliving their past enabled them to negotiate their past and new identities and make sense of their lived experiences, while for others, reliving their pasts was clearly still very raw. McAdams (2006) argues that reliving painful experiences enables someone to make sense of the past in relation to later behaviours and current anxieties. Therefore, if we are to draw from McAdam's theory, painful narratives can share profound memories of intimacy in people's lives as those times when they shared with others deep sadness and pain. The importance of this concept is the psychosocial process of forging new identities through narratives of trauma and healing within different environments.

Conclusion

There is a contrast within the participant's narratives whereby some feel revisiting their pasts enabled them to make sense of their journeys while others are clearly traumatised. Only two participants within the sample of xxx said they found learning to be a negative experience, but their powerful narratives do shed some light on an underexplored area of the pains of desistance and supports Nugent and Schinkel's argument of the need for further in-depth analysis in this area. For others, learning and entering the higher education community as students was central to their psychosocial transformations as the environment allowed them to escape their surroundings but also develop a 'replacement self'. McNeill (2016) argues that this involves becoming part of a moral community. The cognitive changes combined with the process of learning and social environmental factors enabled a psychosocial process whereby the participants were able to forge new identities.

At the foreground of my research, the main argument contends that desistance does not have a beginning and an end goal but rather an ongoing set of complex challenges and in many cases is a journey without an end because of the constant challenges that desisters encounter. These include stigmatisation, rejection and a continuous need for some to keep reinventing themselves in order to fit in to society. This position is generated from my own circumstances as a desister, where I experienced a lifetime of challenges and which was reinforced after my experiences as a researcher, when it became clear to me that my desistance journey was ongoing. I do not mean this in the sense that I was still involved in criminal activity, that ended over 20 years ago, but rather the psychosocial transitions that encompass psychological transformations and sociological transitions which are a major part of the desistance process.

There are many complexities and diversities within the desistance process which require more in-depth analysis and this has been highlighted in recent studies relating to prisons and desistance (McNeill and Schinkel 2016; McLean et al. 2017), the pains of desistance (Nugent and Schinkel 2016) and liminality and desistance (Healy 2010, 2014). Desistance theory requires a more varied, revised and nuanced approach that includes the concept of 'identity desistance' (Nugent and Schinkel 2016, p. 570), which focusses not on the movement away from offending but rather a continual psychosocial transition. This suggests that in many instances, self-transformation takes priority over abstaining from crime, which has been evidenced in studies relating to recovery and desistance (see Colman and Vander Laenen 2012). And also resonates with Nugent and Schinkel's

(2016) theory of the pains of desistance, whereby desistance became a set of painful crises as people leaving custody attempt to reintegrate back into society. But as this study identified, the continual obstacles which led to a crisis of the self also led to positive transformations which highlighted the importance of identifying with painful as well as positive experiences (McAdams 2006). The movement from one stage of life to another often involves a rite of passage (Maruna 2001), which usually involves some form of inauguration or ceremony such as university graduation, marriage or employment. Some of the participant's rite of passage included entering generative occupations as counsellors and substance abuse advisors which also facilitated redeemability (Maruna 2001). This was one of the most compelling transformations where participants saw themselves as 'wounded healers' (Maruna, p. 102) who could help others that were experiencing issues with substance abuse and homelessness as they once had.

References

Becker, H. (1963). *Outsiders*. New York: Free Press.

Braithwaite, J. (1989). *Crime, shame, and reintegration*. Cambridge: Cambridge University Press.

Browne, K. (2005). Snowball sampling: Using social networks to research non-heterosexual women. *International Journal of Social Research Methodology, 8*(1), 47–60.

Colman, C., & Vander Laenen, F. (2012). "Recovery came first": Desistance versus recovery in the criminal careers of drug-using offenders. *Scientific World Journal, 2012*, 1–10.

Cooley, C. H. (1902). *Human nature and the social order*. New York: Scribners.

Crooks, D. (2001). The importance of symbolic interaction in grounded theory in women's health. *Health Care for Women International, 22*, 11–27.

Davies, W. (2015). Unique position: Dual identities as prison researcher and ex-prisoner. In R. Earle, D. Drake, & J. Sloane (Eds.), *The Palgrave handbook of prison ethnography* (pp. 463–478). Basingstoke: Palgrave Macmillan.

Douglass, F. (1851). *Narrative of the life of Frederick Douglass, an American slave*. Written by himself. London: H.G Collins.

Farrall, S. (2005). On the existential aspects of desistance from crime. *Symbolic Interaction, 28*(3), 367–386.
Faugier, J., & Sargeant, M. (1997). Sampling hard to reach populations. *Journal of Advanced Nursing, 26*(4), 790–797.
Giordano, P., Cernkovich, S. A., & Rudolph, J. L. (2002). Gender, crime, and desistance: Toward a theory of cognitive transformation. *The American Journal of Sociology, 107*(4), 990–1064.
Goffman, E. (1963). *Stigma and social identity. Stigma: Notes on the management of spoiled identity.* s.l.: Prentice Hall.
Graham, K. (2014). Does school prepare men for prison? *City, 18*(6), 824–836.
Healy, D. (2010). *The dynamics of desistance: Charting pathways through change.* London: Routledge.
Healy, D. (2014). Becoming a Desister: Exploring the role of agency, coping and imagination in the construction of a new self. *British Journal of Criminology, 54*(5), 873–891.
Honeywell, D. (2018). *Ex-prisoners and the transformation of self through higher education.* PhD thesis, University of York.
Jewkes, Y. (2011). Autoethnography and emotion as intellectual resources: Doing prison research differently. *Qualitative Inquiry, 18*(1), 63–75.
Jones, R. S., Ross, J. I., Richards, S. C., & Murphy, D. S. (2009). The first dime. A decade of convict criminology. *The Prison Journal, 89*(2), 151–171.
Laub, J. H., & Sampson, R. J. (2003). *Shared beginnings, divergent lives: Delinquent boys to age 70.* Cambridge, MA: Harvard University Press.
Liem, M., & Richardson, N. J. (2014). The role of transformation narratives in desistance among released lifers. *Criminal Justice and Behavior, 41*(6), 692–712.
Maruna, S. (2001). *Making good: How ex-convicts reform and rebuild their lives.* Washington, DC: American Psychological Association.
McAdams, D. P. (1993). *The stories we live by: Personal myths and the making of the self.* William Morrow & Co.
McAdams, D. (2006). *The redemptive self: Stories Americans live by.* New York: Oxford University Press.
McLean, R., Matra, D., & Holligan, C. (2017). Voices of quiet desistance in UK Prisons: Exploring emergence of new identities under desistance constraint. *The Howard Journal, 56*(4), 437–453.
McNeill, F. (2016). Desistance and criminal justice in Scotland. In H. Croall, G. Mooney, & M. Munro (Eds.), *Crime, justice and society in Scotland* (pp. 200–216). London: Routledge.

McNeill, F., & Schinkel, M. (2016). Prisons and desistance. In J. Bennett, B. Crewe, & Y. Jewkes (Eds.), *Handbook on prisons* (pp. 607–621). Cullompton: Willan Publishing.

Nugent, B., & Schinkel, M. (2016). The pains of desistance. *Criminology and Criminal Justice, 16*(5), 568–584.

Pollard, A. (2009). Field of screams: Difficulty and ethnographic fieldwork. *Anthropology Matters Journal, 11*(2). https://doi.org/10.22582/am.v11i2.10.

Presser, L. (2009). The narratives of offenders. *Theoretical Criminology, 13*(2), 177–200; 1362–4806.

Presser, L., & Sandberg, S. (Eds.). (2015). *Narrative criminology: Understanding stories of crime*. New York: New York University Press.

Sykes, G. (1958). *The society of captives: A study of a maximum-security prison*. Princeton: Princeton University Press.

Sykes, G. M., & Matza, D. (1957). Techniques of neutralisation: A theory of delinquency. *American Sociological Review, 22*(6), 664–670.

Weaver, B. (2013). Desistance, reflexivity and relationality: A case study. *European Journal of Probation, 5*(3), 71–88.

6

Prisoner Experiences of Prison Health in Scotland

James Fraser

In November 2011, prisoner healthcare in Scotland became the combined responsibility of a partnership between the Scottish Prison Service (SPS) and the National Health Service (NHS) (Royal College of Nursing 2016). Although there were stakeholder events to explore the issues surrounding this change, it was striking that the end users of the service, that is prisoners detained in Scotland, were not consulted on this. Also, very little is known about the experience of male prisoners with regard to their healthcare while in prison and immediately following release. With this in mind I conducted a study for a Doctor of Philosophy degree entitled "An exploratory study of male ex-prisoners' experiences of health and healthcare in prison and the community". Against the backdrop of organisational restructure, the purpose of this study was to investigate the experiences of male prisoners in order that future policy developments can be more grounded in their experience.

As regards the methodology, the study was conducted from a phenomenological perspective. Data was gathered from semi-structured

J. Fraser (✉)
NHS Scotland, Edinburgh, UK

© The Author(s) 2021

M. Maycock et al. (eds.), *Issues and Innovations in Prison Health Research*, Palgrave Studies in Prisons and Penology, https://doi.org/10.1007/978-3-030-46401-1_6

interviews with male ex-prisoners in the community. Interviews were audio-recorded and transcribed where consent was given; detailed field notes were taken in interviews where consent was not given for audio-recording. Transcripts of the recorded interviews and field notes were analysed using inductive phenomenological analysis.

Twenty-nine ex-prisoners participated in semi-structured interviews with nine consenting to being audio-recorded. An inductive thematic analysis revealed the following themes:

1. **The meaning of health**. Participants experienced their own health predominantly as a physical phenomenon related to their ability to function physically in the world. Mental ill-health had been experienced and was spoken about in terms of stigma and ensuring/maintaining personal safety. Substance misuse was not seen as a health issue but more as an issue of poor service provision.
2. **Access to and use of healthcare provisions in prison and the outside community**. Problems were experienced regarding medication and the prescribing practices of doctors. Participants' experience of accessing healthcare services in prison was of a difficult and frustrating process that was controlled by nurses whose attitudes and use of power were perceived as a major factor in prisoners' ability to access and use the services available. All participants described professionals' high level of mistrust in them and the issues surrounding their health status as a result of the phenomenon known as the credibility gap (Butterfield 2015, p. 152). What this means in this context is that, from the participants' accounts, healthcare workers, prison staff and the general public make judgements about their character, whether they can be trusted and believed, and also the motivations for their healthcare requests.

   The general attitude being that prisoners are liars and that their accounts cannot be trusted. This appeared to impact upon their perceived ability to access healthcare whilst in prison and the outside community.
3. **Difficulties in interagency communication of care**. Participants expressed experience of an increasingly bureaucratic process of access to health services characterised by form-filling. This was perceived to

disadvantage and discourage prisoners and those with literacy difficulties. Participants expressed that new complaint procedures were not explained and appeared to be designed in a way to deliberately discourage and delay complaints. Participants expressed that the access arrangements for healthcare appointments were also bureaucratic, slow and perceived to be designed to discourage them from accessing healthcare services.

4. **Vulnerability and hope.** The role of the family and the support that they can provide following liberation was stated to be important and helpful in preventing relapse into former health threatening behaviours. Although it is worth recognising that in some instances family members may promote poor health behaviours post-release. Such support was also described as helping to prevent participants from becoming embroiled in a revolving door syndrome of release and reoffending. The important mechanisms were identified as a source of accommodation and a permanent address, which was essential to access a number of healthcare services and benefits. Planned, consistent throughcare and opportunities were identified as helpful, especially those from third sector organisations.

In conclusion, ex-prisoner participants' experiential accounts raise problematic issues relating to the effectiveness of 2011 policy changes. These changes were intended to ensure equity in health services for prisoners and ensure that they received improved opportunities to benefit from National Health Service care. The changes have not translated into an improved experience for prisoners during and following their incarceration. The overriding conclusion of this study is that the participants' experiences of healthcare differ from the rhetoric of the UK and Scottish Governments, NHS and SPS policy. This is with particular reference to prisoners' accounts differing from policy with regard to equity of service provision and especially with regard to health promotion and education, prisoner involvement with their care and links with the community and public sector. Ultimately a renewed commitment to providing equivalency of opportunity in healthcare for prisoners is required.

Methods and Ethics

A qualitative approach for the study was deemed most appropriate, as it was suited to exploring in depth participants' own subjective experiences. The participants gave their experiential accounts that raised the themes summarised above. These themes help to illuminate the way the participants experienced the healthcare system. What emerged were the four themes that are intertwined and unite the participants' experiences.

Aim

The aim of the study was to investigate the health and healthcare experiences of liberated men who have served a prison sentence and seek out how they view their health and use of healthcare services.

In order to meet the aim there was only one question for the study:

> What are ex-prisoners' experiences of health and healthcare in prison and in the community?

Design

A qualitative, phenomenological study using interpretive phenomenology (Heidegger 1962) was performed, which utilised participants' narratives of their healthcare experiences as the source of data. Their stories were obtained using semi-structured interviews.

Setting and Participants

NHS Tayside serves a population of approximately 415,000 and is composed of the councils of Angus, the City of Dundee and Perth and Kinross (NHS Tayside 2017). It is a region which has urban and rural areas. The major population centres are the cities of Dundee and Perth. There are two prisons with Tayside: the closed secure prison at Perth (678 prisoners) and the only open prison in Scotland at Castle Huntly (285 prisoners) located outside Dundee. While participants had served time in prisons across Scotland, all had been housed in one of the two in Tayside prior to their release.

Participants were recruited within the Tayside region via three centres; a GP practice in Perth and a health centre and a substance misuse service centre in Dundee. In this study a purposive sample with inclusion/exclusion criteria was utilised. The inclusion criteria for participants were that they were males over the age of 18 years and had served a prison sentence greater than three months within a prison in Scotland. Excluded from the study were females, anyone under 18 years of age and those that had not served a sentence of at least three months within a Scottish prison.

Participants were interviewed in the community within six weeks of their liberation from prison.

Ethical Considerations

Ethical approval to conduct the study was obtained from the ethics committees of Abertay University and East of Scotland Research Ethics Service (Part of NHS Scotland).

Participants' gave written consent to participate, to record the interviews and for their quotations to be used pseudonymously within any related publications. Participants were also advised that they should not divulge any material about any criminal activities as this would be passed on to the relevant authorities.

Recruitment

Recruitment centre managers were given details of the study including inclusion criteria. Potential participants were identified in the GP practice and health centre by the GP personally using the NHS computerised patient's records system while the substance misuse service used their initial assessment process documents. Potentially eligible participants were provided with study information including a contact phone number for the researcher.

Data Collection

Semi-structured interviews were used for collecting data between April 2014 and April 2015. It is acknowledged that although the data was relevant during this time, things may, of course, have improved or deteriorated since then.

Prior to commencement, participants were given the opportunity to ask any remaining questions about the study and provided written informed consent. All interviews were performed by the researcher. A semi-structured interview schedule was utilised with the main questions. The order of the questions varied depending upon the participant and their individual experiences. Interviews lasted approximately one hour.

Interviews were audio-recorded if consent was given to do so, and contemporary written notes taken where consent for audio-recording not given. Audio tapes were transcribed verbatim, with the transcriptions creating the text for analysis together with written notes. Recordings and transcripts were kept securely on a password protected University computer drive.

Data Analysis

Data analysis was guided from a phenomenological perspective informed by Heidegger (1962) and Binswanger (1958). As there is a complex interaction between the world in which a person lives and their understanding of it, narratives are particularly suitable for portraying how people experience their position as "Embedded in people's stories we hear their feelings, thoughts and attitudes" (Etherington 2004, p. 75), hence the value of this kind of research which is phenomenological in its approach. In trying to understand human experiences, Binswanger (1958) suggested a model of existential analysis with three basic levels based upon Martin Heidegger's description of the Umwelt, Mitwelt and Eigenwelt (Heidegger 1962, p. 113). The Umwelt is a person's awareness of physical environment, in the sense of an ordered arranging of tools or equipment, which are directly accessible to the objectives and practical tasks of the people within it. The Mitwelt is how a person exists in the world with other people and is how they relate to others and develop relationships, and as such is the social component of existence. The Eigenwelt is an introspection or reflection performed in trying to make sense of our lives and experiences by reflecting on our behaviour, values and desires. These three levels are the basis of Binswanger's (1958) model. This model is used as a framework for categorising and portraying experiences, in particular due to the symbiosis of the model with Heidegger's phenomenological framework and the strong agreement on the core elements of the Umwelt, Mitwelt and Eigenwelt.

Analysis was performed by organising the data into meaningful groups. This step in the process is known as microanalysis of data (Strauss and Corbin 1998). As Wainwright (1994, p. 44) states "Microscopic line by line analysis (or coding) is necessary to achieve a detailed interpretation of the data and to unravel the complexity of the phenomenon studied and making convincing sense of it". Code words or labelled concepts, as they are called by Strauss and Corbin (1998), were written in the wide margins of the transcript for easy identification next to phrases, words or comments in the text.

This coding was performed manually by systematically working through all the transcripts. The purpose of this was to match up the identified codes with data extracts that demonstrated that code. Whilst completing this task it was important to ensure that all data extracts were coded, and collated together within each code.

After coding had been completed, the analysis re-focused at the broader level of searching for themes. This involved methodically sorting the different codes into potential themes, and collating all the relevant coded data extracts within the identified themes. Essentially, this was an analysis of the codes and considering how different codes might combine to form a theme. It became clearer, as I progressed through this process, that there were four distinct themes contained within the transcripts that were coherent, clear and identifiable with distinctions between them. In the following section I discuss how the results from these themes compare with the literature.

Discussion of Themes

A literature review identified that there is a dearth of relevant literature about male prisoners' own views about their involvement in health services and they are rarely asked their opinion or given much choice regarding the services they require. To date there has been no study in Scotland that has explored ex-prisoners' healthcare experiences in prison and the community using their own narratives.

Prison Health Studies That Resonate With My Study

Plugge et al. (2008b) explored female prisoners' concepts of health and illness by conducting focus groups in two English prisons. They found that the women were enthusiastic about contributing to research but, similar to this study, it was discussed that doubts are cast over the contributions of prisoners to research and policy development. Despite the differences in the participant sample and data collection method, the findings of this study are largely congruent with that of Plugge et al. (2008a). What this study adds is that men were followed up in the community and included their experiences with community healthcare services in their accounts. Plugge et al. concluded that the women in their study had a good understanding of the health issues surrounding female prisoners in England and Wales. The women had highlighted illegal drug use, mental illness, self-harm and sleeplessness as the main issues. The men in my study did not mention sleeplessness or self-harm but they did talk at length about the illegal drug use in prison and in the community, albeit no observable comparison was made between incarceration and liberation regarding this issue. Mental illness was also voiced but was framed in terms of participants maintaining their personal safety from those who had a diagnostic label of mental illness. Physical conditions were given a greater priority over mental health and well-being by the participants in the study, pointing towards a gendered difference in this area.

Although there are many similarities in the results of the studies in the literature review, my study did not attempt to generalise the main health issues within the whole prison population but highlights those issues that participants chose to give priority to and focus on in their accounts. The lack of control, power and choice that participants voiced with regard to their ability to access and interact with healthcare staff, substance misuse services, health promotion and complaining resonates with the studies by Condon et al. (2007, 2008), which included both men and women participants. These studies conclude that a lack of prisoner autonomy and access to health promotion strategies available more widely in the community were major barriers in ensuring that prisoners' health needs were fully met and limited their ability to maintain or improve their health. Similar to the conclusions by Condon et al. (2008), participants in my study voiced that opportunities to make healthy choices varied between prisons, particularly in relation to diet and exercise. Thus, whilst imprisonment offers prisoners an opportunity to access health promotion services, in the priority areas identified in Choosing Health (Department of Health 2004), prisoners are often prevented from making healthy choices by the prison setting. Barriers exist within the prison setting which limit the ability of prisoners to maintain and improve their health due to the points immediately outlined above.

Similarly, the sense of vulnerability and isolation brought about by those with a mental illness and the lack of social and/or family support, are in keeping with the study by Samele and Keil (2009). This study revealed that mental health issues for liberated females contributed to their sense of isolation and difficulty to cope in the community.

From the participants' accounts it would appear that healthcare workers in the prison did not plan, or were not involved in, an individual's discharge from prison to community. As a consequence, participants felt they had been left to care for themselves to a great extent after release. This is congruent with research by Binswanger et al. (2011), in which former prisoners reported poor transitional preparation preceding release and inadequate or absent continuity of mental and physical healthcare. Binswanger suggested that improved release planning and greater communication between the health and criminal justice systems may help to reduce the risk of poor health outcomes for the prison population. My study also supports this point.

Participants in my study voiced that being prescribed certain medications made them feel vulnerable and open to bullying as medication was used as a currency within prison (National Guideline Centre (UK) 2016). This occurred not only in prison but also in the community. They also talked about the problems of storing their medications within prison. This is congruent with the findings of Hassan et al. (2012) who explored prisoners' views of holding their own medication in prison and concluded that risk management needs development within the prison. I would also agree with their conclusion that there is still some way to go before in-possession medication policies are fully embraced in prison authorities. The critical issue here is one of balance between allowing the autonomy to manage their own medication and to maintain prison organisational protocols to deter bullying. Although some staff and prisoners recognise its benefits, some remain uneasy around the perceived risks.

Participants talked of feeling like "second class citizens" because they felt that they were negatively labelled by healthcare workers for having been sent to prison. If they were observed associating with ex-prisoners in the community, for example in pharmacies, then this appeared to reinforce these feelings. Ex-prisoners also perceived that they were judged by healthcare personnel in the community, especially when trying to register with a general practitioner. As a consequence of the transition of health from the SPS to the NHS, it is interesting that those working in GP practices and NHS establishments can now view computer records that will inform them if a person has been in prison, whereas prior to November 2011 this was not possible. This means that those that have been in prison are potentially more prone to labelling, stigmatization and discrimination when in contact with the NHS in the community. This would appear to be contrary to the aims of the primary healthcare changes made in November 2011, which were to bring about equity of healthcare provision.

Participants voiced how they felt that access to healthcare and prescribing of medication were heavily influenced by nurses and that this could be reflected by the nurse's attitudes and those of prison officers. As a result, participants voiced that they felt many nurses did not care and were only concerned with their career. Participants interviewed reflected that this led to a mistrust of nurses and doctors with some prisoners subsequently seeking alternative means of treatment by acquiring and using illicit drugs. This is in keeping with results found by Howerton et al. (2007), in which a lack of trust emerged as one of the most prominent themes in male prisoners' not seeking help from healthcare workers.

However, it is not the remit of healthcare services to worry about retribution. It is their job to provide healthcare within an ethical framework of beneficence, fairness and respect for autonomy. There is also the argument that in the community people have to wait for varying lengths of time to get an appointment to see their GP, so why should prisoners receive any level of service that is better? However, the issue here is that in the community people have choices as to where they can access healthcare, whereas those in prison do not. For example, the public can change their GP, access accident and emergency departments and out of hours' services, access private healthcare companies, visit pharmacies and so forth, which prisoners cannot, although prisoners do have access to accident and emergency if they need it.

Participants in my study did not mention anything about staff training as mentioned in the studies by Howerton et al. (2007) and Burnett et al. (2009), but some did express their opinion as to the knowledge, skills and abilities of healthcare staff. In keeping with a conclusion by Burnett, a number of participants in my study did state their observations of a proportion of the prison population who, from their experience, were not troubled by imprisonment and loss of liberty as prison provided for all of their needs.

This theme was congruent with the studies of Jordan (2012) and De Viggiani (2007). Jordan concluded that the prison milieu impacts upon prisoners' perspectives of their mental healthcare within prison. In my study, I argue that the themes are intertwined and that health is a complex concept that prisoners are constantly dealing with in the prison environment and in the community. In effect, it becomes "a world of health" and is a "cat and mouse game". Over time, thus, with the routines and ambience of prison culture, health starts to take a different identity, which is related to the issues of custody. Compare the meaning of health in prison with that of the community, that is the constant battle of risk assessment and problematic consumption by people, be it alcohol, smoking, drugs, exercise, sugar, etc. How this manifests itself in my study is that the meaning and world of health that participants form inside the prison is carried over into the community upon liberation, thus the constant battle to try to initiate change in behaviours. Similarly, De Viggiani (2007) argued that the health of prisoners is integrated within the structure of the prison system through issues such as the prison regime, staff relations, attitudes and lack of opportunities for education and training. In addition to De Viggiani (2007) the participants' accounts from my study provide evidence that the effects of the prison regime continue post liberation. These are all issues that participants in the study have stated as having an influence upon their healthcare.

De Viggiani (2007) also argued that the term "healthy prisons" was an oxymoron. In contrast, some studies such as those by Burnett et al. (2009) and Yu et al. (2015) concluded that prisoners perceived their health as being better in prison. Three participants in my study concur with this conclusion and talked positively about being in a better state of health as a result of having been in prison. It was interesting that they talked of this in terms that gave the impression they viewed their health as a form of "social capital", i.e. it was a commodity and being healthy made it easier to make new friends, have relationships with the opposite sex and get a job. The participants felt that this was something that they wished to keep and it gave them a focus for their future lives and helped to prevent them from turning their attentions to criminal behaviours. This is congruent with one of the theory of desistance proposed by Laub and Sampson (2001), who highlighted a number of factors that are associated with desistance from crime. These included starting a family and gaining employment.

Small (2006), in his case study of a prisoner's experience with addiction services, concluded that the services had failed the prisoner and prejudiced subsequent court proceedings. Although the participants in my study did not go as far as to say that healthcare had influenced any court proceedings, they did outline that the attitudes of healthcare staff had influenced their care while in prison and could cause differences in the approach to care they experienced from different staff members. In this sense, it could be argued that healthcare services are failing to provide a consistent standard of care to this group.

Although participants talked about drug use in prison and the substance misuse services available, the study did not focus on any particular disease unlike many of the studies in the literature, such as those by Lichtenstein (2000), Scheyett et al. (2009), Small et al. (2005, 2009), but rather on their overall experience. However, the conclusion by Scheyett et al. (2009) that prisoners have difficulty in accessing support with treatment in the community is congruent with opinions expressed by participants in my study. Small et al.'s. (2009) study was based upon the experiences of a specific group of prisoners requiring treatment for HIV in Canada. The conclusion from Small et al.'s study was that there was a need for better coordination of healthcare services between the prison and community. This was reached as participants in the study were usually liberated with a supply of the HIV medications they would require to continue their treatment in the community. However, some participants reported that they received inadequate quantities of their HIV medications to bridge the period until they were able to access HIV care in the community. As a result, participants stated that the difficulties in continuity of care upon liberation could have a negative impact upon their adherence to HIV treatment. In addition, liberation back to the community could pose hazards for participants dealing with addictions, as drug use upon liberation was noted to have a particularly negative effect on their ability to obtain care and treatment. Although this is based upon a specific group and condition in a country with a different healthcare service, the general conclusion is compatible with the opinions expressed by the participants in my study. Similarly, in the study by Small et al. (2005), the authors concluded that more harm-reduction strategies were required in prison to prevent further health problems for the population. This is congruent with the participants in my study, who stated that there were few health promotion/education strategies within the prison environment.

For example, Richard had this to say about health promotion:

JF. What classes can you get about health or health promotion?

Richard. Um … I think it's just like um …. what was it again. It's just like …. I think a coach comes in and you could do em … you get this wee monitor on your side and you could do swimming and then steps. Do running on a beep test thing. But that's only. that's only. there's only like ten people could do that.

JF. So it's not for the whole prison.

Richard. Eh yeh. It's for the whole prison. ten at a time …. every six months.

The striking implication from Richard's account is that, from his experience, health education/promotion was not performed or given a high priority within the prison.

What Richard was referring to was a cardiac fitness programme that was facilitated by the physical training instructors within one of the Tayside prisons. Although it is a health promotion initiative, as he explained, the numbers that could actually participate in it were extremely limited, with only ten men twice a year being able to take part. This is disappointing given that the prison holds seven hundred men.

Based on analysis of my participants' accounts, my summation was that they embraced planned, consistent throughcare along with health education/promotion and life skills training and opportunities when these were available. Whilst the participants may not have articulated policy style discourse, they nonetheless sought a focus upon liberation and beyond for a means to improve their lives, desist from crime and training opportunities, especially those from the voluntary sector.

Some of the findings of my study are in keeping with those by Rae and Rees (2015), who performed a study in order to gain a greater understanding of the perspective of the homeless about their healthcare experiences. Although this study was not performed directly with offenders, it is highly relevant as many prisoners have been homeless before. The study was also an interpretive phenomenological inquiry in which interviews were semi-structured and recorded. Data analysis identified three major themes; expressed health need, healthcare experiences and attitudes to healthcare. Some of the findings were similar in that participants reported difficulty in registering with a general practitioner, being treated with prejudice and receiving substandard care. Similarly, the author recommended that there is a need to address the apparent inconsistency of care and promote greater interdisciplinary communication from prisons to hospitals.

If we look at the accounts given in my study, we can see that participants reported that some prisoners would feign illness in order to get prescription medications.

This was confirmed by one of the participants, Mark in his interview, when we were discussing what prisoners did if they had little or no money, he said:

> *Mark: Yes .... Yep .... Or they'll go and try and access ... some sort of medication ... which is currency ... to get themselves ... eh tobacco and things like that. I've seen that happen.*
>
> *JF: So what things are currency then?*
>
> *Mark: Diazepam, dihydrocodeine, gabapentin, eh ... mirtazapine, seroquel ... eh ... oh there's even other things that ... wouldn't even .... Eh what are they things called ... oh ...?*
>
> *JF: Don't get too hung up on that because I appreciate that some of the names can be tongue twisters.*
>
> *Mark: Amitriptyline and things like that as well eh.*
>
> *JF: So to get on to the medications people have to access healthcare don't they?*
>
> *Mark: Yeh and go and see the doctor and say whatever. They say, "I can't get to sleep or ...."*
>
> *JF: Right and is that all thought out beforehand?*
>
> *Mark: Oh yeh it's all pre ... premeditated eh ... stories what they're going to say before they go in or they'll go and ask somebody ... who's on something, "Oh how are you on them" and they will try and say the same story ... to the doctor.*
>
> *JF: So getting drugs gives you a currency?*
>
> *Mark: Yep.*

Although sleep problems were not stated by the participants, it is possible that this may be one of many problems presented to medics. The use of drugs reported by Nesset et al. (2011) is congruent with the accounts given in my study.

Prison Health Studies That Conflict With My Study

The treatment or a provision for older age prisoners was not mentioned by any of the participants in my study and therefore there are no similarities with the study by Jennings (2009). The exploration of the healthcare experiences of older age prisoners is one of the recommendations for further study presented in my thesis as the study reflected rising numbers of prisoners over the age of 50 years within the SPS (Couper and Fraser 2014).

The studies by Condon et al. (2007), Plugge et al. (2008a, b) and Jordan (2012), while looking at specific service provision and outcomes, took patients' overall experiences of the healthcare system into account. Although these studies were conducted within the UK, they were all performed in England where the NHS responsibility for prisoner healthcare took place six years before it happened in Scotland. The vast majority of research studies cited here were conducted within the prison environment and looked at primary care provided by doctors and nurses, mental health or addiction services. However, only three studies interviewed offenders about their experiences inside and outside of the prison: Samele and Keil (2009) looked at the resettlement needs of women offenders in the UK, Howerton et al. (2007) explored the help seeking behaviour in men in UK and Haley et al. (2014) studied the care given to those with HIV after liberation in the USA. My study, specifically exploring offenders' healthcare experiences, is the first to have been performed in the UK since 2012 and certainly the only one that has taken a phenomenological approach. It is also the only study that explored the offenders' use and experience of other health services such as dentist, optician, chiropody and physiotherapy in the prison or community.

For example, when talking about gaining access to services allied to health, Michael said:

> *Aye, you would be able to see an optician but a dentist, it could take months. Even if you have a killer toothache, it could take months.*

While discussing waiting lists for the dentist, Mark expressed that access to the dental service was severely limited if on remand.

JF: How long do you wait on a dentist?
Mark: If you're a remand prisoner … you will not get to see the dentist.
JF: So remand can be up to 140 days.
Mark: 140 days.

Strengths and Limitations of the Research

The main strengths of my study are that, firstly, it is one of a limited number of studies worldwide that have explored prisoners' healthcare both in the prison and community, as well as exploring the implications of the transition from custody to the community. Secondly, it is also the first study in Scotland, and one of the very few internationally, that has explored the healthcare experiences of ex-prisoners by involving them in the research process. This involved participants taking part in the interviews providing the data and also checking the accuracy of interview transcripts which contributed to the authenticity and credibility of the interviews. Thirdly, the participants' accounts have raised themes, which tie in with much of academic literature. In addition, these accounts give an insight into how the participants in this study have experienced health in custody and the community and how this differs from the rhetoric of policy. As a result, there are implications for considering operational and wider healthcare policy for this vulnerable group.

The methodology used for this study was similar to others in that it was a qualitative study exploring the healthcare experiences of prisoners using semi-structured interviews to collect data, which was analysed from a phenomenological perspective. The study methods and analysis were presented earlier in the chapter. However, most studies interviewed participants within the prison environment, raising a number of ethical issues (Moser et al. 2004), whereas I interviewed them in the community shortly after liberation from prison. This ensured that participants were able to fully consent to their participation without any institutional influences. It also ensured that they were able to speak freely without fear of retribution from others and helped to minimise the effects of "research fatigue" that can be experienced by participants/respondents within the prison environment (Ben-Nun 2008).

As with many research studies, my study has its limitations. One of the first limitations is that due to the small size, the study findings are not statistically generalisable. However, my study sought an insider perspective that offered access to the participants' accounts of their experiences. Their accounts "trouble" the official policy line. This was reflected by the theoretical perspective and research design.

The study is about the healthcare experiences of ex-prisoners. Experience is the product of a person's beliefs, attitudes, knowledge and other personal variables that is interpreted by the individual, in order to make sense of the world and the situations that they find themselves in, and then expressed through their narratives.

As a result, the same situation may be interpreted in many different ways by different people as they draw upon different experiences, beliefs, etc. In this study there are issues pertaining to the veracity of the accounts given by participants due to the credibility gap and stigma of having been in prison.

The findings of the study illustrate that although there were differences between the participants' experiences, there were similarities, which constitute a common experience. As a result, it could be expected that their experiences have some similarities with those of other ex-prisoners. The voices of the study participants add an understanding and provide a counterweight to the official bureaucratic policy. This means that the results of this study can be used to inform those working within the NHS/SPS to the possible experiences of their patients' while acknowledging that they are not generalisable or rather there was less concern in the notion of representativeness of views. This is the case as this form of research is based upon the notion that people possess a particular set of views or attitudes that are relatively fixed and can be accessed through, for example, a questionnaire. Ultimately, this study sought an insider perspective that gives the reader access to the participants' experiences.

It is acknowledged that the interviews that yielded the narrative data for the study are socially and historically situated. As a result, the data was constructed within a social context between the participants and me at a certain time. This means that the data obtained in this study cannot be reproduced.

The findings of this study constitute a still frame of the participants' experiences of healthcare within the prison and the community. The significance of this data is not to try to represent the whole picture of their reality but to bring to light the issues that are presented within the participants' accounts of their experience.

A potential limitation to the study was the "credibility gap". This is a journalistic term adopted in order to describe features of a story which lacks certain details often used, for example, in the media or in responses offered by politicians. Thus, taking part in a research study raises the potential of a credibility gap in listening to participants' accounts, as their experience of an event and the way in which they describe it may be quite different to the accounts others may offer about the same experience. Participants in this study may be offering a truthful account but, given their past, will it be believed or merely condemned by others? This poses a question for the researcher: How to be sure that they have given a truthful account? In simple terms, one hundred per cent certainty that participants' accounts are truthful cannot be assured and the researcher can only deal with the accounts that have been given. It is not possible for others to gauge the veracity of the accounts given to them by others, whether they be from an ex-prisoner or not. This was my main concern while conducting the interviews, that of unintentional judgement. However, while conducting the interviews I became aware that the men were deferential towards me. This was clear from the observable meek conduct and language of the participant group. For example, many of the participants would use phrases such as "honest", "I would swear on my mother's life …", "in my humble opinion", "not that my opinion matters", "I could be wrong", "you will understand it better than me" and repeat themselves even though I had acknowledged the point they had made. There are a number of possibilities for why this demeanour was present in their conduct. This factor may be relevant as some of the men may have been trying to overcome any credibility gap, which they themselves are conscious of; they have been called liars and had their accounts challenged by many, throughout their journey in the Criminal Justice System and prison. Several participants described having been treated as a "junkie" by SPS and NHS staff. One participant had experienced being labelled due to his associating with "ex-prisoners" or "junkies" and expressed having been treated as a "second class citizen." However, I made it clear to the men before commencing that I respected their experiences, what they had to say and that the exercise was not imposed and held no threat to their identity or future credibility. However, at times I felt that some participants were being careful in the way they were positioning themselves within the interview context. This could have influenced the way in which they told their stories as they may have felt that they had to make them credible and authentic to me.

It is also important to acknowledge the issue of reflexivity in my study because in my efforts to be empathetic to the participants during the interviews, it was easy to forget about my influences on the process. However, I acknowledge that my experiences of the NHS and SPS could have influenced decisions and interpretations during the study. Examples include the order and wording of questions before and during the interview and the issues that I emphasised in my interview notes and subsequent analysis of findings.

A crucial point to acknowledge in my study was the possibility that I could project my own feelings into the interview. In other words, I could imagine that is how I would feel if I were in the same situation as my participants. However, I understood that their experience of health and relationship with healthcare services will be unique, and very different to that of my own. As I have generally only positive experiences of working in the NHS and of the interactions I have had nursing prisoners within it, this may have influenced the study as I was keen to ensure that the participants' experiences were heard and that this may help bring about positive change for their healthcare. I also acknowledged that my reactions to participant's answers may have influenced the way in which I asked the question and how they asked questions of me. This may have also influenced the answers that were given. My own feelings towards health and healthcare for prisoners could have influenced the analysis and findings of the study. I reflected upon these issues and their potential influence upon the study. Having recognised them, I made an effort to try to minimise their influence while conducting the interviews, and the study as a whole.

I utilised a number of practical techniques to address reflexivity in the study in relation to participant interviews. The first of these was that I allowed enough time between interviews in order that I could critically reflect upon them, discuss the content with other researchers and consider different perspectives. This was useful as it forced me to look at issues from different angles that I could have overlooked or dismissed without due consideration. Secondly, I kept a diary of how I was feeling while performing the study. This proved to be useful as it allowed me to reflect on my emotional state and other significant events on the days I performed the interviews. When it came to writing up the findings, I was able to refer back to the diary, which helped me make allowances for the way I was feeling. I found this to be particularly useful as I conducted the interviews on my own and sometimes had not been able to discuss them with a colleague. Thirdly, during the writeup of the findings chapters of my thesis, I reflected on how I had interpreted what I heard during the interviews and considered how my life experiences influenced the analysis of data. An example of this is I remember when I was writing my thesis, feeling real sorrow for a participant because of the poverty and life experiences they had described to me. Had I not reflected on how my relatively comfortable experience of life and my feelings towards this, I could have unintentionally stressed the powerlessness of the participant in the thesis. Lastly, prior to conducting the interviews I had practised my technique with a colleague in which we both made notes on how I had come across while conducting a mock interview. We took account of what I said, how I said it and what my body language and facial expressions were at the time. After the interview, we discussed the notes we had made which increased my self-awareness and allowed me to improve my interview technique. An example of how I utilised this was that I have a tendency to make many facial expressions that indicate approval when listening to accounts, which could be interpreted by a participant as encouragement to tell me more than they may have done otherwise. Had I not been made aware of my facial expressions I may have conducted an interview and thought that the participant was engrossed with the experience that they were giving when they had just been doing what they thought I wanted them to do.

Conclusion

Criminal justice systems are politically sensitive places and this can be challenging for the prison staff. The public's views on prisoners and the experience of imprisonment can be misrepresented in the media (Jewkes 2007), which tends to concentrate on notorious prisoners, stories of prisoners receiving undue privileges, and sentences deemed to be too lenient. As a consequence, health initiatives in prison run the risk of being perceived as too good for prisoners, who are portrayed as undeserving.

My study has found that participants found it difficult to access healthcare services. They expressed problems with their self-esteem and self-worth due to their experiences of stigma to which they ascribed their low expectations of healthcare and dissatisfaction with life in general. Although the participants in this research were all liberated men who did not foresee themselves ever returning to the prison environment, they had experience of many men who saw prison as a way of life that provided them with all that they required and were caught up in "the revolving door" of prison and liberation.

Accessing healthcare services, particularly seeking a consultation with a doctor, was a difficult experience for participants that could be exacerbated by the nurses who were perceived to be the most powerful group of healthcare staff. Participants voiced that nurses could not only control when they were given an appointment for a doctor's consultation but that they could also heavily influence the outcome of the consultation with particular reference to the medication that may be prescribed.

In prison healthcare, the relationship with the nurses was central to accessing and receiving care, as they were perceived to be the major gatekeepers. However, although it might be expected that they would experience this relationship as being helpful, many found that many nurses did not appear to care and their autonomy was influenced by the interventions and actions of prison officers. Participants expected that nurses would be aware of their vulnerabilities and help ensure their safety, advocate for them and their care, but often found that this was not the case and that a punitive attitude was displayed towards them. When these expectations were not met, for whatever reason, participants felt that nurses did not care and were merely doing a job. This resulted in disappointment and frustration towards individuals but also the healthcare system as a whole, which resulted in complaints.

Structural issues such as the prison routine, staff attitudes and nurse control of the prison healthcare system made it difficult to access healthcare services. Participants also stated that there were limited opportunities to take part in health promotion and education initiatives to help them improve their health. Issues such as medication and a lack of money could also make them vulnerable to bullying and lead to them accumulating large debts while in custody.

Participants had little expectations of the healthcare system catering for their needs. However, many voiced hope for the future. Healthcare was highlighted as having helped three of the twenty-nine participants break free of "the revolving door" of prison and liberation. This is an aspect of healthcare that requires further research and evaluation as it may be of great benefit to society as a whole.

References

Ben-Nun, P. (2008). Respondent fatigue. In P. Lavrakas (Ed.), *Encyclopedia of survey research methods* (pp. 743–744). Thousand Oaks, CA: SAGE Publications, Inc.

Binswanger, L. (1958). The case of Ellen West. In R. May, E. Angel, & H. F. Ellenberger (Eds.), *Existence: A new dimension in psychiatry and psychology* (pp. 237–364). New York: Simon & Schuster.

Binswanger, I. A., et al. (2011). From the prison door right to the sidewalk, everything went downhill. A qualitative study of the health experiences of recently released inmates. *International Journal of Law and Psychiatry, 34*, 249–255.

Burnett, R., et al. (2009). The consolations of going back to prison: What 'revolving door' prisoners think of their prospects. *Journal of Offender Rehabilitation, 48*(5), 439–461.

Butterfield, J. (2015). *Fowler's concise dictionary of modern English usage*. Oxford: Oxford University Press.

Condon, L., et al. (2007). Users' views of prison health services: A qualitative study. *Journal of Advanced Nursing, 58*(3), 216–226.

Condon, L., Hek, G., & Harris, F. (2008). Choosing health in prison: Prisoners' views on making healthy choices in English prisons. *Health Education Journal, 67*(3), 155–166.
Couper, S., & Fraser, A. (2014). Is the Scottish Prison Service looking after its older and frail prisoners? *Scottish Justice Matters, 2*(2), 9–12.
De Viggiani, N. (2007). Unhealthy prisons: Exploring structural determinants of prison health. *Sociology of Health & Illness, 29*(1), 115–135.
Department of Health. (2004). *Choosing health: Making healthy choices easier.* London: Department of Health.
Etherington, K. (2004). *Becoming a reflexive researcher: Using ourselves in research.* London: Jessica Kingsley Publishers.
Haley, D. F., et al. (2014). Multilevel challenges to engagement in HIV care after prison release: A theory-informed qualitative study comparing prisoners' perspectives before and after community re-entry. *BioMed Central Public Health, 14*, 1253.
Hassan, L., et al. (2012). Prisoners holding their own medications during imprisonment in England and Wales: A survey and qualitative exploration of staff and prisoners' views. *Criminal Behaviour and Mental Health, 22*(1), 29–40.
Heidegger, M. (1962). *Being and time.* New York: Harper and Row.
Howerton, A., et al. (2007). Understanding help seeking behaviour among male offenders: Qualitative interview study. *British Medical Journal, 334*(7588), 303–306B.
Jennings, L. K. (2009). *Aging in a confined place: An exploration of elder inmate health and healthcare.* Doctoral dissertation. University of Alabama USA.
Jewkes, Y. (Ed.). (2007). *Handbook on prison.* Tavistock Devon: Willan Publishing.
Jordan, M. (2012). Patients'/prisoners' perspectives regarding the National Health Service mental healthcare provided in one Her Majesty's Prison Service establishment. *The Journal of Forensic Psychiatry & Psychology, 23*(5–6), 722–739.
Laub, J. H., & Sampson, R. J. (2001). Understanding desistance from crime. *Crime and Justice, 28*, 1–58.
Lichtenstein, B. (2000). HIV risk and healthcare attitudes among detained adolescents in rural Alabama. *AIDS Patient Care and STDs, 14*(3), 113–124.
Moser, D. J., et al. (2004). Coercion and informed consent in research involving prisoners. *Comprehensive Psychiatry, 45*(1), 1–9.

National Guideline Centre (UK). (2016). *NICE guideline, No. 57. Physical health of people in prison: Assessment, diagnosis and management of physical health problems*. London: National Institute for Health and Care Excellence (UK).

Nesset, M. B., et al. (2011). Health care help seeking behaviour among prisoners in Norway. *BMC Health Services Research, 11*(1), 301–301.

NHS Tayside. (2017). Director of public health 2016/17 Annual Report. Retrieved from https://www.nhstaysidecdn.scot.nhs.uk/NHSTaysideWeb/idcplg?IdcService=GET_SECURE_FILE&dDocName=PROD_284941&Rendition=web&RevisionSelectionMethod=LatestReleased&noSaveAs=1.

Plugge, E., Douglas, N., & Fitzpatrick, R. (2008a). Imprisoned women's concepts of health and illness: The implications for policy on patient and public involvement in healthcare. *Journal of Public Health Policy, 29*(4), 424–439.

Plugge, E., Douglas, N., & Fitzpatrick, R. (2008b). Patients, prisoners, or people? Women prisoners' experiences of primary care in prison: A qualitative study. *The British Journal of General Practice, 58*(554), 630–636.

Rae, B. E., & Rees, S. (2015). The perceptions of homeless people regarding their healthcare needs and experiences of receiving health care. *Journal of Advanced Nursing, 71*(9), 2096–2107.

Royal College of Nursing. (2016). *Five years on: Royal College of Nursing Scotland review of the transfer of prison health care from the Scottish Prison Service to NHS Scotland* (p. 6). Edinburgh: Royal College of Nursing.

Samele, C., & Keil, J. (2009). The resettlement needs of female prisoners. *The Journal of Forensic Psychiatry & Psychology, 20*(S1), S29–S45.

Scheyett, A., et al. (2009). From the "streets" To "normal life": Assessing the role of social support in release planning for HIV-positive and substance-involved prisoners. *Journal of Offender Rehabilitation, 48*(5), 367–387.

Small, D. (2006). Patient, prisoner or person? *Harm Reduction Journal, 3*(1), 23.

Small, W., et al. (2005). Incarceration, addiction and harm reduction: Inmates experience injecting drugs in prison. *Substance Use & Misuse, 40*, 831–843.

Small, W., et al. (2009). The impact of incarceration upon adherence to HIV treatment among HIV-positive injection drug users: A qualitative study. *AIDS Care—Psychological and Socio-Medical Aspects of AIDS/HIV., 21*(6), 708–714.

Strauss, A., & Corbin, J. (1998). *Basics of qualitative research: Techniques and procedures for developing grounded theory*. Thousand Oaks, CA: Sage.

Wainwright, S. P. (1994). Analysing data using grounded theory. *Nurse Researcher, 1*(3), 43–49.

Yu, S. V., et al. (2015). Self-perceived health improvements among prison inmates. *Journal of Correctional Health Care, 21*(1), 59–69.

7

Building Health and Wellbeing in Prison: Learning from the Master Gardener Programme in a Midlands Prison

Geraldine Brown, Elizabeth Bos, and Geraldine Brady

Introduction: Setting the Scene

In this chapter, we share key findings from a recent study examining a horticultural prison intervention. The chapter starts by locating this research and evaluation within the wider body of literature which explores the benefits of horticulture, in particular as a therapeutic approach. Whilst our study population are men with a substance misuse issue in prison, previous

G. Brown (✉)
Centre for Agroecology, Water and Resilience, Coventry University, Coventry, UK
e-mail: hsx520@coventry.ac.uk

E. Bos
Centre for Business in Society, Coventry University, Coventry, UK
e-mail: e.bos@coventry.ac.uk

G. Brady
School of Social Sciences, Nottingham Trent University, Nottingham, UK
e-mail: geraldine.brady@ntu.ac.uk

© The Author(s) 2021

M. Maycock et al. (eds.), *Issues and Innovations in Prison Health Research*, Palgrave Studies in Prisons and Penology, https://doi.org/10.1007/978-3-030-46401-1_7

research has recognised that horticulture can be a useful rehabilitative tool with patients and with other groups. Having introduced the background, we move on to describe the particularities of the prison context before discussing the aim and objectives of the study. We took an action research approach to working alongside the programme participants and staff delivering the programme and used a wide range of innovative methods to capture the experiences of participants. The data presented demonstrates how the holistic approach of the Master Gardener (MG) programme allows time, space and has realistic expectations of progression and recovery. Our contribution to this book draws attention to the therapeutic value and strengths of an indirect approach to encouraging improvements in physical and mental health and wellbeing; there are many rewards when attention is paid to the social as well as the individual level and goals are shared, when working within the context of prison.

Horticulture as a Therapeutic Intervention

Horticulture has been viewed as a form of therapy and therapeutic activity for many years in many rehabilitation facilities (Riordan 1983). 'Horticulture therapy' therefore "includes a broad range of services, settings, and populations served" (Haller 1998: 43). Horticultural activities can take place within institutional or community settings (Fontaine 2017), and for Hefley (1973), the ultimate goal of horticulture therapy programmes is to improve the mental and physical health of the individual (with benefits seen in four areas—intellectual, social, emotional and physical development Hefley 1973). Seen across every type of healthcare and social service setting, Haller (1998) summarises horticulture therapy services as: vocational (a rehabilitative model for employment), therapeutic (a medical model for recovery from illness or injury) or social (a wellness model for quality of life). Therefore, horticulture therapy or horticulture for rehabilitation is a broad area, comprising different types of programmes, with different purposes, goals and programme designs (Haller 1998). Horticulture as a form of therapy can broaden the practice of counselling for trauma, grief, death, addiction and life-changing experiences (Fontaine 2017) and is therefore an attractive form of therapeutic activity.

Benefits of Horticultural Interventions Such as Gardening for Rehabilitation

Studies generally report on the role of gardening interventions and their positive impact on participants, particularly in terms of health, wellbeing and social interaction (Grabbe et al. 2015; Sempik et al. 2014; York and Wiseman 2012). Firstly, at the individual level, participating in gardening activities is identified as being able to increase self-efficacy, self-confidence and empowerment (Brandt-Meyer and Butler 1999; Pearce and Seals 2006). Grabbe et al. (2015: 258) found that gardening activities interrupted "participants' negative ruminations, offering stress relief and elements of social inclusion and self-actualization." (Grabbe et al. 2015: 258). Across a variety of gardening programmes for different patients or users, participation in horticultural activities, such as gardening and access to nature, was found to reduce stress (Lehmann et al. 2018; Millet 2009; Adevi and Martensson 2013; Kam and Sui 2010) and for those in prison, in the context of substance misuse treatment, it is identified to reduce cravings (drugs, alcohol), insomnia, anxiety and depression (Lehmann et al. 2018; Kam and Sui 2010). Providing opportunities for those in secure settings to take on some degree of responsibility and initiative serves to increase confidence; as such, horticulture therapy is also found to promote 'coping skills' for people to better cope with future daily strain (Millet 2009; Rappe et al. 2016).

The process of gardening and the gaining/development of related skills often offer a satisfying and meaningful method of recovery (York and Wiseman 2012). Not only does the aspect of nature provide positive sensory experiences and enhanced wellbeing (physical and psychological), but the symbolism of nature which is associated with personal growth and the passing of time (Adevi and Martensson 2013) can be beneficial for people undergoing any form of therapy. This is alongside such activities encompassing a collective dimension which facilitates additional benefits, through its ability to bring people together (Fontaine 2017). For example, the 'connectedness' offered through horticulture activities promotes constructive interactions with other participants and care givers, which helps to build relationships with others, contributing towards coping skills and increased confidence (Fontaine 2017; Adevi and Martensson 2013; Rappe et al. 2016). This connectedness, and positive interactions with both nature and people, takes place in a garden environment—a safe arena for recovery, and considered better than many other environments for promoting human wellbeing as the cornerstone of recovery/therapy (Adevi and Martensson 2013; Millet 2009; Harris et al. 2014). Therefore, through the generation of 'interactional meanings', 'group experience', and 'personal and emotional meanings' (Brandt-Meyer and Butler 1999), the opportunities for social interaction through horticultural activities may, therefore, promote social inclusion and community belonging among vulnerable and isolated groups (Sempik et al. 2014; Harris et al. 2014). In addition, Grabbe et al. (2015: 258) assert that "[g]ardening is an inexpensive and positive intervention for a population with a high incidence of mental illness." Hence, horticultural activities and programmes are often low cost and a simple way to provide exposure to gardens and nature, and to promote patient participation and engagement in decisions about their healthcare which results in better treatment experiences and outcomes (Lehmann et al. 2018).

Transferring the Master Gardener Programme into a Prison Environment

The Master Gardener (MG) programme is led by Garden Organic with an aim to promote organic growing for all through campaigning, advice, community work and research.[1] Initially the MG programme was launched as a pilot in 2010, funded as one of the Big Lottery 'Making Local Food Work' programmes and was initially designed to be delivered in a community setting, one of the overall Programme's 'Beacon projects' (the largest grant available). The aim was to "provide communities with a form of local support and advice for growing food" (www.mastergardeners.org.uk). More recently, Public Health England have supported the delivery (and continuation) of the programme and expanded its reach in

[1] See https://www.gardenorganic.org.uk/ourwork.

a number of different areas, recognising the health and wellbeing benefits the programme delivers. The Master Gardener programme was uniquely expanded to HMP Rye Hill, in Rugby, with funding from Public Health Northamptonshire, to work with prisoners with a substance misuse issue. HMP Rye Hill is a private training prison run by G4S, which opened in 2001 and houses men who have been sentenced to over four years and have at least 12 months left to serve on their sentence. Whilst horticultural interventions in HMP Rye Hill, in line with other prisons, are not rare (Dartmoor (category C), Suffolk (category D) and Market Harborough (category B)), HMP Rye Hill prison is the first prison in the UK to adopt the Master Gardener model as an intervention to work with substance-misusing prisoners (www.hmpryehill.co.uk, 2014).

What Is Known About Substance Misuse and Substance Misuse Services in Prison?

Since 2011, the responsibility of funding for substance misuse services (SMS) in prisons moved from the Ministry of Justice to the Department of Health (including funding for CARAT[2] and drug and alcohol and compact-based drug testing) with NOMS remaining responsible for mandatory drug testing (MoJ, NHS and DH 2011). In recent years, the issue of drugs in prison has received a plethora of attention, with increasing concern associated with the use of Novel Psychoactive Substances (NPS) (such as 'Spice', a.k.a. Black Mamba) many of which fall outside international drug control conventions and as such are commonly known as 'legal highs' (Wheatley 2016). Substance misuse in prison has come to be viewed in terms of a barrier to recidivism, rehabilitation and more widely as a threat to safety and order for staff and prisoners (HMP Rye Hill 2014; O'Hagan and Hardwick 2017).

At the time of the study, there was concern in regards to the increasing prison population in England and Wales. Current figures show a total

---

[2] Counselling, Assessment, Referral, Advice and Through care worker.

prison population of 82,683 (21 June 2019)[3]—one which has quadrupled in size between 1900 and 2017, approximately half of this increase taking place since 1990 (Sturge 2018). This increase has taken place alongside a reported increasing number of prisoners self-harming. An estimated 36% of 1435 prisoners interviewed in a Ministry of Justice study were considered to have a disability, including a mental health disability.[4] A Ministry of Justice study also reported that 23% of male prisoners were assessed as suffering from anxiety and depression comparable to 12% of the general UK male population.[5] Fifteen percent of men in prison reported symptoms indicative of psychosis—the rate among the general public is about 4%.[6] Sixteen percent of men said they had received treatment for a mental health problem in the year before custody.[7] Moreover, men recently released from prison are eight times more likely than the general population to take their own lives.[8] In addition, levels of drug use are high amongst offenders, with highest levels of use found amongst most prolific offenders. Sixty-four percent of prisoners reported having used drugs in the four weeks before custody.[9] Over half of prisoners (55%) report committing offences connected to their drug taking, with the need for money to buy drugs most commonly cited. Nineteen percent of those prisoners who said they had ever used heroin reported having used heroin for the first time in a prison.[10]

---

[3] 82,683 21st June 2019. https://www.gov.uk/government/statistics/prison-population-figures-2019.

[4] Ministry of Justice (2012) Estimating the prevalence of disability amongst prisoners: results from the Surveying Prisoner Crime Reduction (SPCR) survey, London: Ministry of Justice.

[5] Ministry of Justice (2013) Gender differences in substance misuse and mental health amongst prisoners, London: Ministry of Justice.

[6] Wiles, N., et al. (2006) Self-reported psychotic symptoms in the general population, The British Journal of Psychiatry, 188: 519–526.

[7] Ministry of Justice (2013) Gender differences in substance misuse and mental health amongst prisoners, London: Ministry of Justice.

[8] Pratt, D. Piper, M, Appleby, L. Webb, R. Shaw, J. Suicide in recently released prisoners: a population-based cohort study, The Lancet—Vol. 368, Issue 9530, 8 July 2006.

[9] Ministry of Justice (2013) Gender differences in substance misuse and mental health amongst prisoners, Results from the Surveying Prisoner Crime Reduction (SPCR) longitudinal cohort study of prisoners, London: Ministry of Justice.

[10] Ibid.

Our Study

The study was undertaken over a 12-month period between August 2013 and December 2014. At the outset, the prison was designated a category B mixed prison housing mainstream and vulnerable offenders, which included sex offenders. However, almost six months into the study it was re-designated as a category B prison for men convicted of a sex-related crime. The study was conducted in two phases. The first 6 months with 'mainstream prisoners' (Phase 1) and 6 months with the new prison population (Phase 2).

The study was designed to capture a range of factors that could impact on the experiences of participants. In placing the journey of participants at the centre the intention was to focus on examining:

1. The process of developing and delivering the MG programme,
2. The experiences and outcomes for a range of key stakeholders (prisoners, prison staff, management, drug workers, public health and family members)
3. The relationship between the context, experiences and outcomes reported

Master Gardener Participants

In total, 25 men were recruited to the study (11 men in Phase 1 and 14 men in Phase 2). A pre-requisite for being involved on the MG programme was that the men had to pass a security check, be in receipt of support from a DART worker and be housed on the Drug Recovery Wing. Prior to their involvement in the study, consent for their participation was sought. The men were informed about the aim of study, what their involvement would entail and notified that their involvement was voluntary.

The diversity of participants in the study was dependent on the outcome of the MG programme recruitment process. Figure 7.1 shows the age distribution over the two phases.

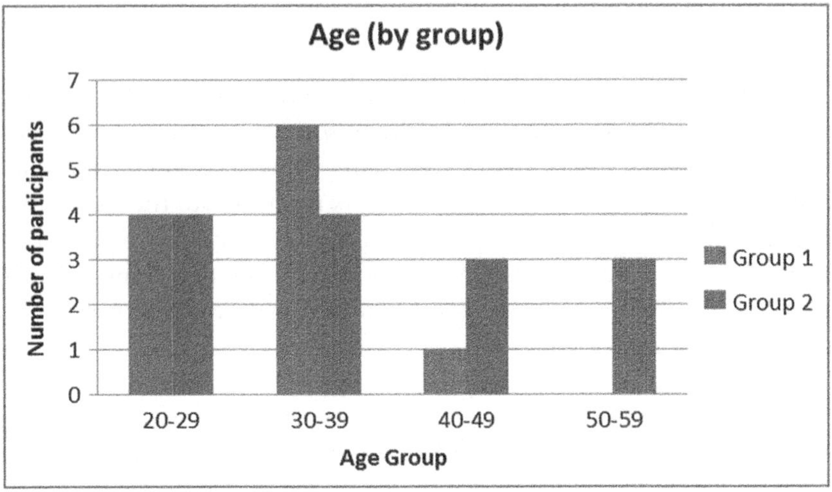

Fig. 7.1 Age

Participants in P1 and P2 were diverse in terms of types of crime committed, number of times imprisoned and type of sentence. Due to the function of the prison at that time, P2 participants were all imprisoned for having committed a sex-related crime and these participants were more ethnically diverse (Fig. 7.1). Just over half (57%) of P2 participants identified as British/English/Welsh/Northern Irish,[11] compared to 91% in P1. In addition, a noticeable difference recorded was the larger number who reported having a mental health need. At the time of conducting the field work in Phase 2, at least three participants were being monitored by staff as they were perceived to be at risk of 'self-harming' or suicide.

Research Tools and Data Collected

Alongside collecting data from men on the gardening programme, in total, the research team:

[11] The remaining P2 participants identified as Irish (21%), Indian (7%), Gypsy or Irish Traveller (7%), and White and Black Caribbean (7%).

Table 7.1 Research tools

Participant observation: This has enabled the research team to spend time with the participants and staff, and to familiarise themselves with the environment at Rye Hill prison. The purpose of participant observations is to observe the delivery of the Master Gardener scheme in a prison setting and to capture first hand participants' views, behaviour and interactions.
Semi-structured interviews: The research team has conducted semi-structured interviews with key stakeholders from Rye Hill prison and Garden Organic. This has included: the coordinator of the Master Gardening programme at Rye Hill, Garden Organic project lead, G4S garden staff, G4S Substance Misuse Lead and a representative from G4S Management. Semi-structured interviews allow the research team to explore issues arising from participant observations and other methods used.
Focus groups: Focus groups were conducted with staff working in the Substance Misuse Team and participants in Group 1.
Portfolio of Work: As part of the Master Gardener programme, participants are required to complete a work-based portfolio. The portfolio contains information related to: personal development—practical, factual and transferable skills learnt or developed as part of the gardening programme worksheets—record of skills covered as part of the gardening intervention, plans and descriptions around areas of work in Phase 2, motivations and expectations in relation to involvement in the gardening intervention, and also included some biographical information.
Reflective Diaries: On a monthly basis participants are asked to complete a reflective diary. The diary is designed to capture individual participants' feelings and experiences about being on the programme. Participants are asked to consider sharing their experiences, feelings, what they feel has changed over the month and generally capture their perceptions about the gardening intervention.
Circle of Change: On a monthly basis participants are asked to record their perceptions about how they feel the programme has encouraged and/or supported them to make changes in areas of their lives.
Prison Data: This is information that is routinely captured as part of the prison management regime. This data includes adjudications, earned privilege level and category.
Demographic Survey: A one-off survey used as a way to gather socio-economic data when participants on the programme consent to take part in the evaluation.
Staff Survey: Used as a way of gaining an insight as to the perceptions of changes observed by members of staff not directly involved in the Master Gardening Programme but who may come into contact with participants as part of their roles; on a bi-monthly basis a short survey is administered to a random selection of staff.
Family Survey: Used as a way of gaining insight as to the perceptions of changes observed by participants' family members; a short survey was administered to family members attending a family event as part of the Master Gardener Programme.

- Spent around 152 hours conducting participant observations
- Facilitated 3 staff focus groups
- Conducted 7 staff semi-structured interviews
- Collected 50 completed staff feedback surveys
- Gathered 58 completed reflective diaries, 46 completed circles of change, 25 demographic surveys
- Analysed 3 prisoner portfolios of work
- Collected 4 family feedback surveys

Phase 1 and Phase 2 used the same methods which yielded similar amounts of data, i.e. a similar number of hours were dedicated to participant observation. The higher number of reflective diaries and circles of change in Phase 2 was due to the increase in Master Gardener programme participants and does not reflect the consistency in collecting this data. Due to the re-designation of the prison, the research team did not collect data from families in Phase 2. Finally, whilst portfolios were analysed in Phase 1, we took the opportunity to include participants' plans and descriptions around areas of work in Phase 2.

Data Analysis

The data was analysed using a system of open coding involving sorting data into analytical categories by "breaking down, examining, comparing, conceptualising and categorising" (Strauss and Corbin 1990: 61). Categories were then compared and contrasted to generate sub-themes which formed the basis for the analysis. In order to organise and analyse the qualitative data effectively, the analytical software tool 'NVivo10' was used. All qualitative data (diaries, reflective circles, observation notes, for example) was scanned and uploaded to NVivo10. The data from all survey responses was entered into and analysed in the quantitative analytical package SPSS (v22).

MG Garden Building Health and Wellbeing

In line with previous research, participants identified wide-ranging therapeutic benefits of the MG programme on their health and wellbeing and recovery journey throughout the data-gathering methods described above. Whilst this chapter focuses on the issues of health and wellbeing, in our report, the data is organised under the following headings.

1. Building an environment that supports recovery and change
2. Building health and wellbeing
3. Building a recovery Master Gardener community
4. Building opportunities for learning
5. The Master Gardener Programme in a prison setting

In organising the data this way, it was important not to ignore the interconnection between each of these areas and how they are all implicated in creating an environment amenable to supporting offenders with a substance misuse issue and their recovery, as demonstrated in Fig. 7.2.

Participants rarely spoke about health, be it physical or mental, without consideration for their general wellbeing or in terms of its relationship to working outside, engaging in purposeful activity and feeling supported by both their peers and staff. The MG programme offered a sense of community in which the men shared responsibility and were able to demonstrate some autonomy resting on a shared goal and ethos. Participants shared how engaging in the MG programme offered an opportunity to get involved in work requiring varying amounts of physical activity.

Engaging in this physical activity contributed to participants reporting improvement in their appetite and health benefits from an improvement in their daily diet[12]:

> *Improvement in my eating habit.* (P1)
> *Healthy and putting on weight.* (P1)

[12] Participant in Phase 1 (P1); Participant in Phase 2 (P2).

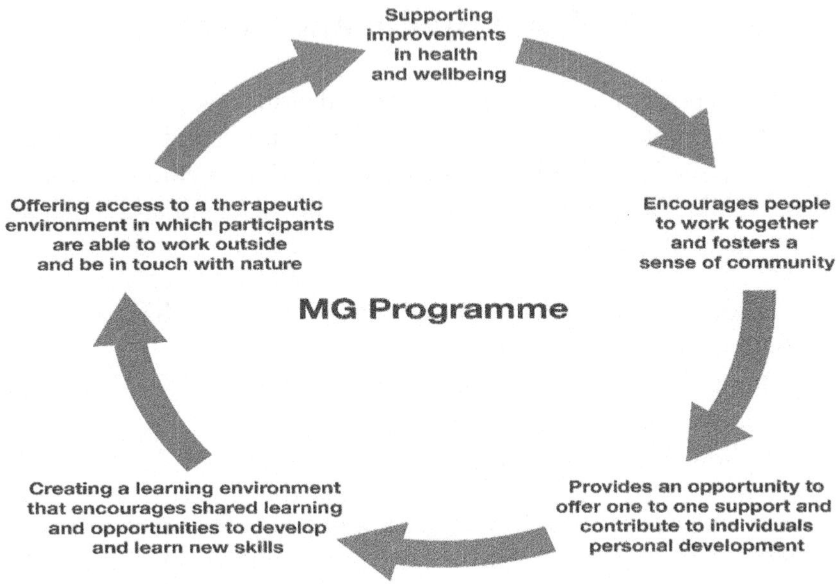

Fig. 7.2 Factors identified as central to the men's recovery journey

The increase in physical activity also led to an improvement in sleeping patterns, in line with research in this area (Grimshaw and King 2002):

I sleep much better after a hard day in the garden. (P1)
Sleep better after a hard days' work and being outside. Also helps with better health and fitness, sense of achievement. (P2)
I couldn't get to sleep before 3am now I can't stay up past 9pm. (P2)

Participants also reported having more energy and motivation since engaging in the programme:

My health is getting better and I'm able to do things I was struggling to do before. (P2)
More motivated to get up and do things. Before we used to get up at 10am or 11am and have lunch and wing work/nothing. (P2)

For some participants, feeling healthier encouraged them to consider adopting other health-related practices, engaging regularly in gym sessions[13] and giving up smoking tobacco. Furthermore, this was perceived as a contributor to increasing their motivation to work and engage in all aspects of the MG programme.

The Master Gardener Programme: A Place for Recuperation

The MG programme was also viewed as conducive to recovery for participants who not only had substance misuse issues but also had been diagnosed with or developed other medical issues. During the evaluation, we were aware of participants with a health-related issue that required being referred to hospital outside of the prison. On their return to the MG programme, they shared how being in the garden and in a supportive environment was beneficial to their recuperation. In their reflective diaries participants wrote how being able to work in the garden, at their own pace and in a calm environment were factors which positively contributed to their physical recovery.

Another example of this is a participant in Phase 2 who was rushed to the hospital with a life-threatening illness. In a group discussion during one of our visits his peers shared how, at the time of being transferred to hospital as an emergency, they were concerned as to whether or not he would survive. In September in his diary he shared how on his return from hospital the first thing he did was to go out into the garden.

> *I'm working on getting my health back to a normal level as I've only been out of hospital a week. … I can't do much work cuz of being ill and it can take up to 12–18 months to get better …*

The following month (October) in his reflective circle he identified feeling an improvement in his health, which he attributed to working in the garden.

---

[13] As part of the MG programme, participants also get additional access to the gym.

Garden at the start of the project

The positive impact and improvement in his health and wellbeing from working in the garden was also reported by a member of staff:

[Name] health had been affected due to being very poorly. [Name] attended and first he was fed up/negative in group. [Name] appears to be more positive and talks about how much he enjoys SMS garden and looks forward to working in the afternoons. … [Name] has since started again and is getting better. (PCO Facilitator, P2)

There was a positive relationship between the MG programme and reported physical health. Being outside, engaged in purposeful and physical activities, working with peers and being able to access support from peers and staff were all factors considered as making a valuable contribution to improving individuals' health. In addition, the MG programme was viewed as supplementing the limitations of the official prison healthcare services. For example, a number of criticisms were levelled at the length of time it could take to receive an appointment, the insufficient amount of space allocated to the service and limitations associated with the care provided:

Health Care leaves the recovery unit till last. I'm trying to stop smoking, as all the drugs I take I smoke. I lasted about 10 days because they stress me out, and I need a smoke when I'm stressed. (P2)

They cram as many people in as they can to save money—6 people were booked in for an appointment at the same time. (P2)

Is it going to take a death before they buck up their ideas? The only time you see a nurse on the wing is when people cut up, or at night when everyone's locked up to dispense night meds. (P2)

Hence, it appeared important to the participants we consulted with that the MG programme offered substance-misusing prisoners access to additional support outside of the prison's health service.

Mental Health

Overwhelmingly, the health benefits reported by participants in Phase 1 and 2 were related to the MG programme and mental health. Across the data, there are numerous entries in participants' diaries, reflective circles and noted in our observations in which participants identify how they perceive the relationship between the MG programme and their mental wellbeing:

It's a great emotional journey for me, as someone who has a number of underlying mental health issues its had a great impact on me, this week so far has been no exception with some new issues going on, it's helped me not to explode. (P2)

Since I've been on the gardens I feel better in myself and have been a lot happier. (P1)

Participants reported how the MG programme was supporting them to manage mental health issues such as depression, self-harming and their suicidal thoughts. In our observations, we were aware that such issues for some participants were ongoing challenges. During one visit, one of the researchers noted the following:

During this visit one of the participants was under observations due to his self-harming and attempted suicide. It appears that the only place he does not

> *appear to self-harm is in the garden. As such, he is allowed to come to work despite being under half hourly observations. I observed how the other participants attempt to support him. They shared with us their feelings about a recent incident which they perceived had contributed to his self-harming. Despite having a particularly bad time, the participant willingly completed his reflective diary (without prompting from the research team) and observed him going out and working independently in the garden albeit under the supervision of GO team.* (P2)

The MG programme became a place considered 'safe' when difficulties were experienced. Over the 12 months we observed how, for participants, it was not only the garden and being outside that was important but this in conjunction with the holistic way in which the MG programme offered support. This holistic support included working outside in the garden, but also access to peer support, flexible and supportive staff, mentoring, purposeful activity and having a sense of safety and a vision for the garden. The holistic way in which the MG programme was delivered meant that staff accepted that recovery was not a linear process and that participants would sometimes encounter challenges that disrupt their recovery. As such, all attempts were made to ensure that participants were aware that as long as they were cleared by security to work in the garden, the MG programme was not a short-term intervention but a programme that was willing to invest the time needed to support participants in their recovery, including periods of relapse:

> *Beginning of the month was really positive but at the moment I am in a dark place of no hope, no light. I am not sure where it will end but I hope soon.* (P2)

> *I had a bad relapse last month where it resulted in me self-harming; it had nothing to do with the gardening project, just life in general—family problems, made myself ill by taking far too many tablets … The garden is looking a bit better; there is a change in myself where I'm not taking nowhere near as much drugs as I was … I had a few problems mentally last month but now I'm feeling a lot better in myself and with my job in the garden I have learned a few new things.* (P1)

Our observation highlighted how the MG programme offered participants an opportunity to access an area within the prison that allowed them a sense of freedom in that they were away from the wing. The MG programme provided an opportunity for participants to engage in a purposeful physical activity, access support, work in calm environment and created an environment in which supportive relationships were established with peers and the staff involved. This was conducive to facilitating an environment where participants were better able to manage their mental health. During one visit a participant shed light on this and shared how the MG programme was important in diverting his thoughts away from self-harm and contemplating suicide. He explained that as someone who has struggled with mental health issues (depression) the physical activity, routine and supportive environment was central to his current health and wellbeing. During our conversation he recounted how he was feeling suicidal as he found dealing with a range of issues related to his sentence challenging. The programme gave him something to focus on and helped him to take his mind off issues he was finding difficult to deal with.

In his diary entry he wrote,

> *This is a bad month due to an anniversary and birthday. I sometimes feel stress coming into the garden but it helps to keep my head clear and is a welcome relief from the nightmares.* (P2)

During our visit the following month his diary entry reported that he was feeling better and this was largely due to the MG programme as he loved the opportunity to work and share his knowledge with others. He described the MG programme as providing him with a sense of 'normality' and as 'saving his life'.

For participants, the MG programme was considered to be unique and different from other programmes in terms of the time and space afforded to listening to participants and taking their views and experiences into account:

> *That we can sit down and discuss our problems and find solutions or just make them aware of them makes you feel better.* (P2)

> *I would like to be open when on the wing as we are in the garden.* (P1)

Alongside this, it was viewed as rewarding as it was delivered in a way in which participants had a level of freedom and autonomy. The MG programme was outside the norm of the prison regime as it encouraged participants to be creative, get involved in a range of activities and take responsibility for decisions related to what they did, when they did it and how.

> *I think it focuses them and diverts their minds from boredom within the prison, they come out to work at 8.30 am in the morning and they've got things to constantly think about, ideas of their own that they can put into practice and their mind is constantly, so that when they go back at lunchtime they're still thinking about what they did in the morning and thinking about what they're going to do in the afternoon and it kind of diverts their attention away from misbehaving and from the substance misuse.* (Staff P2)

To this end, the MG programme helped to divert participants' attention away from their individual health-related issues through engaging them in purposeful activities. Also important is that participants were working towards an individual and shared goal (discussed later in this chapter). The MG programme was delivered in an environment that was viewed to be supportive; this support was provided by peers, programme staff and the wider substance misuse team. A participant's reflections about the relevance of his involvement in work in the garden to his wellbeing:

> *It's the freedom!* (P2)
>
> *I get a positive feeling from working in the garden.* (P1)
>
> *Less stressed, not getting down or responding better when feeling down.* (P1)

Circle of Change

A participant's monthly record detailing his perception about the impact of the MG programme.

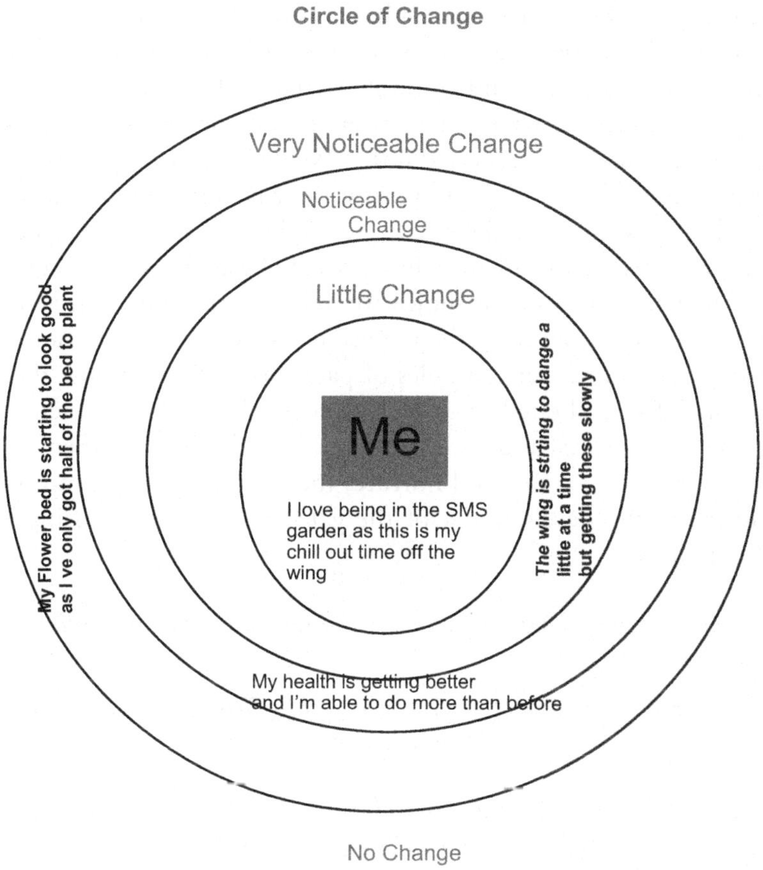

MG Programme and Subjective Wellbeing

Wellness and wellbeing are emerging as major organising concepts used to both analyse and enhance the quality of life of populations, communities, families and individuals. The benefit of capturing data associated with wellbeing is that it allows us to capture notions of health beyond the absence of disease and moves towards a conceptualisation of health that incorporates subjective feelings (Knight and McNaught 2011). Subjective wellbeing (SWB), people's emotional and cognitive evaluations of their lives, includes factors such as happiness, peace, fulfilment and life satisfaction. SWB can be impacted by factors such as personality **dispositions**, life circumstances and cultural variables (Diener et al. 2014). It is a positive concept in which the emphasis rests on social and personal resources as well as physical capabilities. Wellbeing provides a more holistic way of understanding the impact of the MG programme on participants. It is also an essential theme to explore in relation to the data collected as participants identify in a myriad of ways the MG programme as playing a key role in their subjective wellbeing and how this is important in terms of supporting their substance misuse recovery. Across the data there are numerous examples of participants sharing how the MG programme has facilitated access to a space in which they experience positive, mental, physical and social state and how this leads to them having a sense of purpose, a goal and nurtures their willingness and motivation to engage in the development of the garden alongside accessing other SMS activities.

> *No more searching happy, I feel I am positively calm and my wellbeing is good.* (P2)
>
> *Asking for advice instead of bottling it up—(Big Change) more relaxed confident, stress free. More myself, I open up a lot more about how I feel.* (P2)

Staff also reported the MG programme as having a positive impact on participants' health and mental wellbeing. In Phase 1, staff reported that:

> *The prisoners are quieter than they were—calmer and less rowdy or boisterous. One prisoner has demonstrated improved communication skills. Some have even apologised for their behaviour, demonstrating reflection and remorse which was not apparent before. One person has really "come out of his shell". One prisoner is talking more now instead of bottling things up and hurting himself. He's working hard and sleeping.* (*Prison Staff,* P1)

Staff feedback forms were distributed, aimed at all staff in the prison that come into regular contact with the participants but had no direct involvement with the MG programme. Administering the questionnaires was undertaken by the MG programme coordinator, bi-monthly during the first phase of the project. However, the changes to the prison during Phase 2 of the project made collecting meaningful data from staff who were just getting to know the new prison population difficult. The outcome was that only 4 questionnaires were completed during this phase. Notwithstanding, within the questionnaire, staff were asked to report on any changes they had noticed in participants' physical wellbeing, emotional wellbeing, behaviour towards staff, engagement and compliance with prison regimes and interaction with other prisoners. The questionnaire also provided a space for staff to provide specific examples of any of the changes they had noticed in the participant. Focusing on results observed in relation to the whole population, nearly 90% of staff reported changes in participants' general wellbeing and nearly 80% of staff reported changes in participants' emotional wellbeing overall. The majority of staff indicated either a noticeable or very noticeable change in these areas. Generally, low numbers of staff members had noticed no change, or a little change, in participants' general and emotional wellbeing, or were unable to comment ('don't know'). In the survey, staff also shared their views about what they perceived to be changes in the wellbeing of our participants

> *I have seen a lot of change since he has started within the Ryton Gardens Project. He enjoys his time within the gym, mixes well with the other offenders when down here, always polite and compliant to staff. [He] asks a lot of questions about healthy living etc. also enjoys talking about what they do on the gardens!!* (Sports Centre Officer, P1)

> *Looks healthier, … the project offers him more fresh air.* (OCA Officer, P1)

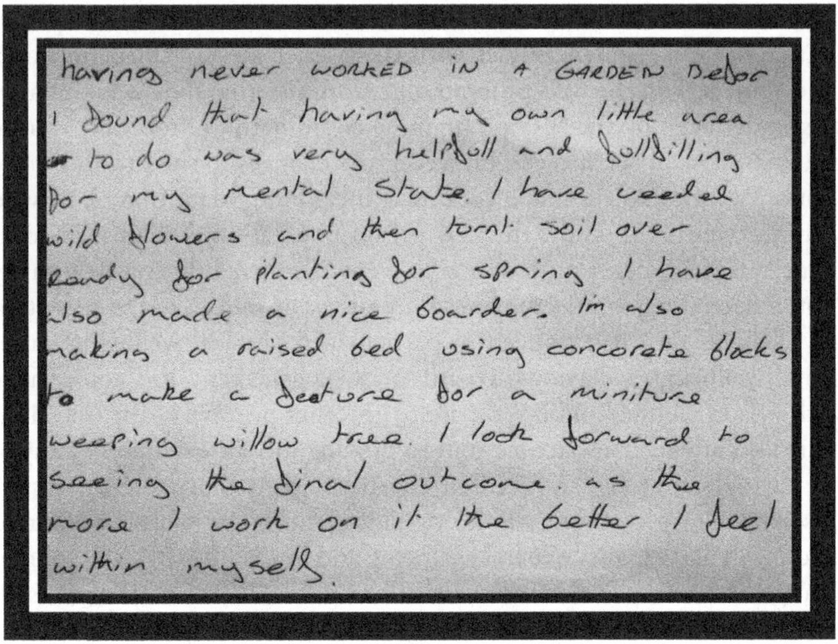
having never WORKED IN A GARDEN befor
I found that having my own little area
to do was very helpfull and fullfilling
for my mental State. I have weeded
wild flowers and then turnt soil over
ready for planting for spring I have
also made a nice boarder. I'm also
making a raised bed using concorate blocks
to make a feature for a miniture
weeping willow tree. I lock forward to
seeing the final outcome. as the
more I work on it the better I feel
within myself.

[Name] has begun to participate in group work and his confidence and self-esteem has increased dramatically; he now organises and runs peer-support groups for other prisoners. (Substance Misuse Nurse, P1)

I have visited Mr [Name] at the garden project. He was very proud of the work he was doing there as part of a team of gardeners. He is clearly finding it a very rewarding experience. His emotional wellbeing in particular appears to have improved. (Offender Supervisor, P1)

Final Reflection: Building Health and Wellbeing in Prisons

Garden at Latter Stages of the Evaluation

There is a growing body of research establishing the link between horticulture and health and wellbeing. Davies et al. (2014) describe the activity of gardening as having a positive impact on individuals' health and

wellbeing due to both the physical activity and the use of the garden as a space for mental relaxation and stimulation. Hence, they argue that the activity of gardening, viewing green space and being in green space, is positive in terms of the support it provides individuals in dealing with mental health issues and stress. In this chapter, we have presented key findings illuminating diverse ways in which participants spoke about the positive benefits they gained from engaging in the MG programme. These benefits go beyond an individualised notion of health to a social notion of health in which interactional meanings, group experience and personal and emotional meanings are experienced on a collective level (Brandt-Meyer and Butler 1999). Our study highlights the interconnections between building a supportive environment, opportunities for men to gain new skills or develop and put to use existing skills, promotes informal and formal peer and staff mentoring and encourages a process of self-reflection. This creates an environment in which common values, group working and a shared responsibility helps in fostering a therapeutic and supporting environment that supplements the men's recovery journey.

The link between health, specifically mental health and substance misuse is commonly acknowledged and, as suggested by Pretty et al. (2011), facilitating nature-based activity and social engagement positively influences health and offers a catalyst for behavioural change (Pretty et al.

2011), The evidence generated through the evaluation acknowledges the MG programme as providing a route to recovery but also points to the significance of the context and interpersonal relationships to the positive outcomes reported. As important as the physical space or activities provided is the interaction between staff delivering the programme, the sense of autonomy prisoners feel and how they are generally treated. Our research shows the inter-connection between each of these areas and the health and wellbeing reported by participants in our study:

Our data reveals that the MG programme is instrumental in supporting participants with their substance recovery journey:

- Building an environment that supports recovery
- Having access to a space in which participants feel a sense of freedom and autonomy and able to access support is important. In conjunction with being outside, it gives participants an opportunity to engage in purposeful activity. Building an environment that is perceived by individuals as supportive and safe helps to restore people's directive attention on their substance-misusing behaviour and behaviour more generally.
- Building health and wellbeing
- Being outdoors in the garden and engaged in growing or other related purposeful activities positively impacts on individuals' physical and mental health and subjective wellbeing. Of equal importance to working in the garden and working with nature is the space that is unlike other parts of the prison estate. This creates opportunities for participants to engage in physical activity, mental relaxation and stimulation (Davies et al. 2014), leading to positive health and wellbeing outcomes.
- Building a recovery Master Gardener community
- Bringing people together to share a vision and goal around the development of the garden offers an opportunity to gain a sense of purpose. Our data shows a relationship between development of the garden and participant's self-perception, confidence and motivation. The MG programme encouraged participants to work together, support each other and to share ideas, views and experiences (in the widest sense).

Building a sense of community was not solely amongst the participants but also extended to staff working on the programme.
- Building opportunities for learning
- Engagement in the MG programme allows participants to gain new skills or develop and apply existing skills. In doing so, this promotes opportunities for informal peer learning (including staff), peer support and mentoring. This is alongside skills that can be transferred to the world of work on release from prison.

The factors listed above together contribute to creating an environment amenable to supporting substance-misusing men in prison, who often present with a range of health-related issues. Our research identifies that the significance of the MG programme was that working collaboratively with key stakeholders, it created a humanising space and promoted self-worth. It provided a root in which the men felt a connection to nature, their peers and staff. This was in tandem with offering valuable opportunities to learn and develop work-related skills. The MG programme offered the men an escape from the harsh realities of prison life and our findings illuminate a myriad of ways in which the MG programme was conducive to positively supporting recovery and change.

There are implications of this research for practice within prison and for future research. Prison drug strategy calls for an integrated and person-centred approach to substance misuse treatment. MG programme is an example of how partnership working can be creative, innovative and bring a fresh approach to responding to complex and multiple needs within prison populations. MG programme offers a valuable insight to how such interventions can make a constructive contribution to improving the prison environment. Prisoners and staff benefit from working within a safe and humanising space, such as the garden; opportunity should be used where possible to create further spaces which also have this function and quality. Significant value was placed on the positive relationships with staff that were created in the garden. Adopting a person-centred approach which prioritised the men's needs, was non-judgemental and recognised their efforts in the garden helped the participants to feel valued, which supported engagement and impacted on their subjective wellbeing.

References

Adevi, A., & Martensson, F. (2013). Stress rehabilitation through garden therapy: The garden as a place in the recovery from stress. *Urban Forestry & Urban Greening, 12*(2), 230–237.

Brandt-Meyer, E., & Butler, S. (1999). Food for people not for profit: Meanings of a farm project for homeless and very poor participants. *Journal of Progressive Human Services, 10*(1), 53–66.

Davies, G., Devereaux, M., Lennartsson, M., Schmutz, U., & Williams, S. (2014). *The benefits of gardening and growing food for health and wellbeing.* Garden Organic and Sustain, UK.

Diener, G., Devereaux, M., Lennartsson, M., Schmutz, U., & Williams, S. (2014). *The benefits of gardening and growing food for health and well-being.* Garden Organic and Sustain UK.

Fontaine, J. (2017). *Horticulture as therapy in Toronto: Unearthing healing and wellness.* Canada: School of Social Work, York University.

Grabbe, L., Ball, J., & Goldstein, A. (2015). Gardening for the mental well-being of homeless women. *Journal of Holistic Nursing, 31*(4), 258–266.

Grimshaw, R., & King, J. (2002). *Horticulture in Secure Settings.* Thrive: Reading.

Haller, R. (1998). Vocational, social, and therapeutic programs. In S. Simson & M. Strauss (Eds.), *Horticulture as therapy: Principles and practice* (pp. 43–68). New York: Food Products Press.

Harris, N., Minniss, F. R., & Somerset, S. (2014). Refugees connecting with a new country through community food gardening. *International Journal of Environmental Research and Public Health, 11*(9), 9202–9216.

Hefley, D. (1973). Horticulture: A therapeutic tool. *Journal of Rehabilitation, 39*(1), 27–29.

HMP Rye Hill. (2014). *About Rye Hill* (online). Available from https://hmpryehill.co.uk/aboutrh_main.htm

Kam and Sui. (2010). Evaluation of a horticultural activity programme for persons with psychiatric illness. *Hong Kong Journal of Occupational Therapy, 20*(2), 80–86.

Knight, A., & McNaught, A. (Eds). (2011). *Understanding wellbeing: An introduction for students and practitioners of health and social care.* Lantern Publishing.

Lehmann, L., Detweiler, J., & Detweiler, M. (2018). Veterans in substance abuse treatment program self-initiate box gardening as a stress reducing therapeutic modality. *Complementary Therapies in Medicine, 36*, 50–53.

Millet, P. (2009). Integrating horticulture into the vocational rehabilitation process of individuals with fatigue, chronic fatigue, and burnout: A theoretical model. *Journal of Therapeutic Horticulture, 19*, 10–22.

Ministry of Justice, National Health Service and Department of Health. (2011). Funding for 2011/12 substance misuse services in prisons. Polmoski, R.F, Johnson, K. M., Anderson, J. C, (1997) Prison.

O'Hagan, A., & Hardwick, R. (2017). Behind bars: The truth about drugs in prisons. *Forensic Research & Criminology International Journal, 5*(3), 00158. https://doi.org/10.15406/frcij.2017.05.00158.

Pearce, C., & Seals, L. (2006). The Importance of Gardening for Homeless Women: A pilot Study. *Journal of Therapeutic Horticulture, 17*, 20–27.

Pretty, J., Barton, J., Colbeck, I., Hine, R., Mourato, S., MacKerron, G., & Wood, C. (2011). The UK National Ecosystem Assessment Technical Report Chapter 23: Health Values from Ecosystems. In: *The UK National Ecosystem Assessment Technical Report. UK National Ecosystem Assessment.* UNEPWCMC, Cambridge in.

Rappe, E., Kajander, H., Vesamäki, J., & Malinen, A. (2016). Horticulture in rehabilitation of inmates. *Acta Horticulturae, 1121*, 19–26.

Riordan, R. (1983). Gardening as a rehabilitation adjunct. *Journal of Rehabilitation, 49*(4), 39–41.

Sempik, J., Rickhuss, C., & Beeston, A. (2014). The effects of social and therapeutic horticulture on aspects of social behaviour. *British Journal of Occupational Therapy, 77*, 313–319.

Strauss, A., & Corbin, J. M. (1990). Basics of qualitative research: Grounded theory procedures and techniques. Sage Publications,

Sturge, G. (2018). *UK prison population statistics*. House of Commons Library.

Wheatley, M. (2016). Drug misuse in prisons. In Y. Jewkes, J. Bennett, & B. Crewe (Eds.), *Handbook on prisons* (pp. 205–223). Oxford: Routledge.

York, M., & Wiseman, T. (2012). Gardening as an occupation: A critical review. *British Journal of Occupational Therapy, 75*(2), 76–84.

8

The 'Dead Zone' in the Stories of People in Prison

Alan Farrier

Introduction

The Healthy and Sustainable Settings Unit, based at the University of Central Lancashire, England, carried out a two-year qualitative evaluation concerning the impact of a prisons-based horticulture and environmental programme on the health and well-being of participants. The qualitative evaluation was designed to complement an existing quantitative study of participants' well-being.

The research team used purposive sampling to select 12 people in prison serving a custodial sentence to be interviewed, all of whom were taking part in the programme. In order to cover a range of prison contexts, people in prison were selected from four UK prisons (category B, C, D and a women's prison). The primary research approach used was the biographic-narrative interpretive method (BNIM). This chapter explores some of the challenges with regard to conducting BNIM interviews with

A. Farrier (✉)
University of Central Lancashire, Preston, UK
e-mail: AFarrier@uclan.ac.uk

© The Author(s) 2021

M. Maycock et al. (eds.), *Issues and Innovations in Prison Health Research*, Palgrave Studies in Prisons and Penology, https://doi.org/10.1007/978-3-030-46401-1_8

people in prison, in particular those who have committed serious offences, in order to build individual case studies. Issues such as the context of the prison setting, ethics, the nature of the participants' offending behaviour, and the strengths and challenges of using this method are discussed. One such case study, with a person in prison serving a life sentence, is used to illustrate the challenges of understanding their story and how we understand notions such as rehabilitation in the participant when the criminal act for which they are serving their sentence is consciously avoided in their story. The chapter demonstrates how, despite some problematic issues, there is value in using such a method in this context.

Background: Prisoner Health and Well-being and Horticulture

Within England and Wales, there are strong links between offending behaviour, a lack of skills and low educational attainment (Prison Reform Trust 2015). Ill health is often exacerbated in prison (WHO Europe 2014), particularly as people in prison are more likely to be diagnosed with poor physical and mental health than the general population (Baybutt et al. 2009). It is estimated that 80% of people in prison have a mental or psychiatric disorder (Prison Reform Trust 2016). Self-harm incidents in prison rose to a record high in 2018 (Ministry of Justice 2019). Studies have shown that rates of self-harm in female people in prison are ten times higher than male people in prison, between 20% and 24% compared with 0.6% in the general population (Hawton et al. 2014). Despite these understandings, traditionally, health-based initiatives in prisons have focused on physical rather than mental dimensions of health and well-being (Woodall et al. 2014), utilising reductionist rather than holistic approaches (Warwick-Booth et al. 2012). Horticulture has arguably managed to escape easy pigeon-holing in this regard, due to the multifaceted nature of the therapeutic benefits which may be gained from active participation (Genter et al. 2015).

Horticulture has a century-long history in prisons, being recognised as early as the 1920s as a "means of creating more humane conditions and as a form of inmate rehabilitation through meaningful work" (Rutt 2016: 182). It has, more recently, been recognised as a mechanism to enable marginalised people to reintegrate into society by facilitating skills development (O'Brien et al. 2011). It has been further argued that investing in health-promoting activities such as horticulture may increase a prisoner's chances of returning to society with improved health and self-efficacy, which may increase their chances for a reduction in reoffending (Flagler 1995).

Horticulture Intervention and Evaluation

Greener on the Outside for Prisons (GOOP) is a therapeutic horticulture intervention. It was initially funded by Big Lottery between 2008 and 2015 and is currently operating in all public sector prisons in the North West of England, with further prisons in the North East, Midlands and Wales beginning to create GOOP projects. The programme is focused on working with people in prison to: establish and maintain outdoor green spaces in prisons; grow flowers, plants and food where space and facilities are available; improve local environments by allowing people in prison to be released on temporary licence (ROTL) to work in local public green spaces; offer training on accredited courses and NVQ Horticulture Qualifications; and link with health staff inside prisons to assess health and well-being of participants (Baybutt and Farrier 2015).

A process evaluation was conducted on GOOP between 2008 and 2012 (Baybutt et al. 2018), followed by an impact evaluation between 2013 and 2015 (Farrier and Kedwards 2015). The latter was a two-year mixed-method evaluation in which, amongst a mixed-methods approach, Biographic-Narrative Interpretive Method (BNIM) interviews were conducted with 12 people in prison from four prisons. The BNIM interviews and the case studies which resulted served a dual function: as well as bolstering existing monitoring and evaluation, which focused on outcome indicators of mental well-being, physical activity and healthier eating, they aimed to understand in more depth how the programme may affect other pertinent issues, such as participants' attitudes towards re-offending and their future lives 'through the gate'. An exemplar case study with one female participant is the focus of this chapter.

Narrative and the Biographic-Narrative Interpretive Method

The increasing recognition of the value of stories in social research is demonstrated by the 'narrative turn' (Kohler Riessman 2008) in research methods in the latter twentieth century, although it has been noted that the emergence of narrative-based research began in the early twentieth century (Goodson and Gill 2011). In an article in *Time* magazine, Lance Morrow spoke of how television and radio have shaped popular culture into being a 'war of myths':

> *Stories are precious, indispensable. Everyone must have his history, her narrative. You do not know who you are until you possess the imaginative version of yourself. You almost do not exist without it.* (Morrow 1992: 78)

This quote suggests a distinction between the 'imagined' version of oneself told through stories and an actual self. BNIM explores such intricacies in people's stories and is concerned with eliciting and analysing narratives (a story with context and time) (Wengraf 2001). It is a psycho-social methodology, concerned with macro (global and national), meso (organisational and institutional), interpersonal (social networks) and inner-worlds (the intra-psychic), and the interplay between these domains (Froggett 2002). BNIM recognises the value of narratives and argues that they can reveal what emotions the participant was feeling in a certain situation; that stories have an inner logic and flow that captures sense making from the participant's perspective; that stories are more authentic than opinions; and finally, and perhaps more contentiously, that allowing participants the time and space to tell their own stories can be therapeutic and possibly even empowering (Wengraf 2001).

BNIM interviews are open ended and structured using frames of reference of beneficiary. They are framed around a single question aimed at inducing narrative (abbreviated to 'SQUIN') that requests that participants tell their story in relation to a particular area of interest. For the GOOP evaluation, we were examining people in prison's experiences of participation in the programme, and in particular those that who coming towards the end of their sentences (going 'through the gate') or moving from one prison site to another, as the study had a particular interest in how the experience of the GOOP programme in a specific prison may be transferred to other locations and environments. Therefore, the opening 'SQUIN' was:

> *Can you please tell me the story of your involvement in the GOOP programme, the events and experiences that are important for you, I won't interrupt you, please take as long as you want, I'll just take some notes in case I have any questions afterwards.*

Participants were subsequently asked follow-up questions related to their initial story (in phases of the interview called 'subsessions'), which push for clarification via further narratives, using not only the participant's frame of reference (language and particular terminology) but also respecting the order in which the story was told in the next subsession.

Interviews were recorded and verbatim transcripts are analysed chronologically in 'data chunks'. In full BNIM, this would then be subject to an in-depth hermeneutic analysis by a panel of individuals (for instance, the researcher and colleagues from their institution). The researcher divides the verbatim transcript text each time there is a change in narrative speech style and these chunks are analysed in sequence. The speech styles detailed by the method are: description (painting a picture); argumentation (offering an opinion); report (a factual explanation); narrative (a specific particular story within the larger interview); and evaluation (similar to argumentation but more truncated and linked to narrative or report in the flow of the participant's story). The purpose being that the panel are able to freely associate and speculate on the data chunks, and a series of hypotheses are created about the particular case, which are confirmed, disconfirmed or elaborated on as the analysis progresses. However, for this study, the funders were not able to allocate a budget sufficient to be able to conduct this comparatively costly analysis. This led the researcher to adapt the method in order that they were still able to produce a range of hypotheses to add to the richness of the analysis, which would traditionally be added by the panel's hermeneutic analysis. The researcher employed a method of leaving a gap of six months between conducting all the interviews and analysing the data. After this time had elapsed, the interviews had faded in the researcher's memory and he found that he remembered surprisingly little from the time of the interview; thus, he was able to analyse the data, creating 'chunks' of data whilst proceeding through a line-by-line analysis of the transcript, hypothesising as he went. He then used a process of code–recode (Anney 2014) to interrogate this analysis at a later stage and challenge original assumptions.

The purpose of this method is to develop rich, detailed chronological narrative case studies, demonstrating the lived experience of individual participants. Wengraf argues that the in-depth analysis of three to six BNIM interviews should be sufficient to compare the dynamics of the 'whole cases', enabling structural themes to be drawn out of each case and allow for cross-case comparison and theorisation (Wengraf 2001). Even this small number, studies in the level of depth the methodology affords, allows for an empirical intimacy (Sandelowski 2002) (sufficient familiarity with each case), and commonalities will emerge from this number of case studies to allow generalisability of key themes. In total, 12 in-depth interviews were conducted with people in prison across four sites and six subsequent case studies were developed (by which point it was felt by the researcher that sufficient analysis had been conducted and the analysis had reached a "point of saturation" (Macdonald 1993: 96). The case study is presented in this chapter was chosen as it reflected the wider effects of the study whilst also containing some specific issues that merit consideration. Approval for the work was given by HMPPS:NRC and the University of Central Lancashire Ethics Committee.

Case Study

In order to preserve the anonymity of the participant, only minimal context will be given: the prisoner in question, who has been given the pseudonym of Karen, is a woman approaching the end of serving a life sentence. She was suggested by prison staff as an individual who was particularly engaged in the GOOP project. After meeting with her several times in the prison gardens to discuss the research I was working on, she consented to let me interview her. I let the people in prison choose the venue of the interview (insofar as prison security would allow) and Karen chose one of the polytunnels.

Affective Connections

Karen's narrative brought in few elements of her life prior to her sentence beginning. The only friend or family member she mentioned in her interview was her mother, and only in the context of horticulture being an activity that they shared together.

> *My mum, she's always done her gardening and stuff. So I'd go and do like little bits of gardening and things like that. And then for my eighteenth birthday, my mum bought me a red rose because red's my favourite colour.*

This anecdote appeared to be recalled with fondness. Karen seemed connected with her mother in this moment, but no attempt was made to link with the present day in her narrative. This anecdote referred to events that occurred at least 20 years ago and it was not made clear if her mother was still alive or if horticulture was still something they bonded over. Rather it appeared an attempt to ground her interest in gardening as something personally resonant, rather than as simply a way to pass the time on her sentence.

Reimagining of Self

The polytunnel Karen chose to be interviewed in was one of several in the prison grounds. During the interview, she explained that she spent a lot of time working in this particular polytunnel, and showed me the variety of flower and fruit beds with a palpable degree of pride:

I tell you now, I wish I'd have done all this at school, right, because it has been the making of me. I absolutely love it. Because it's like, when you put a seed in the soil ... and then you watch it, and it's like, you're growing with that seed.

This part of Karen's story was told with an apparent element of wistfulness, as she considers an alternative path she might have taken she been exposed to horticulture to this degree whilst she was a child. She discussed her experience of the programme as a reshaping of her identity: as a caring person. It appears to help her forget her identity as a prisoner serving a life sentence and reimagine herself as a horticulturalist.

Harmful Behaviour Change

Self-harm is a significant part of Karen's story, but it is told implicitly: she describes her self-harming behaviour as being prior to moving to her current prison, where she has been for a decade:

I used to be a prolific self-harmer. And in the last...nine years, I don't self-harm no more.

Karen never makes the explicit link between participation in GOOP and her ceasing of self-harm behaviour; however, in the chronology of her story these two events coincide, as this change in behaviour closely aligns with GOOP's presence in the prison (GOOP was just entering its ninth year in the prison at the time of the interview). This information is offered immediately after she gives her previous 'growing' metaphor.

Green Space and Well-being

The particular prison related to this case featured a large, well-maintained gardens area, which was by all accounts a pleasant environment in which both people in prison and prison staff went to relax. The open nature of the house within the prison Karen was living in meant that GOOP participants were able to spend a full day working in the gardens, even eating their lunch on benches surrounded by plants and flowers, only returning to their rooms to sleep. The large polytunnels helped further obscure the location for Karen.

> *It's just getting away from everything and it's like, sometimes I don't even see that fence* [points out of the polytunnel door] *because I'm … I don't even see it. To me, most of the time, until I really look on where it is, I forget where I am.*

Positive Visioning

Karen's story ended with her current preoccupation with moving through the gate into supported housing which was located outside of the prison walls, but within walking distance. In this new accommodation, Karen would be able to leave during working hours, and it is her intention to begin volunteering:

> *There was a lady who come in…and gave me an interview. I shown her…my portfolio of all the pictures of the tunnels and that. And they don't normally take people on for community work. And she said, I'm more qualified than the lads that she's got!*

Participation in GOOP has evidently increased Karen's skills and abilities in horticulture, she is now receiving recognition for her work and this has increased her confidence levels, which enables her to imagine a more positive future.

Discussion

Case Study

Reflecting on the case study of Karen, a number of key themes emerged, which were both central to her story and also reflected wider generalisability of the benefits of horticulture. Firstly, the affective connections observed. This worked on two levels. Firstly, a connection with nature, identified as the biophilia hypothesis (Wilson 1984); that is, that humans have a connection with nature that is innate and that this desire to nurture plants, vegetables and flowers has a psychological benefit. Secondly, that horticulture allows connections to be made with other people. In the BNIM interviews, this was described more often than not as family members, with some intergenerational dynamic being at play (either a desire to take up horticulture with participants' children or parents). Working with horticulture appeared to entail people in prison reimagining their identity and was therefore highly congruent with the notion of a narrative 'redemption script' described in desistance theory. That is, the notion that there is an element of "renewal, gaining strength and realizing their true selves" (Maruna 2010: 576) in the process of such change. This is a metamorphosis on a deeper level than merely changing one's name or appearance, but rather as a repositioning of oneself from criminal and prisoner to a useful and valuable member of the group and potentially, wider society and to demonstrate this to others (Toch 2010). For the participant in the case study presented in this chapter, Karen's metaphor of growing with the seed underlines this process of change she is describing.

Although the overarching structural hypothesis of the cross-case comparison was similar, there were some distinct differences that were gender-based—particularly in relation to self-harming behaviour. This is perhaps unsurprising, as this is such a recognised issue (Völlm and Dolan 2009) that in the women's prison studied, they have their own dedicated unit for women at risk of self-harm. Even in the small number of interviews conducted in this study (n = 12), narratives of self-harm and suicide attempts were only present in female participants' stories (n = 3), but not in the male participants' stories (n = 9). In relation to GOOP, some of the participants made direct links to participation and a reduction in self-harm and suicidal behaviour. In this case, the link was made implicitly (i.e. her reduction in self-harming behaviour coincided with her enrollment on a GOOP project). For others the link was made more explicit, but in a more muted way. For example, stating that GOOP is not a panacea for their mental health issues regarding self-harm and suicide, but it does at least help to reduce these thoughts and feelings. However, this was also present in other case studies, in the form of a change of behaviour and an emotional maturation that occurred in the process of becoming immersed in horticultural work. For example, observations of a reduction in aggressive behaviour by other people in prison considered to be violent.

It is well documented that exposure to green space has beneficial effects on well-being, both in terms of physical benefits (Pretty et al. 2007) and mental health (Clatworthy et al. 2013; Richardson and Hallam 2013). In the gardens in the prison, it appeared that there was another layer which was specifically pertinent to this context: it enables people in prison to temporarily forget that they are incarcerated. It appears that both the physical cocoon of the polytunnel and the absorption in the horticultural work helps Karen to forget—at least for a short time—that she is in prison, serving a life sentence.

The scale of ambitions for future life 'through the gate' varied amongst the BNIM participants, but a commonality was a sense of positivity. This could be something as minor as spending time bonding with a child in the garden to setting up a self-employed business selling their own fresh produce. Whether the more ambitious aims are realistic is perhaps not as important as whether or not their involvement in the GOOP project opens up a 'potential space' of visioning a positive future which is beneficial to the participant's mental well-being and enables them to cope more effectively with the harsh realities of prison life. GOOP offers an opportunity for creative apperception, which "makes the individual feel that life is worth living" (Winnicott 1999: 65).

The case study featured in this chapter falls somewhere in the middle in terms of the ambitions of the participants. Volunteering work, which will benefit local communities as well as enhancing employment prospects for ex-offenders is both a realistic and achievable aim that GOOP participants moving 'through the gate' should be able to take part in. This requires effective links between prisons, probation and community organisations which were well coordinated in the prison in question, but which aren't always present in prisons generally.

Cross-Case Comparison: The 'Monomyth'

When analysing the data using BNIM, one of the distinctive features of the method is the development of a structural hypothesis of each case. After several cases are analysed and case studies developed, a saturation point is reached. Therefore, although 12 interviews were conducted, it was after six cases had been analysed, despite the distinct experiences of the individual participants and the variation between gender, age and length of custodial sentence, a commonality in the stories emerged.

In many ways, the stories seemed to echo Vogler's concept of the hero's journey or 'monomyth', reflecting on Joseph Campbell's 'The Hero With a Thousand Faces' (Campbell 2012) and concern's a heroic narrative in which "the hero enters a central space in the Special World and confronts death or faces his or her greatest fear" (Vogler 1985: 1). What is of course different in the cases of our protagonists is that, legally and in society's view, they are villains, most sympathetically to be seen as anti-heroes. However, due to the unstructured and non-judgemental nature of the BNIM interview, the participants are allowed to be the hero of their own story, freed from these other constraints.

This does, however, create some interesting dilemmas for the participant when telling their story. As a methodological and ethical consideration for the research, participants were not questioned on their actual offences, but rather allowed to tell their story in the way they wished. Karen chose not to mention her offence, either within the formality of the interview, or the informality of the rapport building that took place prior to it. Accessing the prisoner files concerning their offences and sentences was also consciously not part of the study design, so the researchers had no ability to compare and contrast any objective 'lived life' data concerning the cases with the 'told story' data from the interview. Hence for the case study in this chapter, the only information that the researcher had prior to the interview was that Karen was coming to the end of serving a life sentence.

The 'Dead Zone' in Participants' Stories

For the most part, the stories told by the participants mirror the template of the 'hero's journey'. For example, in Karen's story it involves travelling from the known into the unknown (from freedom to prison life), a 'death and rebirth' resulting in a transformation (from suicidal prisoner serving a life sentence to skilled horticulturalist) and an impending 'return' to freedom as Karen comes to the end of her sentence and prepares for life 'through the gate' as a volunteer. However, Karen's decision to avoid making any reference to her offence directly creates a hole in her story, which I have called the 'dead zone'.

The phrase 'dead zone' has a multitude of applications in everyday parlance, from different academic fields, referring to everything from polluted areas of the ocean to damaged areas of smartphone screens. It resonated as an appropriate metaphor for not only Karen's story but also other cases developed in the study in which the participants' offences were seemingly consciously not discussed. It appeared that if the participants felt comfortable with sharing their crime, if it was deemed to be acceptable, palatable, or perhaps even exhilarating to the researcher (bank robberies and marijuana farming were both mentioned openly in other cases with male people in prison). As Karen was serving a life sentence, one could argue her offence is actually a pivotal, inescapable element of her story. The fact that Karen could tell her story without mentioning this, meant that she was either working very hard on her narrative to avoid it, or that she has managed, over time, to create a narrative of her life where her crime, and the multiple ways it has affected her—are compartmentalised into this 'dead zone'. The offence is no longer part of her story. Seemingly, she has managed to 'split' off this unpalatable aspect of herself as a defence mechanism against a version of herself that she cannot tolerate (Klein 1997).

This may be considered both a constraint for the research (if the nature of the offence may illuminate the case in some regard) and a source of amelioration for the participant, who is often, due to the nature of their surroundings and their identity as a 'prisoner', defined by their offence. One might argue that one of the strengths of the BNIM is that by not asking any direct questions about the nature of the people in prison' offences, it liberates the prisoner as storyteller and serves a potentially important function for prisoners' well-being with the ameliorative potential: to forge a 'through the gate' rebirth to create new identity for themselves. However, conversely, the lack of engagement with the offence means that this creates a 'dead zone' in the narrative, in which both the journey into the unknown lacks a 'call to nature' (other than being sentenced and sent to prison for an undefined reason), and perhaps more crucially, lacks a quality of 'atonement' when moving back from the 'unknown' to the 'known'. In psychosocial terms, Karen's narrative is missing some intrapsychic processes of moving from her identity of the perpetrator of a crime that was deemed serious enough to warrant a life sentence to a skilled and valued horticulturalist.

Due to the ability to ask follow-up questions in later subsessions of the interview, there were certainly opportunities to push for narratives concerning offences, but our ethical application stated that the study design was focused on the experience of GOOP, rather than the participants' offences. The researcher was also aware that when participants completely avoided the subject, it would not be true to her narrative to start steering towards this topic.

I would also argue, as a strength in the methodology, that allowing the prisoner participant the freedom to avoid discussing their offence reduces potentially problematic defence mechanisms in the researcher. In Karen's case, the researcher later discovered the specifics of the crime the participant had committed (which will not be discussed to preserve the participants' anonymity) and commented on this in their reflective notes:

> *I actually subsequently saw Karen when visiting the prison when meeting another prisoner for a further BNIM interview. She was friendly and familiar with me, having already done the interview, but I found the interaction uncomfortable, unable to block out what I'd read about her.*

It is therefore not unreasonable to suggest that the BNIM interview might have had a different form had the researcher had access to Karen's offending history, and that this may also have been the case in other interviews. As people in prison are within "stigmatized groups" (Schlosser

2008: 1500) who are often defined by their criminal offences, the opportunity to tell their story and define what the parameters of the story are gives the participant a sense of agency that they will often be lacking in their environment. Although interviewing people in prison is a task beset with "methodological landmines" (1522), it is helpful to consider the stories constructed in the interviews as a set of multiple realities (Ewick and Silbey 1995) constructed not only by the researcher's presence but also their relationship with other women enrolled on the GOOP project, the gardens staff and the wider prison institution on the whole.

For the participants who took part in the BNIM interviews, the *bildungsroman* of the study (a German term referring to the psychological and moral growth of the individual (Lynch 1999)), was identified as being essentially similar to the 'monomyth', with the only clear distinction being that in certain cases, including the one presented in this chapter, the story was problematised by the existence of a 'dead zone' created by the storyteller. When viewed through the lens of criminal justice, and in particular how it is perceived by the larger public, this also creates certain challenges. One argument would be that part of the rehabilitative process requires that the offender needs to accept some kind of responsibility for their crime (the 'atonement' present in the 'monomyth'), and this is not evidenced in these stories.

For researchers interested in employing BNIM or congruent narrative-based methods in prisons research, it is important to raise the issue of gaining ethical approval to do such work. This particular study was significantly delayed due to being initially rejected by National Offender Management Service (NOMS) (now HMPPS: National Research Committee). Part of the reason it was denied approval on the first application was due to the open-ended research method. As the study was framed around the participants' health and well-being, it was deemed that the method was not sufficiently impact focused. In resubmitting the application, the research team emphasised how elements of health and well-being can be drawn out of stories, even when they are told from the participants' perspective and questions are asked in an open-ended way, without a specific health and well-being focus. The second application received approval and the rationale for the method was borne out in a subsequent paper derived from the study focusing on mental health and well-being and illustrated using quotes from the BNIM case studies (Farrier et al. 2019). Although not mentioned explicitly, it could be argued that there is a degree of anxiety around prisons-based research using BNIM or congruent methods.

Storytelling is inherently risky, so to agree to put oneself in the role of storyteller, as BNIM requires, is to place oneself in a position of "intentional vulnerability" (Nairne and Thren 2017: 117). In the second research application to NOMS, the focus on horticulture, health and well-being was emphasised, and it was emphasised that we would not pursue any threads of the participants' narrative related to any criminal activity in the subsequent subsessions.

Conclusion

Although this study imposed certain challenges in opting to use BNIM in a prison setting, specifically in not picking up on threads concerning offending behavior and therefore not being able to access the 'dead zone' of participants' stories, the study revealed the importance of telling stories for the participants. This is exacerbated in prison, where the individual is deprived of so many material objects that are available in the outside world that an individuals' 'story' takes on added dimensions of value: as a way to exert power, to protect oneself from other people in prison, to endear oneself to staff (and researchers).

As BNIM is experience-near, it enables a more holistic understanding of people in prison and their well-being, unencumbered by the usual research and evaluation they are subjected to (staff commented that the people in prison are often asked to complete questionnaires for monitoring and evaluation purposes). It certainly appeared that enabling people in prison to tell their story was empowering. Perhaps in part this was due to the constraints of the study design and ethics, but nevertheless the participants appeared to welcome a non-judgemental space in which to tell their story. It could even be argued that the potential space offered by participating in the BNIM may have had ameliorative qualities for the participants in terms of enabling them to envision a more optimistic and positive future 'through the gate'.

There is also value in the method in terms of compatibility with the rehabilitative function of prisons. Studies have demonstrated that there is little value in shaming offenders regarding their crimes (Tangney et al. 2012), and BNIM gives the participants the opportunity to reflect on their behaviour on their own terms, without enforcing an ultimately unhelpful agenda. In this regard, the method is akin to restorative justice insomuch as it allows reflection, which may lead to rehabilitation. In terms of the 'monomyth', this would be the process of 'atonement', which is often absent from the stories but may have been experienced by the participant in the formulation of their story. Furthermore, there are other contexts in a prison environment in which the participants may be able to discuss and reflect on their offence (e.g. personal officer or custody manager). We may also know important elements of their history (e.g. being a prolific self-harmer) without the cause or intention of such behaviour ever being clearly articulated in the story. Although it would be illuminating as researchers to hear a life story that involved the participants' offences, their decision to mention these offences or not is an important element in their shaping of their own story, particularly as they are preparing for life 'through the gate', which is arguably more beneficial to the participant and therefore society as a whole.

Acknowledgement The author would like to thank the participants in prison who placed themselves in a position of intentional vulnerability by telling their stories; the prisons and prison staff involved in the study who helped facilitate the BNIM interviews; and delegates at the Carceral Bodies: Prisons Research Symposium 2017 in Belfast who gave feedback on an early version of this paper given as an oral presentation.

References

Anney, V. N. (2014). Ensuring the quality of the findings of qualitative research: Looking at trustworthiness criteria. *Journal of Emerging Trends in Educational Research and Policy Studies, 5*(2), 272–281.

Baybutt, M., & Farrier, A. (2015). *Greener on the outside for prisons: A guide to setting up and delivering a prison-based GOOP project.* UCLan/Big Lottery Fund. Manual. UCLan, Preston.

Baybutt, M., Hayton, P., & Dooris, M. (2009). Prisons in England and Wales: An important public health opportunity? In J. Douglas et al. (Eds.), *A Reader in Promoting Public Health: Challenge & controversy* (p. 134). London: Open University Press.

Baybutt, M., Dooris, M., & Farrier, A. (2018). Growing health in UK prison settings. *Health Promotion International.* ISSN 0957-4824.

Campbell, J. (2012). *The hero with a thousand faces* (3rd ed.). Novato, CA: New World Library.

Clatworthy, J., Hinds, J. M., & Camic, P. (2013). Gardening as a mental health intervention: A review. *Mental Health Review Journal, 18*, 214–225.

Ewick, P., & Silbey, S. S. (1995). Subversive stories and hegemonic tales: Towards a sociology of narrative. *Law and Society Review, 29*(2), 197–226.

Farrier, A., & Kedwards, J. (2015) *Impact report: Greener on the outside for prisons.* Project Report. Groundwork UK, Manchester.

Farrier, A., Baybutt, M., & Dooris, M. (2019). Mental health and wellbeing benefits from a prisons horticultural programme. *International Journal of Prisoner Health, 15*(1), 91–104.

Flagler, J. S. (1995). The role of horticulture in training correctional youth. *Horticultural Technology, 5*, 185–187.

Froggett, L. (2002). *Love, hate and welfare: Psychosocial approaches to policy and practice.* Bristol: Policy Press.

Genter, C., Roberts, A., Richardson, J., & Sheaff, M. (2015). The contribution of allotment gardening to health and wellbeing: A systematic review of the literature. *British Journal of Occupational Therapy, 78*(1), 593–605.

Goodson, I. F., & Gill, S. R. (2011). The narrative turn in social research. *Counterpoints*, 386, Narrative Pedagogy: Life history and learning, 17–33.

Hawton, K., Linsell, L., Adeniji, T., Sariaslan, A., & Fazel, S. (2014). Self-harm in prisons in England and Wales: An epidemiological study of prevalence, risk factors, clustering, and subsequent suicide. *The Lancet, 383*(9923), 1147–1154.

Klein, M. (1997). *Envy and gratitude and other works, 1946–1963.* Random House.

Kohler Riessman, C. (2008). *Narrative methods for the human sciences.* Thousand Oaks: Sage Publications.

Lynch, J. (1999). Glossary of literary and rhetorical terms. Rutgers University (Last revised 3 August 1999). Retrieved June 28, 2019, from https://andromeda.rutgers.edu/~jlynch/Terms/index.html.

Macdonald, S. J. (1993). *Towards a sociology of dyslexia: Exploring links between dyslexia, disability and social class*. Muller: VDM Verlag Dr.

Maruna, S. (2010). Redemption scripts and desistance. In F. T. Cullen & P. Wilcox (Eds.), *Encyclopedia of criminological theory* (pp. 574–583). Thousand Oaks, CA: Sage Publications.

Ministry of Justice. (2019). Safety in custody. *Quarterly Bulletin*. December 2018. Retrieved July 1, 2019, from https://www.gov.uk/government/statistics/safety-in-custody-quarterly-update-to-december-2018.

Morrow, L. (1992). *Folklore in a box*. Time (21 September 1992), 78–79.

Nairne, D. C., & Thren, J. (2017). Storytelling: A unique approach to developing partnerships with students. *The Vermont Connection, 38*, Article 15. Retrieved June 28, 2019, from http://scholarworks.uvm.edu/tvc/vol38/iss1/15.

O'Brien, L., Buris, A., Townsend, M., & Ebden, M. (2011). Volunteering in nature as a way of enabling people to reintegrate into society. *Perspectives in Public Health, 131*, 71.

Pretty, J., Barton, J., Colbeck, I., Hine, R., Sellens, M., South, N., & Griffin, M. (2007). Green exercise in the UK countryside: Effects on health and psychological wellbeing, and implications for policy and planning. *Journal of Environmental Planning and Management, 50*(2), 211–231.

Prison Reform Trust. (2015). *Bromley Briefings prison factfile: Autumn 2015*. London: Prison Reform Trust, London.

Prison Reform Trust. (2016, November). *Bromley briefings factfile: Autumn 2016*. (No. 1). London: Prison Reform Trust.

Richardson, M., & Hallam, J. (2013). Exploring the psychological rewards of a familiar semi-rural landscape: Connecting to local nature through a mindful approach. *The Humanistic Psychologist, 41*(1), 35–53.

Rutt, D. (2016). Prison horticulture. In T. M. Waliczek & J. M. Zajicek (Eds.), *Urban horticulture* (pp. 179–204). CRC Press.

Sandelowski, M. (2002). Reembodying qualitative inquiry. *Qualitative Health Research, 12*(1), 104–115.

Schlosser, J. A. (2008). Issues in interviewing inmates: Navigating the methodological landmines of prison research. *Qualitative Inquiry, 14*(8), 1500–1525.

Tangney, J. P., Stuewig, J., & Hafez, L. (2012). Shame, guilt and remorse: Implications for offender populations. *The Journal of Forensic Psychiatry & Psychology, 22*(5), 706–723.

Toch, H. (2010). 'I am not now who I used to be then': Risk assessment and the maturation of long-term prison inmates. *The Prison Journal, 90*, 4–11.

Vogler, C. (1985). A practical guide to the hero with a thousand faces by Joseph Campbell. Retrieved May 30, 2018, from www.parklandsd.org/web/peters/files/.../a_practical_guide_to_the_hero-campbel.doc.

Völlm, B., & Dolan, M. (2009). Self-harm among UK female people in prison: A cross-sectional study. *Journal of Forensic Psychiatry and Psychology, 20*(5), 741–751.

Warwick-Booth, L., Woodall, J., South, J., Bagnall, A., Day, R., & Cross, R. (2012). *An evaluation of Sunderland Health Champions Programme*. Leeds: Centre for Health Promotion Research, Leeds Metropolitan University.

Wengraf, T. (2001). *Qualitative research interviewing: Biographic narrative and semi-structured methods*. London: Sage.

Wilson, E. O. (1984). *Biophilia: The human bond with other species*. Cambridge: Harvard University Press.

Winnicott, D. (1999). *Playing and reality*. London and New York: Routledge.

Woodall, J., Dixey, R., & South, J. (2014). Control and choice in English prisons: Developing health-promoting prisons. *Health Promotion International, 29*(3), 474–482.

World Health Organisation Europe. (2014). *Prison and health fact sheet*. WHO Europe, Copenhagen. Retrieved June 28, 2019, from http://www.euro.who.int/__data/assets/pdf_file/0020/250283/Fact-Sheet-Prison-and-Health-Eng.pdf?ua=1.

9

Evaluation and Reflections from the Use of Implementation Science to Accommodate a Community Mental Health Awareness Programme to a Prison

David Woods and Gavin Breslin

Chapter Aims

Implementation research is the scientific study of methods to promote the uptake of research findings and other evidence-based interventions into practice, and, hence, to improve the effectiveness of health provision and care (Eccles and Mittman 2006). New research continually produces findings that can contribute more effectively to the care of the public; however, in many cases research cannot change health outcomes if effective services shown in research are not transferred or introduced into

D. Woods (✉)
School of Sport at Ulster University, Belfast, UK
e-mail: dg.woods@ulster.ac.uk

G. Breslin
School of Psychology at Ulster University, Coleraine, UK
e-mail: g.breslin1@ulster.ac.uk

© The Author(s) 2021

M. Maycock et al. (eds.), *Issues and Innovations in Prison Health Research*, Palgrave Studies in Prisons and Penology, https://doi.org/10.1007/978-3-030-46401-1_9

practice (Brownson et al. 2012). Implementation science includes the study of what influences health care provision and organisational behaviour and provides the basis on which to take an already effective programme such as State of Mind Sport (SOMS), a successful mental health awareness programme available in the community, and trial it within a new environment such as a prison.

In this chapter, our overall aim is to demonstrate and reflect on a process in which implementation science has been used to improve mental health awareness of prisoners. To do so, we present an overview of mental health issues and challenges faced by prisoners. We describe the rationale for adapting an evidence-based SOMS community programme and present a critical overview of the implementation process through an evaluation of the programme using quantitative and qualitative research methods. We then present our reflections on five critical steps within the research implementation process experienced throughout the integration and evaluation of SOMS within the prison environment. Throughout the chapter, we provide recommendations for conducting future mental health awareness evaluation research in prisons with a focus on the practical implementation of suitable research methods, designs and measurement tools.

Overview of Mental Health Issues in Prison

The rehabilitation of prisoners has been identified as the primary purpose for prisons, to be prioritised over separation and confinement from society, punishment for crime, and correction (Cullen and Gilbert 2012). Critical to successful rehabilitation is prisoner health and well-being; however, the need for prioritising security and discipline can often undermine the perception of individual prisoners as patients (Spencer 2007). Likewise, over a decade ago the World Health Organisation (WHO) (2007a) suggested in their Guide to Health in Prisons that the prison service is not sufficiently recognised in society as a public service, with a remit to support and improve prisoner health and well-being. To address this imbalance, it was suggested that the focus of prisons could be extended to better serve the public need by recognising: (a) good prison health is essential to good public health; (b) good public health will make good use of the opportunities presented by prisons; and (c) prisons can contribute to the health of communities by helping to improve the health of some of the most disadvantaged people in society. The principle of equivalence also highlighted by the WHO states that prison health care should aspire to equivalence of care between standards inside and outside of prison, although this is rarely achieved (WHO 2014). Lines (2006) goes further, suggesting that due to the complex health issues presented in prison, in particular mental health issues, more intensive and integrated services than those available within community settings are required; shifting the principle from equivalence in standards in health provision to equivalence in objectives and outcome.

Reports from across multiple jurisdictions highlight poor mental health within the prison population as endemic (United Kingdom—Mental Health and Criminal Justice Report, [Durcan] Durcan 2016; United States—Travis, Western, and Redburn, Travis et al. 2014; Australia—Australian Institute of Health and Welfare 2015). It is commonly estimated that within the United Kingdom, up to 90% of prisoners aged 16 years and over are mentally unwell (Durcan 2016). Fraser, Gatherer and Hayton (Fraser et al. 2009) suggest that mental illness such as depression, anxiety and stress-related symptoms affect the majority of prisoners. Leigh-Hunt and Perry (2015), accounting for variations in methodology and definitions used, estimate 30–75% of prisoners suffer from depression and anxiety. Blaauw et al. (2000), in their analysis of mental disorders in European prisons, estimated up to 12% of the prison population would require transfer or urgent psychiatric attention with the remainder benefiting most from health care services and mental health promotion. Although definitive mental health figures are hard to ascertain (National Audit Office 2017), consistently researchers have demonstrated a higher prevalence of poor mental health within the prison population when compared to those within the community (Steadman et al. 2009; WHO 2014).

Factors contributing to the higher prevalence of mental ill-health in prisons are multiple and complex with many prisoners having suffered from or been subjected to adverse health determinants. These include poor educational attainment, illiteracy, substandard housing, high unemployment and childhood abuse or neglect (MacNamara and Mannix-McNamara 2014; WHO 1999). This increased vulnerability may then be exacerbated by hostile prison conditions including overcrowding, interpersonal distrust, bullying, marginalisation, social withdrawal, decreased sense of self-worth, stigma, discrimination and a lack of purposeful activity and/or privacy (Ferszt et al. 2009; WHO 2014; Wildeman and Wang 2017). Prisoners with poor mental health are also at greater risk of suicide, self-harm, violence and victimisation (Fazel et al. 2016). These factors are plausibly co-existing contributory factors to suicide, as in 2016, the Prisons and Probation Ombudsman found that 70% of prisoners who had committed suicide between 2012 and 2014 had mental health needs. It was unclear how many of these people were receiving mental health services. In England and Wales, the number of reported self-harm incidents in 2016 (40,161) increased by 73% between 2012 and 2016. There were also 120 self-inflicted deaths reported in prison in 2016, almost twice the number in 2012, and higher than any previous year on record. Improved mental health awareness and treatment provisions are therefore drastically required.

Dumont et al. (2012) reported that for many adults within the United States, prison health care is their first experience of accessing preventative and chronic medical care. Therefore, an opportunity exists across the prison system for diagnosis and the provision of targeted health promotion activities to those with high need and limited prior exposure (Wildeman and Wang 2017). Historically, health-related interventions within the prison have focused on treating acute pathologies rather than formulating preventative measures which might buffer against the negative impacts on mental health prevalent in prisons (De Viggiani 2007). This is at odds with the Trenčín Statement which highlighted that "promoting mental health and well-being should be central to a prison's health care policy" (WHO 2007b, p. 6). The identification of appropriate prison-based interventions supported with evidence-based outcomes, leading to improvements in prisoners' mental health and an associated reduction in rates of self-harm and suicide are therefore much needed (Fazel et al. 2016; Joint Committee on Human Rights (JCHR) 2017; Woodall 2016). Alongside the lack of innovative evidenced-based mental health interventions in prisons, a complicating factor is that many prisoners who would benefit from appropriate health interventions do not wish to engage with treatment (Stewart 2008). This refusal to engage with standard interventions encouraging help-seeking behaviours is often linked to stereotypical prison masculinities and a weighing up of the risks to personal safety associated with such disclosures that highlight human fragility or weakness (Ricciardelli et al. 2015).

Almost two decades ago, the WHO (1999) judged access to sport and fitness facilities to have high potential to positively impact prisoners' mental health and well-being. During the intervening period, research on the impact of sport in prison has grown dramatically and demonstrated that sport can offer a more acceptable means to engage prisoners in health and well-being promotion (Meek and Lewis 2014; Meek 2018). Similarly, Woods, Breslin and Hassan (Woods et al. 2017) conducted a review of the perceived benefits of sport-based interventions on the psychological well-being of people in prison. The review highlighted reductions in depression, stress and anxiety, alongside increases in self-confidence, self-esteem and pro-social identities, all factors contributing to improved mental health. Sport-based interventions therefore appear to offer an innovative and attractive approach to engage prisoners and improve their mental health. However, in a study conducted in England and Wales (Meek and Lewis 2012) only 23 of the 142 secure estates surveyed were running sport or physical education programmes explicitly aimed at improving mental health. A disconnect therefore exists between the potential for improved mental health awareness promotion through sport-based interventions and the implementation of programmes.

Implementation Science

Implementation science is useful for improving understanding of the challenges or barriers to integrating mental health promotion programmes across settings. It serves to broaden our understanding of the real-world factors that may impact programme implementation (Peters, Tran & Adam, Peters et al. 2013). To our knowledge, implementation science has not been used previously to inform the adoption of a mental health awareness programme for prisons. For implementing a mental health awareness programme in prison, implementation science allows us to determine what needs to be put in place to increase the likelihood of achieving planned outcomes, with specific factors highlighted as a result of research evaluation and reflections. In the case of prisons where there are strict regimes for prisoners and a culture that suggests little autonomy, introducing a programme that has demonstrated success in terms of research outcomes, but was developed for a non-prison community, may present challenges. As implementation science has not been introduced to prison research, it is reassuring that the process draws on a wide variety of research approaches and disciplines including pragmatic trials, effectiveness–implementation hybrid trials, quality improvement studies and participatory action research. According to Peters et al. (2013), p. 10) in implementation research, the 'question is king', and it is the question that determines the method used. Implementation research questions are often complex, reflecting the wide array of variables and contextual factors that can influence implementation, and requiring continuous adaptation by programme designers and implementers. Embracing that complexity expected in a prison environment requires considerable flexibility on the part of researchers, particularly in regard to the complex and dynamic nature of mental health in prisoners and the prison environment.

Rationale for the State of Mind Sport Community Programme

Included within the United Kingdom's national suicide prevention strategy, the Ministry of Justice published a policy paper entitled 'Preventing Suicide in England' (Department of Health 2017). State of Mind Sport (SOMS) was highlighted within the paper as a community-based mental health and well-being initiative, raising awareness, tackling stigma, and encouraging individuals to seek help when needed. To assist prisons in successfully meeting WHO recommendations of becoming environments which promote positive mental health and well-being (WHO 2007b, 2014), researchers have highlighted the need to better consider and integrate appropriate community-based initiatives (Fazel et al. 2016; Leigh-Hunt and Perry 2015; Portillo et al. 2017). Therefore, in response to the requirement for innovative mental health promotion in prisons, and in recognition of the attractive platform sport can offer to achieve this, State of Mind Sport (SOMS), a community mental health awareness programme, was adapted, implemented and evaluated within a prison based in England.

State of Mind Sport Programme Content

SOMS is a 75-minute programme aimed at raising awareness of, and promoting, mental well-being and resilience, tackling stigma, and highlighting the importance of signposting to appropriate services, with the overall aim of preventing suicide. Originally developed as a community-based intervention, the State of Mind team worked with Her Majesty's Prison and Probation Service (HMPPS) to take account of the risks presented within the prison environment. SOMS was delivered within the prison by a mental health and substance misuse nurse, and two elite-level rugby players who had previously experienced mental health problems. It was the first time the SOMS programme was delivered within a prison. Through collaborative working with the Suicide and Self-Harm project group within HMPPS, the programme was tailored to include a mixture of the original content (delivered to over 25,000 people in sports clubs, universities, construction and office workplaces), alongside specific contextual information relevant to the prison environment previously highlighted. This included, for example, the risks associated with high levels of interpersonal distrust, bullying, marginalisation and social withdrawal.

The content of the programme included: (a) risks men face in relation to mental health and psychological well-being; (b) risk factors such as stigma, macho-cultures, avoidance of help-seeking behaviours and negative coping strategies; (c) markers of stress and positive coping strategies; and (d) well-being and resilience (both an understanding of the concepts and practical steps to improve). To support understanding of mental health, case-studies were presented by former elite rugby league players who suffered from poor mental health and who also considered taking their own lives, prior to seeking help. Key messages from the intervention included:

- Seek help/advice from someone you trust.
- It is a strength, not a weakness to seek help.
- Respond to a mate who may be feeling down.
- Set achievable goals and celebrate upon achievement.
- We are all part of a team.

Evaluation of the State of Mind Sport Programme

The effects of the SOMS programme were evaluated wherein prisoners' knowledge of mental health, intentions to seek help, levels of well-being and resilience were compared to a waiting-list control group (Woods, Meek, Leavey and Breslin, In press). The following questionnaires were completed at three time points, pre-intervention, immediately post-intervention, and during an 8-week follow-up: (1) Mental Health Knowledge Schedule (MAKS) (Evans-Lacko et al. 2010); (2) Reported and Intended Behaviour Scale (RIBS) (Evans-Lacko et al. 2011); (3) The Short Warwick Edinburgh Mental Well-being Scale (SWEMWBS) (Stewart-Brown et al. 2009); and (4) The Brief Resilience Scale (Smith et al. 2008). Prisoner views of programme content and feasibility were also examined via focus groups. Areas explored in the focus group were (a) well-being impact of SOMS; (b) benefits of exploring mental health and well-being using sport examples; (c) suitability of SOMS content to prisoners; and (d) how the programme could be further enhanced.

A total of 75 male prisoners volunteered to participate in the study (*M*age = 37.30, *S.D.* = 11.01), 47 prisoners (*M*age = 38.3, *S.D.* = 11.4) received the intervention, while 28 (*M*age = 35.3, *S.D.* = 10.2) were in a control group. All participants completed the same questionnaires. Fifteen volunteered to take part in focus group.

Immediately following the State of Mind Sport programme, prisoners in the intervention group demonstrated a greater increase in their knowledge of mental health and ability to correctly classify types of mental illness (stress and drug-addiction), compared to those in the control group. These findings demonstrate that knowledge of mental health issues can be increased following a brief awareness program. Importantly, the findings provide encouraging evidence-based outcomes in response to the need for innovative mental health promotion within prisons (Keogh et al. 2017; MacNamara and Mannix-McNamara 2014). There was no significant increase in psychological well-being and resilience immediately post-intervention. On reflection, this non-effect is not surprising as the SWEMWBS, focused on participants' positive core 'functioning' more than subjective 'feeling' (Tennant et al. 2007). A significant increase in participant levels of psychological functioning, based on their perceived value and meaning in life (Huta 2016), was therefore unlikely following a 75-minute program. Similarly, it would be reasonable to expect any increases in resilience to require more time to become embedded. Our view is supported in that increases in psychological well-being and resilience were observed at the 8-week follow-up. However, this was true for both the intervention and control groups, and could not be attributed to the SOMS intervention. The increases in mental well-being and resilience for both the control and intervention groups were likely due to the broader efforts across the prison to raise awareness of mental health issues in response to the poor mental health and self-harm reported across the secure estate (JCHR 2017; NAO 2017). Upon reflection, extending an invite to those in the control group to participate in focus groups exploring their views on mental health awareness and promotion in the prison would have benefitted the study. Their qualitative input may have provided an insightful source of contrasting themes to those emerging from the intervention group, alongside improvements to future implementation of the SOMS programme within the broader support provided within the prison.

In contrast to the increased mental health knowledge observed immediately post-intervention, results from the 8-week follow-up study failed to demonstrate any sustained impact on knowledge of mental health, with a slight decrease evident at follow-up. Therefore, one-off sessions do not appear to be sufficient to sustain an increase in the mental health knowledge of prisoners, pointing to the need for ongoing awareness campaigns to be made available. An example of this can be seen in the peer-led self-management project implemented at HMP & YOI Parc (Mental Health Foundation 2017). Results from the qualitative analysis of the current study highlighted a participant desire for programme hand-outs and follow-up materials not provided in the pilot intervention, which could assist in the maintenance of increased knowledge of mental health.

Toxic hegemonic masculinities, for example the need to compete with and dominate others, can be pervasive within prisons (Kupers 2005) leading to the discouragement of openness regarding emotional distress (Ricciardelli et al. 2015). In contrast, focus group data revealed an encouraging theme of prisoners' willingness to discuss their vulnerabilities as a positive coping mechanism following the information presented in SOMS. However, there also remained a persistent concern that being more open regarding personal feelings could result in stigmatisation from both fellow prisoners and the prison system. For example, a negative impact on parole hearings was cited as a concern, reflecting previous research (Howerton et al. 2007; Skogstad et al. 2006). This was despite the program specifically addressing stigma concerns and why they should not act as barriers to adopting behaviours which may lead to improved mental health within the prison. Upon reflection, this provides a useful insight into the unique challenges when transferring innovative programs from the community into the prison, in this case the heightened potential for stigma and increased difficulties in personal disclosures without family or loved ones surrounding. Increasing the likelihood of programs successfully delivering their message(s), therefore, depends on a deep understanding of the contextual nuances within prisons, achieved through working in partnership with prison management and service users throughout design and implementation. An example suggestion for improvement from the focus groups was the inclusion of prisoner testimonies, alongside those of the athletes, to positive outcomes derived from adopting new help-seeking behaviours and improved coping mechanisms within prison. It is suggested this role modelling would serve to increase help-seeking efficacy in prison when faced with the challenges of mistrust and stigmatisation.

As highlighted within the introduction, sport-based interventions have been considered an innovative and attractive route to engage prisoners in mental health promotion and improve buy-in to new coping strategies. As part of the research into feasibility, the focus groups addressed this point specifically, with positive views expressed by participants. A theme developed that SOMS, a mental health awareness programme originating from the masculine sport of rugby league, was well positioned to contribute to the broader efforts tackling the harmful outcomes associated with poor mental health in the prisons. The personal life stories shared by the ex-professional rugby league players regarding perceived conflicts in their identity as macho athletes privately dealing with vulnerabilities resonated with the participants. The shared athlete experiences increased the validity of the prisoners' feelings and concerns and allowed their own lived experiences to be framed in a less toxic, more enabling narrative. Overall, themes from the focus groups demonstrated participants were favourable to the implementation of mental health promotion through sport. Crucially, it was perceived as acceptable and credible regardless of whether those attending held a prior interest in sport.

Reflections and Recommendations

In a recent scoping review of qualitative research within prisons, Abbot et al. (2018) noted that it is uncommon for authors to include substantial reflexive detail on the research process within peer-reviewed articles. This tendency to omit greater reflexive accounts may be a result of what Becker (2008, p. 90) describes as the requirement for impersonal, passive writing commonly regarded as "scientific", but lacking in the detail that many readers of prison research are keenly interested in. There are many examples of insightful reflexive accounts of prison research; however, rather than inclusion in an evaluative research paper, they are often written up as separate reflexive accounts (see Qualitative Inquiry, Volume 20, Issue 4, Special Section: Doing Prison Research Differently).

The purpose of this section is to add to the available resource of prison research reflexivity, sharing experiences encountered during SOMS research implementation process, whilst remaining respectful of the privileged access granted and the candidness of the participant prisoners. It is hoped these shared experiences can act as a source of tangible advice to prison researchers when faced with the unique sets of obstacles and methodological landmines of which inexperienced prison researchers may be unaware (Schlosser 2008). The approach adopted follows that advised by Edge (2011), considering both the effect of the researcher on the research and that of the research on the researcher. Using this approach, we focus and reflect on five critical steps within the research implementation process experienced throughout the integration and evaluation of SOMS within the prison environment.

Research Co-Production

The SOMS evaluation presented in this chapter was completed as the final study within a programme of prison research submitted for doctoral thesis. As a result, a deeper understanding of the challenges involved in gaining ethical approval and access had developed from a standing start during the intervening 18 months (see Woods and Breslin 2019). One of many lessons learned was that for unknown or inexperienced researchers, access issues often lie primarily in establishing connections and relationships with gatekeepers (Noakes and Wincup 2004). Therefore, when designing the SOMS evaluation, which was situated in a new geographical location from the research team's previous prison studies with new gatekeepers, building strong relationships prior to ethics application was an area where considerable effort was focused. The research team established a working group comprised of representatives from Her Majesties Prison and Probation Service (HMPPS), the State of Mind delivery team, the prison site Governor and the Head of Physical Education. The aims and design of the research were fully and openly debated, facilitating discussions related to the inclusion of vulnerable prisoners, logistical and security concerns, the rationale for a control group which was an additional logistic/resource demand on the prison and how prisoners could be involved to increase autonomy. These discussions ensured that upon submission of the ethics application, stakeholders were fully bought into the rationale for the research design and implementation, they had anticipated where logistical difficulties might lie and put in place contigency plans. For researchers keen to implement their first prison study, this gatekeeper identification and relationship-building step can appear exaggerated and exhaustive in comparison to research in other fields. However, it is important to be mindful that these gatekeepers are in place as the proposed research is to be conducted with a high-risk and stigmatized population, consequently and correctly treated as a highly protected group (Schlosser 2008). Ethics and access, if subsequently granted, therefore provides the prison researcher with privileged access.

The access considerations outlined could be perceived as a very "top-down" approach to the co-production of research, with input sought from prison management, researchers and intervention delivery staff, but no input from the potential participants. The inclusion of an inmate liaison council to emphasise mutual goals throughout the research (Apa et al. 2012), was not considered prior to the implementation of the research and may have increased attendance at the SOMS program, voluntary participation in the research and/or the maintenance of baseline participant numbers at the 8-week follow-up. Prisoners were involved in the design of the flyers for the intervention subsequently delivered to all potential participants, allowing for some "bottom-up" inclusion in the research recruitment process. On reflection, within the overall design and implementation process, this input was minimal and discrete. Those embarking on prison research should therefore give thought to innovative ways in which prisoners may provide more collaborative and participatory inputs, an approach already becoming more common (Martin et al. 2018). Although there will be a possible knock-on effect in design and planning time, this would potentially be offset with strong dividends not just in participant recruitment, but also for prisoners' sense of autonomy a basic psychological need linked to improved mental well-being (Woods et al. 2017).

Prison Intermediaries and Research Control

Having secured ethical permission to conduct research within the prison, a key facilitator in the implementation phase became the allocated single point of contact (SPOC) within the prison. Due to geographical distances and access restrictions, the SPOC took responsibility for several tasks, for example, ensuring flyers advertising the intervention were delivered to prisoners in their cells, monitoring the numbers of those wishing to attend, identifying the control group within the agreed criteria and collating the anonymous questionnaire returns from central drop-off points at the 8-week follow-up period. These responsibilities were additional to the SPOC's daily remit; however, possibly in light of the governor's strong commitment to the research, the working relationship between the research team and the SPOC was excellent, with frequent communications. Inherent in this working relationship was a subsequent loss of direct control by the research team over several tasks which caused small moments of concern in relation to the fidelity of the research. Although the use of research intermediaries is common practice in prison studies due to daily access restrictions, it can have implications for maintaining the ethical research protocol as proposed in the application (Abbott et al. 2018; Kristensen and Ravn 2015). Risks for researchers to be aware of may include coercion at recruitment, privileging research participation or blocking access to silence difficult voices. Based on the strong working relationships developed, the research team was confident in the equity of opportunity to participate afforded to all prisoners. In light of the required reliance on research intermediaries often experienced in prisons, it is recommended that researchers dedicate substantial effort to developing high-trust working relationships with their intermediaries to secure intervention fidelity and maximise the reliability and validity of their outputs.

Implementation Science Data Collection: Quantitative

Implementation science draws on a wide variety of research approaches, including mixed methods as utilised in our evaluation. A potential issue when adopting these multiple methods is that the data collected can appear contradictory, as happened in our evaluation. However, when framed within an implementation science approach, this provided useful learning with regard to conducting future health research in prisons. The issue identified was that our analysis of the data from the Reported and Intended Behaviour Scale (RIBS) did not show any rise in participant intentions to engage and offer support to those with mental health concerns immediately post-programme or at follow-up. However, focus group results suggested that following the SOMS programme, prisoners were more willing to listen to others, combined with an increased willingness to share thoughts and feelings with others. When reflecting on the possible reasons for the variance in outcomes on the same topic across research methods, the suitability of the RIBS measure in its original format for the prison context was examined further. Individual items of the RIBS enquire about the respondent's intentions to: "live with", "work with", "work nearby" and "continue a relationship" with someone suffering from a mental illness. Within prison, there is minimum autonomy in relation to these variables (De Viggiani 2012). Also, the point at which prisoners may be released and able to make these choices can be many years away and therefore considered abstract and hard to tangibly answer. These factors may have combined to impact the validity of the RIBS questionnaire for the prison context, despite having sound psychometric properties when used in the community and having been agreed as appropriate with the prison education department for comprehension. When implementing similar studies, researchers should consider a tailored version of the RIBS, presenting more common interactions within the prison environment. This is indicative of a broader consideration for researchers embarking on prison studies, that questionnaires regardless of robust psychometric properties should be closely scrutinised for suitability and, where appropriate, modified.

Implementation Science Data Collection: Qualitative

During evaluation, the qualitative method adopted took the form of focus groups immediately following the 75-minute SOMS intervention, to examine feasibility and appropriateness. The organisation and implementation of the focus groups within a prison environment provided a good example of the unique issues and methodological challenges nuanced to prison research.

The primary issue encountered was the cancellation of the first of the three focus groups due to prisoner unrest in another wing, namely an attempt to access the prison roof. This decision was made just as participant questionnaires had been completed and focus group volunteers identified. From a research perspective this was simultaneously frustrating and disappointing and naively appeared unnecessary as the unrest was in a completely different wing. Immediate thoughts were centred on how difficult it had been to secure access and organise the focus group, the improbability of rescheduling and a feeling of denying the participants their opportunity to express their views as promised. This experience was encapsulated by Abbott et al. (2018) who noted that prison research is complicated by the restrictions of imprisonment and the inherent controls. The controls in this scenario meant that regardless of the location of the unrest, the prison was on lock-down until safety and security was resumed, which of course took priority over the research plans. A key learning from this was that however frustrating, the process of accepting these incidents may occur is an integral part of conducting prison research alongside being constantly mindful that the privileged access granted is at all times subject to change for safety and security.

The focus groups proceeded the following day, which provided critical data collection and further reflexive learnings. One learning point centred on an unexpected need to manage the input and impact of prison management to facilitate the collection of unedited, reliable and valid views of the prisoners during the focus group. A visiting prison governor, with a special-projects remit related to mental health in prisons, who had played a facilitative role in securing access for the current project, requested to sit in and observe the focus group. The response was shaped by the desire to maintain civility to our hosts in the field and in recognition of the imposition the research requests had made. After agreeing to the request to observe in return for the prison access granted (albeit implicit) felt like the correct approach to take. The presence of staff in or close to the prison research setting is a common occurrence, a trade-off between researcher security and participant privacy (Eldridge et al. 2012); however, this presence usually takes the form of prison guards who maintain a working distance and are not particularly focused on the discussion. Also, although the agreement of the participants on observation of the focus group was sought, Hanson et al. (2015) comment that prisoners may not feel they are in a position to refuse research requests due to the power imbalances within prison.

On balance, the view was that progressing with the close observation of the visiting governor would not risk the authenticity of the data collection. The room was comfortably large enough and previous experience had been that prisoners were not afraid to speak freely in front of prison management. As the focus group evolved with honest and open inputs from participants, an unexpected interruption occurred when the observer disagreed and challenged a collective view being presented by the group on current health care provision. Conscious that a direct closing down of the challenge may have created a scenario perceived as a play for power between an "outsider" and an "insider" (Rowe 2014), the participants were briefly afforded time to respond to the individual despite this going off-topic. To regain control and turn attention back to the SOMS evaluation, everyone was reminded of the tight timeframes and a requirement to focus on the agreed-upon topics. This indirect approach appeared to work well in the moment, satisfied all parties and maintained the required focus. However, it did highlight the need to anticipate and put clear boundaries in place for future requests. Facilitating focus groups, particularly in prison, provides an outlet in which the participants can speak candidly about their lived experiences and as the researcher providing that outlet, it is important that every effort is made to ensure it is not unintentionally contaminated or shut down.

Impression Management in Prison Research

A final critical step identified during implementation, although in reality it runs concurrent to all others from the first moment a researcher enters the prison, is how he or she manages the impact of their surroundings on them. Jewkes (2014, p. 389) describes prisons as "peculiar places from a sensory perspective, managing to deny and deprive while, sometimes simultaneously, overloading the senses". As a result, common research activities such as facilitating a focus group can prove challenging when, for example, having to manage a mix of unanticipated emotions.

During the co-production phase with all stakeholders, there was a commitment that the SOMS intervention would be offered to all prisoners. Specifically, this should include those prisoners considered vulnerable or at-risk from fellow prisoners because of their crimes. Whilst it was acknowledged this would introduce logistical difficulties, the inclusion of this at-risk population was: (a) deemed particularly appropriate given the aims of the intervention, to promote positive mental health and coping, and reduce stigma; and (b) equitable prisoner access to research participation is consistent with the principle of equivalence in prison health care (Charles et al. 2016). Due to a focus on managing the logistics, deliberate thought had not been afforded to how personal feelings and emotions may be affected when facilitating a focus group of predominantly older sexual offenders and empathising with their concerns and views on mental health and well-being. Outside of this unique research setting, this was not a scenario that would ever have been presented. Upon processing the immediate thoughts and feelings prior to beginning of the focus group, a brief reflection in action (Schön 2017) reassured that for the same reasons cited in the previous example (non-contamination of data collection), there was no reason why this focus group should cause any uneasiness or demand a change in approach based on their categorisation. Goffman's view of impression management (Goffman 1959) contends that people engage in "front stage" and "back stage" performances in different spheres of life and that as social actors we behave differently when an audience is present. The audience in this research sphere were the focus group participants, and the front stage performance demanded that any uninformed personal judgement be suspended, with priority given to their right to effective health care and effectively facilitating a role for them in shaping this.

Schlosser (2008) noted that operating within the prison environment requires the researcher to constantly adapt and change the way they regard themselves and present themselves to others. Upon reflection, it is not always possible to anticipate or fully imagine the scenarios which might challenge oneself or cause mixed emotions. Seeking out specific learnings from experienced prison researchers regarding similar challenges will assist, alongside a strong belief in the core rationale for your research and the positive influence it may have on those involved.

Conclusion

The prevalence of poor mental health in prisons combined with the deficit in ambitious, innovative mental health promotion interventions led to the adoption of implementation science, incorporating a mixed-methods evaluation of a pilot State of Mind Sport programme. This chapter has presented an overview of the primary outcomes and detailed an open and honest reflection of the ethical and methodological issues and difficulties encountered, with associated recommendations for those embarking on research in prisons with the aim of implementing programmes to improve health and well-being. The results from the evaluation support the use of implementation science both as an effective delivery methodology and process for reflective learning, and for sport as an attractive way to engage, innovate and deliver mental health promotion within prisons. Through our reflections, further improvements have been recommended to sustain benefits arising from similar mental health awareness programmes.

The World Health Organisation (2007a) has commented that society does not sufficiently recognise that the prison service is a public service with a significant role to play in societal health provision. Health researchers have a unique opportunity to play their part through the application of their knowledge, skills and abilities to challenging research projects. Subsequently, these opportunities can produce robust evidence-based outcomes which may impact the health and well-being of many of the most vulnerable in our society. The privileged access to this unique environment and trust placed in the researcher by these high-risk, highly stigmatised participants, demands that high levels of patience and planning are executed in equal measure. It is hoped the reflections and recommendations presented in this chapter alongside the novel use of implementation science in prisons will assist researchers deliver on these requirements and contribute to the improved health and well-being of prison populations.

References

Abbott, P., Di Giacomo, M., Magin, P., & Hu, W. (2018). A scoping review of qualitative research methods used with people in prison. *International Journal of Qualitative Methods, 17*, 1–15.

Apa, Z. L., Bai, R., Mukherejee, D. V., Herzig, C. T., Koenigsmann, C., Lowy, F. D., & Larson, E. L. (2012). Challenges and strategies for research in prisons. *Public Health Nursing, 29*(5), 467–472.

Australian Institute of Health and Welfare. (2015). *The health of Australia's prisoners 2015*. Canberra: AIHW.

Becker, H. S. (2008). *Writing for social scientists: How to start and finish your thesis, book, or article* (2nd ed.). Chicago, IL: University of Chicago Press.

Blaauw, E., Roesch, R., & Kerkhof, A. (2000). Mental disorders in European prison systems: Arrangements for mentally disordered prisoners in the prison systems of 13 European countries. *International Journal of Law and Psychiatry, 23*(5–6), 649–663.

Brownson, R., Colditz, G., & Proctor, E. (Eds.). (2012). *Dissemination and implementation research in health: Translating science to practice*. Oxford University Press.

Charles, A., Rid, A., Davies, H., & Draper, H. (2016). Prisoners as research participants: Current practice and attitudes in the UK. *Journal of Medical Ethics, 42*(4), 246–252.

Cullen, F. T., & Gilbert, K. E. (2012). *Reaffirming rehabilitation*. Routledge.

De Viggiani, N. (2007). Unhealthy prisons: Exploring structural determinants of prison health. *Sociology of Health & Illness, 29*(1), 115–135.

De Viggiani, N. (2012). Trying to be something you are not: Masculine performances within a prison setting. *Men and Masculinities, 15*(3), 271–291.

Department of Health. (2017). *Preventing suicide in England: Third progress report of the cross-government outcomes strategy to save lives*. Retrieved from https://assets.publishing.service.gov.uk/government/uploads/system/uploads/attachment_data/file/582117/Suicide_report_2016_A.pdf.

Dumont, D. M., Brockmann, B., Dickman, S., Alexander, N., & Rich, J. D. (2012). Public health and the epidemic of incarceration. *Annual Review of Public Health, 33*(1), 325–339.

Durcan, G. (2016). *Mental health and criminal justice: Views from consultations across England & Wales*. London: Centre for Mental Health.

Eccles, M. P., & Mittman, B. S. (2006). Welcome to implementation science. *Implementation Science, 1*(1). https://doi.org/10.1186/1748-5908-1-1.

Edge, J. (2011). *The reflexive teacher educator: Roots and wings*. New York, NY: Routledge.
Eldridge, G. D., Robinson, R. V., Corey, S., Brems, C., & Johnson, M. E. (2012). Ethical challenges in conducting HIV/AIDS research in correctional settings. *Journal of Correctional Health Care, 18*(4), 309–318.
Evans-Lacko, S., Little, K., Meltzer, H., Rose, D., Rhydderch, D., Henderson, C., & Thornicroft, G. (2010). Development and psychometric properties of the mental health knowledge schedule. *The Canadian Journal of Psychiatry, 55*(7), 440–448.
Evans-Lacko, S., Rose, D., Little, K., Flach, C., Rhydderch, D., Henderson, C., & Thornicroft, G. (2011). Development and psychometric properties of the reported and intended behaviour scale (RIBS): A stigma-related behaviour measure. *Epidemiology and Psychiatric Sciences, 20*(3), 263–271.
Fazel, S., Hayes, A. J., Bartellas, K., Clerici, M., & Trestman, R. (2016). Mental health of prisoners: Prevalence, adverse outcomes, and interventions. *The Lancet Psychiatry, 3*(9), 871–881.
Ferszt, G. G., Salgado, D., DeFedele, S., & Leveillee, M. (2009). Houses of healing: A group intervention for grieving women in prison. *The Prison Journal, 89*(1), 46–64.
Fraser, A., Gatherer, A., & Hayton, P. (2009). Mental health in prison: Great difficulties but are there opportunities? *Public Health, 123*, 410–414.
Goffman, E. (1959). *The presentation of self in everyday life*. London, England: Penguin.
Hanson, B. L., Faulkner, S. A., Brems, C., Corey, S. L., Eldridge, G. D., Johnson, M. E. (2015). Key stakeholders' perceptions of motivators for research participation among individuals who are incarcerated. *Journal of Empirical Research on Human Research Ethics, 10*, 360–367.
Howerton, A., Byng, R., Campbell, J., Hess, D., Owens, C., & Aitken, P. (2007). Understanding help seeking behaviour among male offenders: Qualitative interview study. *BMJ, 334*(7588), 303.
Huta, V. (2016). Eudaimonic and hedonic orientations: Theoretical considerations and research findings. In *Handbook of eudaimonic well-being* (pp. 215–231). Springer International Publishing.
Jewkes, Y. (2014). An Introduction to "Doing Prison Research Differently". *Qualitative Inquiry, 20*(4), 387–391.
Joint Committee on Human Rights. (2017). *Mental health and deaths in prison: Interim report.* Retrieved from https://publications.parliament.uk/pa/jt201617/jtselect/jtrights/893/893.pdf.

Keogh, B., McBennett, P., de Vries, J., Higgans, A., O'Shea, M., & Doyle, L. (2017). Prisoners perceptions of a mental health wellness workshop. *International Journal of Prisoner Health, 13*(2), 81–90.

Kristensen, G. K., & Ravn, M. N. (2015). The voices heard and the voices silenced: Recruitment processes in qualitative interview studies. *Qualitative Research, 15*(6), 722–737.

Kupers, T. A. (2005). Toxic masculinity as a barrier to mental health treatment in prison. *Journal of Clinical Psychology, 61*(6), 713–724.

Leigh-Hunt, N., & Perry, A. (2015). A systematic review of interventions for anxiety, depression, and PTSD in adult offenders. *International Journal of Offender Therapy and Comparative Criminology, 59*(7), 701–725.

Lines, R. (2006). From equivalence of standards to equivalence of objectives: The entitlement of prisoners to health care standards higher than those outside prisons. *International Journal of Prisoner Health, 2*(4), 269–280.

MacNamara, C., & Mannix-McNamara, P. (2014). Placing the promotion of health and wellbeing on the Irish prison agenda—The complexity of health promotion in Irish prisons. *Irish Journal of Applied Social Studies, 14*(1), 49–59.

Martin, R. E., Turner, R., Howett, L., Howard, T., Hanberg, D., Buxton, J. A., et al. (2018). Twelve committed men: The feasibility of a community-based participatory HIV-prevention intervention within a Canadian men's correctional facility. *Global Health Promotion, 25*(3), 6–14.

Meek, R. (2018). *A sporting chance: An independent review of sport in youth and adult prisons.* Retrieved from https://assets.publishing.service.gov.uk/government/uploads/system/uploads/attachment_data/file/733184/a-sporting-chance-an-independent-review-sport-in-justice.pdf.

Meek, R., & Lewis, G. (2012). The role of sport in promoting prisoner health. *International Journal of Prisoner Health, 8*(3/4), 117–130.

Meek, R., & Lewis, G. E. (2014). The impact of a sports initiative for young men in prison: Staff and participant perspectives. *Journal of Sport & Social Issues, 38*(2), 95–123.

Mental Health Foundation. (2017). *Parc Prison: An evaluation of peer-led self-management training within a prison setting.* Retrieved from https://www.mentalhealth.org.uk/publications/parc-prison-impact-report.

National Audit Office. (2017). *Mental health in prisons.* Retrieved from https://www.nao.org.uk/wp-content/uploads/2017/06/Mental-health-in-prisons-Summary.pdf.

Noakes, L., & Wincup, E. (2004). *Criminological research: Understanding qualitative methods.* London: Sage.

Peters, D. H., Tran, N. T., & Adam, T. (2013). *Implementation research in health: A practical guide*. World Health Organization.

Portillo, S., Goldberg, V., & Taxman, F. S. (2017). Mental health peer navigators: Working with criminal justice–involved populations. *The Prison Journal, 97*(3), 318–341.

Ricciardelli, R., Maier, K., & Hannah-Moffat, K. (2015). Strategic masculinities: Vulnerabilities, risk and the production of prison masculinities. *Theoretical Criminology, 19*(4), 491–513.

Rowe, A. (2014). Situating the self in prison research: Power, identity, and epistemology. *Qualitative Inquiry, 20*(4), 404–416.

Schlosser, J. A. (2008). Issues in interviewing inmates: Navigating the methodological landmines of prison research. *Qualitative Inquiry, 14*(8), 1500–1525.

Schön, D. A. (2017). *The reflective practitioner: How professionals think in action*. Routledge.

Skogstad, P., Deane, F. P., & Spicer, J. (2006). Social-cognitive determinants of help-seeking for mental health problems among prison inmates. *Criminal Behaviour and Mental Health, 16*(1), 43–59.

Smith, B. W., Dalen, J., Wiggins, K., Tooley, E., Christopher, P., & Bernard, J. (2008). The brief resilience scale: Assessing the ability to bounce back. *International Journal of Behavioral Medicine, 15*(3), 194–200.

Spencer, A. (2007). *Rethinking imprisonment in Scotland: The dilemma for prison reform and the challenges beyond*. Retrieved from https://www2.gov.scot/resource/doc/1102/0056826.pdf.

Steadman, H. J., Osher, F. C., Robbins, P. C., Case, B., & Samuels, S. (2009). Prevalence of serious mental illness among jail inmates. *Psychiatric Services, 60*(6), 761–765.

Stewart, D. (2008). *The problems and needs of newly sentenced prisoners: Results from a national survey*. London: Ministry of Justice.

Stewart-Brown, S., Tennant, A., Tennant, R., Platt, S., Parkison, J., & Weich, S. (2009). Internal construct validity of the Warwick-Edinburgh mental well-being scale (WEMWBS): A Rasch analysis using data from the Scottish Health Education Population Survey. *Health and Quality of Life Outcomes, 9*, 7–15.

Tennant, R., Hiller, L., Fishwick, R., Platt, S., Joseph, S., Weich, S., et al. (2007). The Warwick-Edinburgh mental well-being scale (WEMWBS): Development and UK validation. *Health and Quality of Life Outcomes, 5*, 63.

Travis, J., Western, B., & Redburn, F. S. (2014). *The growth of incarceration in the United States: Exploring causes and consequences*. National Academies Press.

Wildeman, C., & Wang, E. A. (2017). Mass incarceration, public health, and widening inequality in the USA. *The Lancet, 389*(10077), 1464–1474.

Woodall, J. (2016). A critical examination of the health promoting prison two decades on. *Critical Public Health, 26*(5), 615–621.

Woods, D., & Breslin, G. (2019). Reflections on implementing the Active Choices Rugby Programme to enhance mental health and wee-being of young men in prison. In G. Breslin & G. Leavey (Eds.), *Mental health and well-being interventions in sport* (pp. 128–143). Abingdon, Oxon: Routledge.

Woods, D., Breslin, G., & Hassan, D. (2017). A systematic review of the impact of SBIs on the psychological well-being of people in prison. *Mental Health and Physical Activity, 12*, 50–61.

Woods, D., Leavey, G., Meek, R. & Breslin, G. (In press). Developing mental health awareness and help seeking in prison: A feasibility study of the State of Mind Sport programme. *International Journal of Prisoner Health.*

World Health Organization. (1999). *Mental health promotion in prison: Report on a WHO meeting*. World Health Organisation, Regional Office for Europe, Copenhagen

World Health Organization. (2007a). *Health in prisons: A WHO guide to the essential in prison health.* Copenhagen: World Health Organisation.

World Health Organization. (2007b). *Trenčín statement on prisons and mental health.* Copenhagen: WHO Regional Office for Europe.

World Health Organization. (2014). *Prisons and health.* Retrieved from http://www.euro.who.int/__data/assets/pdf_file/0005/249188/Prisons-and-Health.pdf.

10

Oral Health as a Door to Promoting Psychosocial Functioning for People in Custody: Lessons Learnt from the Development of the Mouth Matters Intervention

Ruth Freeman

Introduction

Of the nearly 8,300 people in custody in Scottish prisons on a given day, 80% are from the 5% most deprived communities in Scotland (Scottish Prison Service 2019a). A large proportion have had adverse childhood experiences including childhood violence, witnessing domestic violence and being in residential, foster and/or secure care. Nearly a third have mental health problems, use substances and have literacy and numeracy difficulites (Carnie et al. 2017). People liberated without employment are twice as likely to reoffend (Carnie et al. 2017). To address these inequalities, the Scottish Government reformed The Rehabilitation of Offenders Act 1974 (1974): 'To make a contribution to:

R. Freeman (✉)
University of Dundee, Dundee, UK
e-mail: R.E.Freeman@dundee.ac.uk

© The Author(s) 2021

M. Maycock et al. (eds.), *Issues and Innovations in Prison Health Research*, Palgrave Studies in Prisons and Penology, https://doi.org/10.1007/978-3-030-46401-1_10

- Reducing underemployment,
- Increasing the proportion of young people in learning, training or work,
- Improving mental well-being,
- Reducing reconviction rates,
- Reducing the proportion of individuals living in poverty' (Scottish Government 2018a).

The 1974 Act reform reflected the Scottish Government's National Performance Framework (Scottish Government 2018b) and Scottish Prison Service's aims (Scottish Prison Service 2019b) for human rights, health, employment and education.

The aspiration for oral health becoming a human and civil right for people in prison was promoted by the World Health Organisation in their 2014 report (World Health Organization 2014). Their recommendations concerning the oral health of people in prison highlighted the importance of providing holistic dental care within current dental systems (Gray and Gregory 2014). Oral health, Gray and Gregory (2014) proposed, would be couched within general health, would adopt the common risk factor approach and, therefore, prison interventions which targeted smoking, diet and so forth, would automatically have benefits for oral health. The requirement for oral health to be an integral part of general health and preventive programmes was apparent especially in Scotland where oral health is a central tenet of prison health policy (Brutus et al. 2012). The Scottish Executive's Dental Action Plan of 2005 (Scottish Executive 2005) stated clearly the need for oral health interventions for those categorised as, 'priority groups'. Therefore, for people in custody, they directed NHS Boards to, 'develop and deliver oral health care preventive support programmes for adults in most need such as prisoners' (Scottish Executive 2005). Following this directive, the Scottish Oral Health Improvement Prison Programme evolved under direction of the author (RF) and with it, its intervention, entitled, 'Mouth Matters' (Freeman et al. 2014). By 2015, the Scottish Government's policy for oral health improvement for people in prison included the adoption of 'Mouth Matters' within a 'whole prison approach' (Scottish Government 2015).

Despite the recognition of the importance of adopting a whole prison approach (World Health Organization 2014; Gray and Gregory 2014) to oral health preventive programmes, the oral health of people in prison remained poor. Reports have repeatedly shown that the oral health of those in custody is less than that in the general population (Nobile et al. 2007; Cunningham et al. 1985; Jones et al. 2005; Heidari et al. 2008; Freeman et al. 2011). The extent of their dental caries experience being described as rampant caries or extreme oral health represented by the 'so-called cliff-edge of inequality' (Aldridge et al. 2018). In order to understand their extreme oral health, it was proposed that people in prison experienced multiple social exclusions as a consequence of adverse childhood experiences, mental health issues and the stigma associated with exclusion. Therefore, despite the best efforts of Government and policy implementation to promote oral health, these interventions failed because of a lack of understanding that 'people who experience social exclusion and multiple intersecting vulnerabilities face a "triple separation"' (Freeman et al. 2020). For people in prison, this represents a separation from mainstream society, from education, work and family life and from holistic health and social care where health promotion is an active part of everyday life. It was a lack of an appreciation of the multidimensional nature of the poverty together with an unawareness of prisoners' relational deprivation that underpinned failures in oral health promotion (Akbar et al. 2012). An alternative means of development which included an interactive framework, a co-design and co-production philosophy was required. Adopting this approach would be more likely to enable the life stories of those in prison to be an integral part of programme development and permit the promotion of oral health and psychosocial functioning for those in prison.

In order to accept this alternative strategy a number of questions must be answered. This first of these is: what is the content of an intervention that 'enables people to maximise their capabilities and have control over their lives' and 'create [the means for] employment and good work' (Marmot et al. 2010)? The second is: what constitutes evidence-based practice? While the health information provided in health promotion programmes must be evidence-based, other factors such as the stories of people, their life experiences, their ability to access care and the consequences of poor health upon their psychosocial functioning must have the same status as the evidence provided from randomised control trials. Therefore, people in prison, it may be argued, know more than those on the outside, about the importance and effects of their oral health upon their lives and psychosocial functioning. Adopting Friere's critical consciousness (Friere 1970), therefore, permits those who are experts by experience to inform the content of health interventions. It is by accepting and incorporating the above analysis that oral health interventions may provide a portal to psychosocial functioning and the promotion of health in general.

The aim of this chapter is to report on the development of the oral health intervention programme for the Scottish Government, called 'Mouth Matters' (Freeman et al. 2014), and its progression to a peer health coaching intervention to improve the psychosocial functioning of people in prison. Aspects of the development work that gave rise to Mouth Matters will be used to illustrate the links between oral health and psychosocial functioning. Therefore, the first part of this chapter will describe the psychosocial needs of people in prison in Scotland which informed the six Units of the Mouth Matters intervention. The second part will present a reworking of a qualitative exploration of the prisoners' oral health concerns that permitted Unit 6, 'Working with offenders: promoting and supporting oral health behaviour change', to be reconfigured into a peer health coaching programme to promote psychosocial functioning via the portal of oral health. A summary description of the qualitative evaluation of the peer health coaching intervention that promoted psychosocial functioning via the portal of oral health will be provided.

People in Prison: Psychosocial Functioning and Oral Health: Survey Findings

In 2011, over 300 people in prison took part in a survey to examine their health, oral health and psychosocial health. People residing in a male high-security jail, a women's prison and in a young offenders' institution participated. They agreed to an oral health examination and to complete a health questionnaire which included psychometric measures of depression, oral health-related quality of life and dental anxiety. The aim being to provide evidence to inform the development of the Mouth Matters (Freeman et al. 2014) oral health promotion intervention to fulfil the requirements of the Scottish Government's policy initiative for oral health promotion (Scottish Executive 2005; Scottish Government 2015). Specifically, could this survey development work identify any evidence for an association between psychosocial functioning and oral health that could inform the content and improve the ability of an intervention to promote oral health?

Findings showed that dental health and the ability to access dental care was similar to that reported in an earlier survey of 2002 (Jones et al. irritableness with others because of their sore teeth 2005). People had more missing or extracted teeth and fewer filled or restored teeth than those in the general population. They reported experiencing pain and discomfort and difficulties when accessing dental care. Reported barriers to attending for dental treatment during imprisonment included problems arranging appointments, infrequency of dental clinics and difficulties in obtaining, reading and completing prison request forms. Access to dental treatment was strongly connected to quality of life. Those unable to access dental care, reported greater difficulties in eating and speaking; feeling self-conscious, suffering embarrassment and tension about the appearance of their teeth and expressing irritableness with others because of their sore teeth. For those who accessed emergency dental care in prison, the quality of life impact, 'feeling irritable with others' acted as a significant factor in accessing this type of dental care. The connection between psychosocial functioning and oral health was apparent (Freeman and Richards 2019).

The mental health of the participants, based on their reported prescribed medication suggested that the prevalence of mental illness was equivalent to population norms (Scottish Government 2019); however, careful examination of the depression scale data showed that 35% were suffering from typical symptoms of depression. Women prisoners, in addition to their increased prevalence of injecting drug use, had increased depressive symptomatology than younger and older men. A pathway from depression via drug use to missing and decayed teeth was demonstrated, recently for the first time, for this group of people in custody (Arora et al. 2020). This confirmed once more the important links between psychosocial functioning and oral health status.

The prison as a routine and regulated environment promoted the adoption and maintenance of toothbrushing with fluoride toothpaste and denture hygiene practices. However, outside the prison environment prisoners spoke of their difficulties in accessing appropriate dental care and maintaining basic oral health practices. Their experiences suggested that people needed to be empowered with basic life skills and knowledge of how to access dental health services, among others.

The survey, therefore, provided the important evidence for the content for Mouth Matters to be an: 'evidence-informed oral health promotion resource. It has been compiled under expert guidance and is designed …. to meet the specific oral health needs of offender populations in Scotland. Its overall purpose is to raise awareness of the key factors that affect oral health and provide core motivational interviewing skills that can be used to support an oral health brief intervention tailored to offenders.' as stated on page 7 of the Mouth Matters Guide for Trainers (Freeman et al. 2014). Units 1–5 covered all aspects of oral health couched within the common risk factor approach (Sheiham and Watt 2000). In these first Units, the person in prison would learn how to access dental care, prevent oral disease and understand the effect of diet, smoking, drugs and oral sex upon an individual's oral health. The final 6th Unit returned to the evidence-base and the health psychology literature. It included motivational interviewing to promote oral health and delivered a framework to identify and negotiate the most appropriate form of the behavioural intervention. However, while it was 'compiled under expert guidance', the voices of the experts by experience were not incorporated sufficiently to provide a cogent understanding of what was needed to promote health and psychosocial well-being. There needed to be a revisiting of the qualitative exploration of the prisoners' thoughts and experiences of oral health.

People in Prison: Psychosocial Functioning and Oral Health

While the survey information provided strong support to incorporate the recognised dental and psychological evidence-base, the results relating to associations between oral health with quality of life and depression suggested that vital, additional elements needed to be incorporated into the programme. The Mouth Matters programme, because it is a Scottish Government intervention, is implemented by oral health promotion officers employed by the National Health Services (NHS) Boards in Scotland to promote oral health in Scottish Prisons. The reliance of using the NHS Boards' oral health promotion officers to deliver the programme to people in prison, did not, in all situations, provide an appropriate platform to address the psychosocial needs of those in custody. If this was to be achieved, then the relationship between oral health and psychosocial functioning would need to be clearly addressed. It was now necessary to revisit people's stories provided in the qualitative work (Freeman et al. 2011) obtained as part of the developmental work, reformulate their oral health concerns and reconfigure Unit 6 to promote psychosocial functioning via the portal of oral health, to enable this to be achieved.

As part of the development work for Mouth Matters, a series of qualitative interviews were conducted to inform the intervention content. The verbatim quotes provided in the next section are from the qualitative data collected as part of that process. People in custody residing in four of the prisons in Scotland were invited to participate in a series of one-to-one in-depth interviews to explore their felt health needs, oral health self-care, their experiences of dental care and the effect their oral health had upon them. A purposive sample of 42 prisoners, who wished to participate, were interviewed. They represented adult male (n = 8) and female (n = 13) prisoners on long sentences; young offenders (n = 9) and those on remand or on short-term sentences (n = 12) (Freeman et al. 2011). They were assured that the discussions were confidential unless there was a suggestion of violence or harm to others. They could speak about whatever they wished and to bring the interview to a close when they wanted. All interviews were recorded and transcribed later. The qualitative data were analysed using framework analysis. To ensure trustworthiness of the data analysis, the data was examined independently by the author and a researcher. After the data had been scrutinised, they met to discuss the emerging themes they had identified individually. It was agreed that the themes reflected the elements of oral health-related quality of life as conceptualise by Locker (Locker 1988).

For people in prison, therefore, their oral health influenced their quality of life (Locker 1988) (Fig. 10.1). Their poor oral health reduced '*self-esteem*' and '*confidence*', increased feelings of depression, affected their self-worth and how they interacted with others. Repeatedly, people spoke of how their teeth influenced their social interactions. Many spoke of how their '*broken*', '*damaged*', '*ground down*' and '*rotten*' teeth betrayed their violent past and their drug and/or alcohol use. Unable to enjoy eating and communicating with others, hiding '*bad breath*' and fears of being misunderstood by friends and family, exacerbated their social isolation. They felt stigmatised and anxious and were often at the mercy of physical or verbal bullying by others, on account of their teeth. Fears of stigma, prejudice and judgement extended to accessing services, dental treatment and work opportunities on liberation. Views of there being little likelihood of being appointed to a job, when '*teeth were rotten*' were often voiced. People felt that the prison establishment, including dentists, were oblivious of how their teeth affected employment opportunities. As one prisoner who participated in the qualitative work (Freeman et al. 2011), mentioned above, stated clearly; '*I din'nae think they realise that that could be the difference in a guy goin' for a job for an interview, when he gets out of prison.*'

The effect of such '*instant judgements*' or fears of '*the dentist just sees me as drug addict prisoner*', therefore influenced their social interacting and employment possibilities. When accessing dental care, whether inside and outside of prison, they feared criticisms from the dentist and consequently felt that they were treated in some way differently to others. Their anxieties were supported by their impressions that their appointments were hurried, that treatment options were not discussed, and their teeth were extracted abruptly rather than filled. Their experiences and perceptions of dental care reflected othering by the dentist: 'othering' (Todorov 1999), in which, judgements were made about them, where they were

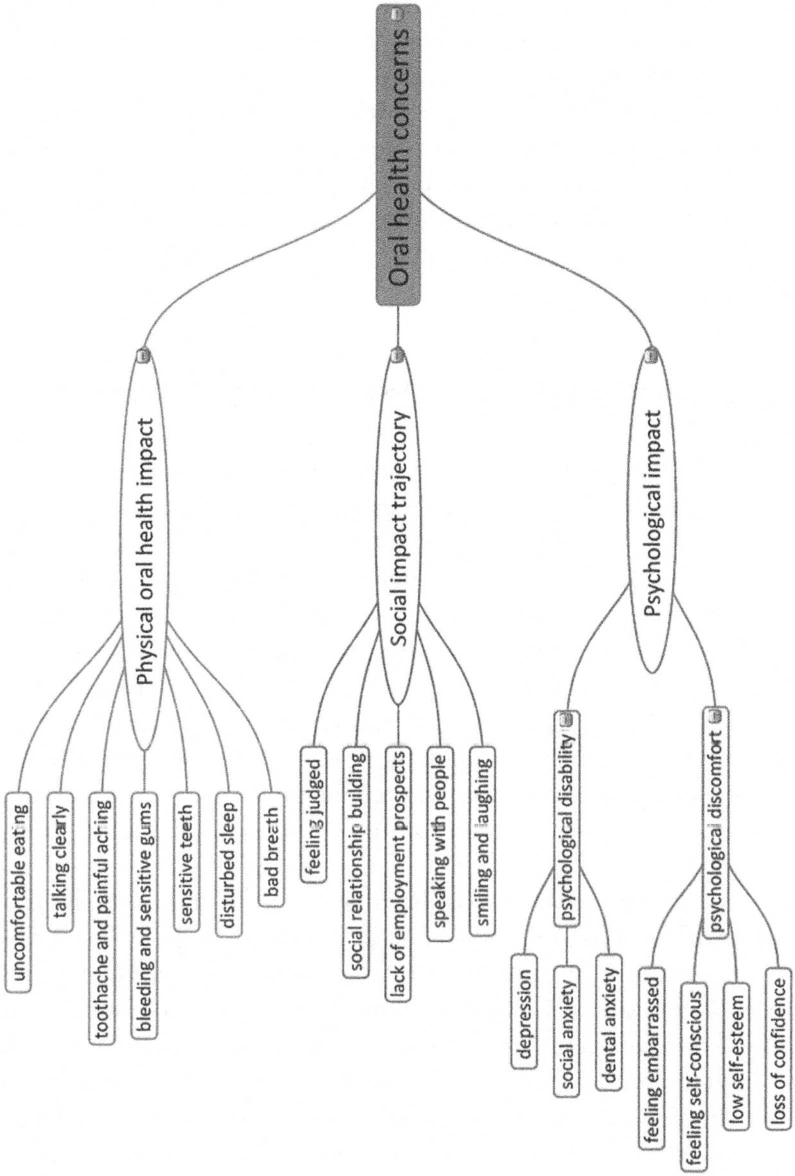

Fig. 10.1 The oral health concerns of people in custody in Scottish prisons

left feeling isolated and misunderstood by the dental health professional they had come to see. Othering, on the part of the dental health professional, therefore, not only maintained the social gulf between them but promoted their social isolation and exclusion.

The findings from the qualitative work revealed the need to incorporate an alternative person-centred approach to complement the motivational interviewing framework of Unit 6 of Mouth Matters. Doing so would promote social interacting, support communication, reduce and improve an understanding of the other, while promoting self-esteem and confidence.

From Mouth Matters to Peer Health Coaching

Health coaching is generally a person-centred approach, with a reliance on personal goal setting to develop personal skills, promote self-esteem, confidence and self-efficacy to maintain health behaviour change (Wolever et al. 2013). Health coaching interventions have been associated with improved dietary behaviours (O'Hara et al. 2012), reduced smoking (Rabius et al. 2007), improved communication (Jimison et al. 2013) and psychosocial functioning (Wolever et al. 2013). In the prison context, health coaching programmes had assisted in 'the transition from prison to the community' (Spaulding et al. 2009). Therefore, the evidence suggested that health coaching could provide both a theoretical and practical framework to promote psychosocial functioning in the prison setting.

Health coaching, however, was dependent on the 'interpersonal relationship with a coach' (Almondes et al. 2017) and since peer health education interventions in prison were associated with positive health outcomes (Almondes et al. 2017), it seemed appropriate to adopt a health coaching format as a peer intervention to promote psychosocial functioning through the portal of oral health (Everington 2013). The policy rationale, for the personal, social and wider political context of peer health coaching reflected the principles of the Scottish Government's reform to provide agency for people in prison to promote self-care, to access health and social care services and thereby transform their lives (Scottish Government 2018a, b; Scottish Prison Service 2019b).

A protocol together with a logic model (Cinar et al. 2017) of a peer health coaching intervention was operationalised initially as the 'People in Prison: health coaching for Scotland' or PeP-SCOT programme (Cinar et al. 2017). The health coaching intervention was implemented in two consecutive years in a male, high-security Scottish prison and was co-designed with stakeholders and the participants in the prison (Cinar et al. 2017). The coaching model and course curriculum focused on leadership coaching with a motivational interviewing element (Cinar et al. 2017). In all, 12 peer health coaches were trained. On completion of the training programme the participants were awarded a Level 1 training certificate from an accredited International Coaching Federation Health Coaching Programme. They also successfully completed the Royal Society of Public Health examination in Understanding Health Improvement.

To evaluate the effectiveness of the peer health coaching intervention, a qualitative assessment was undertaken. The aim was to assess the effectiveness and the sustainability of the programme on the peer health coaches' and their coachees' psychosocial functioning. A researcher from the Scottish Prison Service interviewed six peer coaches individually at 3-monthly intervals following their training over a 12-month period. Six coachees, five personal officers and three residential officers also took part in one-to-one interviews to gauge their views on the peer health coaching programme. All participants were assured that interviews were confidential unless there was a suggestion of violence or harm to others. They could speak about whatever they wished and to bring the interview to a close when they wanted. All interviews were recorded and transcribed by the researcher. The data was analysed using content analysis. The trustworthiness and dependability of the manifest content data analysis was ensured by the author and the researcher reading the transcripts individually. Once they had identified the themes they met to discuss. If a difference occurred, the differences were fully debated to guarantee confirmability of the data analysis. Since the author and the researcher had complementary experience of person-centred interventions and of the prison service, respectively, this meant that the credibility of the data was assured.

The effect of peer health coaching training was apparent from the outset. For instance, the peer health coaches spoke of an increased confidence in approaching and speaking with other people: '*This course has given me an opportunity to improve my language and confidence to contact others.*' Some described how their social interactions had changed and attributed this to their new knowledge of the differences between types of questions and when to use open and closed questioning. Therefore, they felt that the health coach training had informed and strengthened their communication skills and consequently their social interactions. They could now speak openly about health matters and pass on information on sugar and diet, fluoride toothpaste use and self-care. During telephone conversations and family visits some went further negotiating with young relatives to remain at school to get a good job with positive results—'*It's alright, I sorta must have got through cause the next thing I know our Mum was telling me (s)he's going back to school*'.

On completion and several months following the peer health coaching training it was apparent that there had been a strengthening of their psychosocial functioning. They spoke of understanding other people and an awareness that others had '*feelings and emotions*' that also had to be considered. Previous experiences of '*insensitive or offensive words from workers*' that would previously have resulted in an immediate violent '*blow-out*' now were ignored as the peer health coaches had space for '*self- reflection*' and management of their frustrations and anger. '*Improved control over emotions*' and a more positive outlook on life were of central importance when the peer health coaches were placed into situations in which they felt they had failed or were made to feel '*less worthy or silly*'. In these situations, their improved coping skills gave way to earlier and more self-destructive behaviours. In some instances, the peer health coach was able to reflect, problem-solve and take '*ten minutes to chill out*' before providing an explanation, and negotiated a solution, as illustrated in the vignette here:

> I said to him, "*I felt like you just ignored me, just treated me like I was'nae there, and, got a bit upset about it because 'aw I was wanting was the paper and if you'd have been decent with me, I'd have been decent with you … but, just for the sheer fact you sat there and done nothing, and, I apologise for the*

way I spoke to you; I shouldn't have spoke to you that way. I was just upset, eh and it's no an excuse but I'm tryin' to stop smoking—I've no had a smoke for a couple a days," so .... He (residential officer) was like at, "*Aw I'm sorry as well, know what I mean ... I can see where you're coming fae, we'll try not to let that happen again*" ... and that was it.

The ability to problem- solve, to apologise was related to the degree of trust felt by the peer health coach in another individual. Trust emerged as an important factor as the participants spoke of the need of having a safe place to open up, being able to voice opinions without judgement and to be understood when hostile and violent outbursts occurred with their peers and the prison officers. Therefore, while the programme assisted with self-reflection, problem-solving, improved confidence and self-esteem, the issue of trust, being slighted and standing frustration were factors which mitigated against the maintenance of the psychosocial skills attained during and in the first months following completion of the peer health coaching programme. Connected with trust was the individual's social standing within the prison, related to the crime committed, shared identities and personality types. Some peer health coaches admitted that their fellow coaches were less regarded by other prisoners and reinforced their view by naming the peer health coaches they would or would not be associated with. Those participants who referred to themselves as fathers or serving long-term sentences identified with one-another and regarded the others as different. These peer health coaches identified with prison staff who they considered as hardworking and concluded the staff were '*not criminals*'. They further distinguished themselves as '*non-drug users*' and '*the healthy group*'. In this way they could ensure their social standing in the prison was maintained.

Despite the recurring theme of maintaining their social standing within the prison, the peer health coaches worked hard to overcome such thoughts and old patterns of behaviour and used the skills learnt to understand their emotions, feelings and perceptions of themselves and others. For one peer health coach, although acknowledging his tendency to be dismissive and to trivialise others' life experiences, he continually tried to generate alternatives to avoid confrontation with others and '*being landed with a report*'. It seemed that many of the peer health coaches, self-coached (Box 10.1) and informally coached those around, including as mentioned previously, family and friends. This suggested that some aspects of the coaching ethos had pervaded beyond the formal peer-to-peer sessions and into the residential halls in general.

The peer health coaches were vocal in both their praise and complaints about the programme. Factors that enabled informal coaching also exposed the difficulties encountered by the peer health coaches, such as the willingness or unwillingness to coach or, for an individual to be coached, when providing peer-to-peer health coaching in the prison environment. It became apparent that a number of contextual factors constrained the progression from self-coaching through informal coaching to formal peer-to-peer coaching. These factors included:

1. Complaints regarding access to potential coachees. The participants complained that coaching referrals were only permitted from two levels of one residential hall. Since the majority of the peer health coaches were long-term prisoners, coachees had to come from the same flat due to location of coaching sessions being in cells or in recreational areas. The peer health coaches felt there were too many coaches and not enough coachees. Frustration at not being able to apply their newly acquired skills; fears of reduced confidence with coaching skills fading were a recurring theme.
2. Time was listed as another reason for not accessing coachees. The peer health coaches complained about fitting coaching time into daily routines and finding time to set up sessions when they and the coachees were available.
3. Location was cited as a considerable barrier for peer-to-peer coaching. The peer coaches complained of the noise in the residential areas, of their fears of being overheard, concerns of people prying and issues of confidentiality. They called for specific locations for peer-to-peer health coaching within the flat or hall.

In the 12 months following the health coaching training, the peer health coaches' confidence, their self-efficacy together with improved communication skills and social interactions, were sustained. For the majority of participants, this meant that they allowed themselves time to

Box 10.1 Peer Health Coach: Problem-Solving and Goal Setting for Behaviour Change

'When I started thinking about it I thought this could be good for me and for my heart, to stop smoking. I had issues with my blood ... producing too much blood. That was pushing me into a bad area that could potentially kill me so I talked to the doctor and he explained to me, "Your bone marrow is producing too much blood, causing blood clots, causing heart attacks so I was like well what could be causing my bone marrow to produce blood too much, why would it be doing that there's no reason for it to be doing that then when I started thinking about it, it was like smoking, smoking takes it all because you've got the blood, bone marrow produces more blood to give me more oxygen to collect oxygen. So in my head I'd already played it out and went there's my culprit, but I just never put it into action until the Mouth Matters. I thought let's not be a hypocrite and let's do this—I'll be an example. The health coaching sorta, like, it helped me tidy myself up and go like well okay, sort my brain. Life's got to be worth something is it, so ... then I just started like wanting to stop smoking. Then started coaching myself! Setting myself a time frame, working out the good and bad benefits, who am I really doing it for? It benefits everybody but I need to make sure I'm happy, and if I'm not doing it for myself it's never going to happen. So I know what I'm doing, I know what I need to do, I know how to do it and I know why I need to make me believe in myself.'

reflect, to problem-solve and set interim health goals to succeed in changing their behaviours. The following vignette in Box 10.1 is illustrative.

Of the coachees interviewed, many spoke of the problems of being in prison and the detriment this had for their self-esteem, their confidence and communicating with family, friends and others. They found that the one-to-one with a peer coach who understood the prison experience, who had experienced the same issues of trust, of fears of bullying and violence, assisted in their participation in the health coaching intervention. In this working alliance, the coachees related to the communication and goal setting techniques used to help them find their own answers which encouraged and inspired them to engage with the programme.

They reported that their experience of peer-to-peer coaching helped to improve their own communication and reduce their anxieties. For example, changing diet, buying fewer snacks and feeling more comfortable speaking to others resulted, for one coachee, having more money on his phone account to speak to relatives. He felt that making healthier choices and saving money meant that he was able to spend more quality time speaking with his children:

> *So now that I've got that bit extra I'm a bit more lenient with them, I'll just sit and chat to them and it feels good. It's less stressful because when my kids are sitting talking to me about homework or something I used to feel like I was changing the subject so that I had enough to phone them every day.*

The anxieties and the fears shared with the peer health coaches were at times considerable. Worries about returning to drug use on release from prison, or fears of dying were brought to the coaching sessions. The trust built up between coach and coachee meant that one man was able to speak openly of his fears of dying whilst in custody. With the peer health coach, this man was able to speak of his sentence length and his concerns about his family on the outside and started to think about solutions to assist them while he was in custody.

Improvements in the coachees' social interactions with family and friends and hence psychosocial functioning were also related to an increased understanding of general oral health and health issues for the coachees. Some coachees stated that as a consequence of their better knowledge of goal setting and problem-solving, they reasoned that, '*staff needed to learn* [health coaching] *so they* [could] *have better conversations with prisoners!*' It seemed that a shift had occurred in the coachees' psychosocial functioning and in particular with their families and children during phone calls and/or on family visits.

In the following vignette (Box 10.2), the peer health coach interaction permitted this coachee to think about his unhealthy eating pattern and the cause of it. With the coach he identified a series of health goals for dietary behaviour change that resulted not only in weight loss but in a promotion of prosocial behaviours.

Differences in the social interactions between the prisoners were observed by staff both within the residential areas and in the Physical Education Department. The officers spoke of observing a maintenance in participants' '*prosocial behaviour*'. Some of the peer health coaches returned to education to improve computer skills for life on liberation.

Box 10.2 Coachee: Reasoning, Problem-Solving and Improved Well-Being

An individual reported that he had achieved his ideal weight using the reasoning and problem-solving he had learnt during peer health coaching. He recognised that he had used confectionary to solve his boredom and now replaced boredom with actions rather than sweets. He stated that: '*I used to [eat confectionary at night] when I felt like 'aw I'm starvin' but I wasn't really starvin'. I was bored. I was buying, knowing I was gonna be bored—like I was buying sweets and junk food knowing I was gonna be bored at the weekend. Normally I'd be bored because I'm up so late whereas now because you're doing circuits in the gym and you're doing a work out by 10–10.30 pm you're wanting to go to sleep rather than sitting up to 12–1.00 am o'clock in the morning. If you're bored at night, do something different, sit and write a letter ... the coach was just giving advice like that—you choose. So I started putting it into practice. So times like I was sitting feeling hungry, I didn't have the sweets because I stopped buying them, so I'd be sitting feeling hungry and would just write my Missus a letter or my parents, like my Auntie Margaret writes to me sometimes so I sometimes write back to her. Again, I think the coaching helped my family communication as well because they enjoy hearing from me.*'

He explained that the peer-to-peer coaching had provided a time for reflection. This had started with an awareness of what food he ate during meal times and what he was putting inside his body: '*Like in here, you get fed at certain periods of time you know what I mean so you just sort of get fed, have your dinner and that's it, it's done. So you didn't need to think about it, but when you do now. When it's been pointed out to me if you just cut down on this slowly it will help.*'

The peer-to-peer coaching not only enabled him to lose weight but also to recognise his feelings, improve his self-image and psychosocial well-being: '*I feel happy! I don't know why—I just feel a bit happier. I feel like its working and that's maybe why I feel happier. I don't know if secretly, self-consciously like when I was gaining weight, whenever if it was mentioned, I'd say ah it doesn't bother me, and it wasn't but then it started to because more people kept saying it. Men are more insecure than women so secretly it was bothering me as much as I used to say it wasn't. So I feel happy, I just feel overall happy now because although I've not gained my target, it's working so I think that's why I feel happier. Losing the weight has made me feel better about myself, know what I mean? Mentally I feel like more confident and things like that.*'

Others decided to go further with health coaching and completed additional health coaching training and gained the Level 2 award from the same accredited Health Coaching Programme.

The qualitative evaluation of the peer health coaching programme, therefore, showed that short, medium and some long-term benefits accrued to those who acted as peer health coaches and their coachees. While some health behaviours were not maintained, what was retained indicated an improved psychosocial functioning. Therefore, it was noted that the peer health coaches and their coachees experienced enhanced self-efficacy, positive behaviour change and improvements in communication, coping skills, problem-solving and interactions with peers and prison staff, resulting in reduced abusive exchanges.

Conclusions

The work presented here, while showing some elements of success, clearly illustrated that when evidence-based practice is closely adhered to at the expense of evidence from experts by experience, the reductionist nature of the product, while improving oral health knowledge, does little to promote psychosocial factors essential for successful behaviour change, in practice.

What are the practical lessons that may be learnt from the development of this oral health programme and its ability to promote psychosocial functioning for people in custody? To answer this question, it is necessary to return to the place of 'evidence'? At the outset of the programme development, difficulties were encountered with Mouth Matters because of its reliance on the evidence-based approach to fulfil the requirements of the Scottish Government's oral health improvement policies (Scottish Government 2018a, b; Scottish Prison Service 2019b; Brutus et al. 2012). In adopting a narrow evidence-based approach, Mouth Matters (Freeman et al. 2014) served, '*governmental function*', where ready-made and convenient 'goals and targets' were to be achieved (Cinar et al. 2017). But, and in addition, what was ignored was the supplementary evidence obtained in the survey and in the qualitative exploration as being somehow '*unscientific*' (Holmes et al. 2006). Despite the evidence of the interactions between oral health and psychosocial functioning, this additional, supplementary evidence was given less importance in the face of the requirement to put all the evidence-based information on the prevention, for example, of dental caries through reduced frequency of sugary foods and drinks and the twice daily use of fluoride toothpaste. Therefore, Mouth Matters improved oral health knowledge, but was unable to change oral health behaviours or address issues surrounding wider health and psychosocial health. How the people in custody would change their behaviours would be dictated by using the evidence-based motivational interviewing. To shift, Mouth Matters from a reductionist intervention to a pluralistic programme would require an acknowledgement of the equivalence of the supplementary evidence from the people in custody as experts by experience as that from randomized controlled trials. Therefore, it was necessary to reexamine and reformulate the qualitative data. Doing so gave way to the emergence of the co-designed peer health coaching intervention. It represented a pluralistic intervention (Holmes et al. 2006), which used all evidence from experts by experience to cause a sustainable difference in their social interactions with others.

Therefore, in the development of interventions, which may truly promote all aspects of health, it is necessary to adopt a community development approach and to produce, 'evidence-based action plans informed by mixed research methodologies and undergirded by participatory research paradigms in order to privilege the voices and lived experiences of people experiencing social exclusion and extreme oral health' (Freeman et al. 2020). Doing so ensures that psychosocial functioning for people in custody may start at the door of oral health.

Acknowledgement I would like to acknowledge my colleagues past and present from the Scottish Oral Health Improvement Prison Programme, DHSRU, University of Dundee. Special thanks to Denise Downie, Ally Jackson and colleagues from the Scottish Prison Service and to all of the people in prison who took part in the survey, qualitative exploration and the peer health coaching intervention.

References

Akbar, T., Turner, S., Themessl-Huber, M., Richards, D., & Freeman, R. (2012). The health-promoting prison: Can, it improve oral health? An evaluation of an Oral Health Improvement Project for high-security prisoners. *International Journal of Health Promotion and Education, 50*, 169–177.

Aldridge, R. W., Story, A., Hwang, S. W., Nordentoft, M., Luchenski, S. A., Hartwell, G., Tweed, E. J., Lewer, D., Katikireddi, S. V., & Hayward, A. C. (2018). Morbidity and mortality in homeless individuals, prisoners, sex workers, and individuals with substance use disorders in high-income countries: A systematic review and meta-analysis. *Lancet, 391*, 241–250.

Almondes, N., Downie, D., Cinar, A. B., Richards, D., & Freeman, R. (2017). Is health coaching effective in changing the health status and behaviour of prisoners?—A systematic review protocol. *Systematic Reviews, 6*, 127.

Arora, G., Humphris, G., Lahti, S., Richards, D., & Freeman, R. (2020). Depression, drugs and dental anxiety in prisons: A mediation model explaining dental decay experience. *Community Dentistry and Oral Epidemiology*, 248–255.

Brutus, L., Mackie, P., Millard, A., Fraser, A., Conacher, A., Hardie, S., McDowall, L., & Meechan, H. (2012). *Better health, better lives for prisoners: A framework for improving the health of Scotland's prisoners: Volume 1: The framework*. Retrieved March, 2019, from http://www.scotphn.net/pdf/2012_06_08_Health_improvement_for_prisoners_vol_1_Final_(Web_version)1.pdf.

Carnie, J., Broderick, R., Cameron, J., Downie, D., & Williams, G. (2017). *SPS: Prisoners survey 2017*. 16th series. Retrieved November, 2019, from http://www.sps.gov.uk.

Cinar, A. B., et al. (2017). PeP-SCOT a health coaching intervention for people in prisons: intervention protocol. *Community Dental Health, 34*, 97–101.

Cunningham, M. A., Glenn, R. E., Field, H. M., & Jakobsen, J. R. (1985). Dental disease prevalence in a prison population. *Journal of Public Health Dentistry, 45*, 49–52.

Everington, T. (2013). *Healthier people safer communities: Working together to improve outcomes for offenders*. Retrieved from http://www.cjalb.co.uk/uploads/Offender%20Health%20Report%202013.pdf.

Freeman, R., & Richards, D. (2019). Factors associated with accessing prison dental services in Scotland: A cross-sectional study. *Dentistry Journal, 7*, 12.

Freeman, R., Akbar, T., Buls, D., Edwards, M., Everington, T., Richards, D., Themessl-Huber, M., Watt, C. (2011). *The oral health and psychosocial needs of Scottish prisoners and young offenders*. Retrieved January, 2020, from https://dentistry.dundee.ac.uk/sites/dentistry.dundee.ac.uk/files/media/SOHIPP-report.pdf.

Freeman, R., Buls, D., Watt, C., Richards, D., Everington, T., MacFarlane, F., Edwards, M., O'Neill, P., & Jones, C. (2014). *Mouth Matters guide for trainers: Better oral care for offenders*. Edinburgh: NHS Health Scotland.

Freeman, R., Doughty, J., MacDonald, M. E., & Muirhead, V. (2020). Inclusion oral health: Advancing a theoretical framework for policy, research and practice. *Community Dentistry and Oral Epidemiology, 48*, 1–6.

Friere, P. (1970). *Pedagogy of the oppressed*. London: Penguin Books.

Gray, R., & Gregory, S. (2014). Dental health in prisons. In S. Enggist, L. Møller, G. Galea, & C. Udesen (Eds.), *Prison and health*. Retrieved January, 2020, from http://www.euro.who.int/data/assets/pdf_file/0005/249188/Prisons-and-Health.pdf.

Heidari, E., Dickinson, C., Wilson, R., & Fiske, J. (2008). Oral health of remand prisoners in HMP Brixton, London. *Journal of Disability and Oral Health, 9*, 18–21.

Holmes, D., Murray, S. J., Perron, A., & Rail, G. (2006). Deconstructing the evidence-based discourse in health sciences: Truth, power and fascism. *International Journal of Evidence-Based Healthcare, 4*, 180–186.

Jimison, H. B., Klein, K. A., & Marcoe, J. L. (2013, July 3). *A socialization intervention in remote health coaching for older adults in the home*. 35th Annual International Conference of the IEEE Engineering in Medicine and Biology Society (pp. 7025–7028).

Jones, C. M., Woods, K., Neville, J., & Whittle, J. G. (2005). Dental health of prisoners in the north west of England in 2000: literature review and dental health survey results. *Community Dental Health, 22*, 113–117.

Locker, D. (1988). Measuring oral health: A conceptual framework. *Community Dental Health, 5*, 3–18.

Marmot, M., Allen, J., Goldblatt, P., Boyce, T., McNeish, D., Grady, M., & Geddes, I. (2010). *Fair society healthy lives* (The Marmot Review). Retrieved January, 2020, from http://www.instituteofhealthequity.org/resources-reports/fair-society-healthy-lives-the-marmot-review.

Nobile, C. G., Fortunato, L., Pavia, M., & Angelillo, I. F. (2007). Oral health status of male prisoners in Italy. *International Dental Journal, 57*, 27–35.

O'Hara, B. J., Phongsavan, P., Venugopal, K., Eakin, E. G., Eggins, D., Caterson, H., King, L., Allman-Farinelli, M., Haas, M., & Bauman, A. E. (2012). Effectiveness of Australia's get healthy information and coaching service®: Translational research with population wide impact. *Preventive Medicine, 55*, 292–298.

Rabius, V., Pike, K. J., Hunter, J., Wiatrek, D., & McAlister, A. L. (2007). Effects of frequency and duration in telephone counselling for smoking cessation. *Tobacco Control, 16*(Suppl. 1), i71–i74.

Rehabilitation of Offenders Act. (1974). *1974 chapter 53*. Retrieved September, 2019, from http://www.legislation.gov.uk/ukpga/1974/53.

Scottish Executive. (2005). *An action plan for improving oral health and modernising NHS dental services in Scotland*. Retrieved March, 2019, from https://www.scottishdental.org/wp-content/uploads/2015/04/Dental-Action-Plan-2005.pdf.

Scottish Government. (2015). *Oral health improvement and dental services in Scottish prisons*. Retrieved January, 2020, from https://www.gov.scot/publications/oral-health-improvement-dental-services-scottish-prisons/.

Scottish Government. (2018a). *Management of Offenders (Scotland) Bill: Rehabilitation of offenders equality impact assessment*. Retrieved September, 2019, from https://www.gov.scot/publications/management-offenders-scotland-bill-equality-impact-assessment-rehabilitation-offenders/.

Scottish Government. (2018b). *Scotland's national performance framework*. Retrieved September, 2019, from https://nationalperformance.gov.scot/.

Scottish Government. (2019). *Mental health*. Retrieved January, 2020, from https://www.gov.scot/policies/mental-health/.

Scottish Prison Service. (2019a). *SPS prison population*. Retrieved November, 2019, from http://www.sps.gov.uk.

Scottish Prison Service. (2019b). *Unlocking potential and transforming lives*. Retrieved December, 2019, from http://www.sps.gov.uk.

Sheiham, A., & Watt, R. G. (2000). The common risk factor approach: A rational basis for promoting oral health. *Community Dentistry and Oral Epidemiology, 28*, 399–406.

Spaulding, A. C., Sumbry, A. R., Brzozowski, A. K., Ramos, K. L., Perez, S. D., Maggio, D. M., Seals, R. M., & Wingood, G. M. (2009). Pairing HIV-positive prisoners with volunteer life coaches to maintain health-promoting behavior upon release: A mixed-methods needs analysis and pilot study. *AIDS Education and Prevention, 21*, 552–569.

Todorov, T. (1999). *The conquest of America: The question of the other*. Norman, OK: University of Oklahoma Press.

Wolever, R. Q., Simmons, L. A., Sforzo, G. A., Dill, D., Kaye, M., Bechard, E. M., Southard, M. E., Kennedy, M., Vosloo, J., & Yang, N. (2013). A systematic review of the literature on health and wellness coaching: Defining a key behavioral intervention in healthcare. *Global Advances in Health and Medicine, 2*, 38–57.

World Health Organization. (2014). *Europe guide on prison and health*. Retrieved January, 2020, http://www.euro.who.int/en/health-topics/health-determinants/prisons-and health/publications/2014/prisons-and-health.pdf.

11

Health, Arts and Justice

Alison Frater

Introduction: Health, Crime and Justice

Starting with a creative narrative inspired by the experiences of people who have spent time in prison, this chapter argues the need for a reality check. The truth is that repeated findings of poor physical and mental health in prisons have prompted calls for changes to policy and practice that are yet to deliver. It is likely that interventions will only be effective if they recognise the complexity of the relationship between health, crime and justice, and can respond to it. Evidence is presented to suggest that the arts may offer the imagination and reflectiveness needed to help shift the inertia, creating a more health-promoting rehabilitative culture. The arts peer into dark places and see the causes of crime and criminalisation. They have transforming effects on individuals and there is sufficient variability of impact to raise the potential for a humanities-based strategy for health improvement across the criminal justice system. The arts can't hold all the answers but may be where change begins.

A. Frater (✉)
Royal Holloway University of London, Egham, UK
e-mail: Alison.frater@rhul.ac.uk

© The Author(s) 2021

M. Maycock et al. (eds.), *Issues and Innovations in Prison Health Research*, Palgrave Studies in Prisons and Penology, https://doi.org/10.1007/978-3-030-46401-1_11

Long-standing inequalities in health are glaringly apparent when reviewing the health of people in prisons; they raise questions about the effectiveness of government policy for health and justice, making the case for considering a more innovative approach. The requirement to deliver equivalence with services in the community may be falling short of the mark. There are repeated findings of high levels of unmet physical and mental health needs, adverse consequences to health from incarceration and inadequate continuity of care at vulnerable points of transition 'through the gate'. Discriminatory effects in the criminal justice system are likely to exacerbate disparities in health and access to healthcare for people from black and minority ethnic communities (Lammy 2017), for people with disabilities, for women and for those with experience of trauma including poverty, neglect and abuse (Liebling and Maruna 2013).

Against this background, evaluations of the impact of arts on health and well-being are discussed, noting alignment with the treatment aspirations of psychotherapeutic programmes shown to be effective among prisoner populations. The findings demonstrate a value for the arts that goes beyond 'spectator' even where this involves 'seeing' differently. Studies of participation in the arts report positive health benefits including improvements in emotional resilience, a reduction in depressive symptoms, better physical health, motivation and readiness to work with others. Beyond this, it seems, the arts are able to go some way to counter the destruction of empathy inherent in a retributive system of justice. The arts provide people with the tools they need to support their own mental health and well-being while incarcerated and, the deeper the arts are embedded in criminal justice, the greater the benefits seem to be.

Summarising the effects raises the possibility of a holistic arts-informed health strategy for prisons. A central policy question will be how to increase equity of access to the arts across the system. Further research is needed to understand how best to optimise the benefits of this overlooked but potentially far-reaching approach.

The Setting[1]

You remember getting to the prison though not much about the rest of the day. Your solicitor said it would be a community sentence. You hadn't even brought a bag. You thought it must be a dream, a bad one. The sweatbox stopped at the entrance, the driver wound the window down. He shouted to the officer on the gate who pressed a buzzer but the van didn't go forward. You were desperate to pee but they were talking about something, football you think. You're pressing your nails into your hand, to sooth the pain. Then, there's a whine, a metal on metal scream. The gate grinds open and the van moves forward. Hitting the trap at the end the gate's forced back clanging as it goes. Gathering pace it bangs closed on your freedom.

Stepping out you keep thinking this can't be happening. You're in a cage, high fences, barbed wire. There's a house, some huts, people moving about, a dog. They ask questions about drugs and hurting yourself. They tell you stuff you can't remember. It's late so they'll sort everything out in the morning, they say. The officer takes you to a building that's warm but dark and old and damp. You're in a long corridor willing yourself somewhere, anywhere else. There are locked doors and a strip light stuffed with dead flies. One of the bulbs is flashing. The whole place is the sort of grimy that's so far gone even if anyone cared they couldn't clean it up. The officer snaps into his key pouch, rattles the keys, thrusts one into the lock, turns the bolt. The smell of piss hits you. The walls in the room are bare, there's a window, dirty, barred. The little bit of moon that's coming through lights up white marks on the wall, rusty bed frame.

There's a toilet, three beds, two people lying down startled by the noise. The top bunk's free, thin mattress, green sheet, grey blanket. You don't want to be in there and they don't want you. There are no introductions, nobody cares what you all think. One of the people startles, bangs the wall, swears, the other is moaning, quiet at first but then loud like a child sobbing. All three of you lie within bad breath touching, space invading closeness. There are people shouting, alarms, sirens; no-one sleeps.

---

[1] From focus groups including with User Voice and other people with lived experience of prison, compiled to inform the development of a health strategy for women in prison. (Frater et al. 2016).

During the days, the whole prison operates to the rhythm of the regime. In the morning busy people arrive, teachers, trainers, employers, therapists, doctors, nurses, dentists, lawyers, inspectors, monitors, families, friends. They slip through the walls into your locked-up world. If your name's on a list their arrival means you can get out of hated confinement for a few hours. You go to classes or work as a cleaner or in the kitchens. These are things you're required to do. Sometimes they forget about you or there's a mix up and you don't get unlocked. Nothing's ever certain, except the rules.

They're mostly about what you can't do, what you can't wear and what behavior is not acceptable. Rules for things you want to do, like eat your own food or book a family visit are about privileges and how to apply. At first you try to reason with them, then you think you'll do what they ask, maybe get something out of it but the boredom is too much to bear. You get angry but that's not allowed.

You tone it down, you stop feeling, you're dead inside, that's allowed. In fact, everything in here seems designed to make you feel worthless like you don't belong in the world. If you did you wouldn't have done it would you?

Sometimes there aren't enough people with keys to let you out because they're sick or they've left because they just couldn't take it anymore. There's always less staff at weekends so the lock ups are long. When it gets really bad unlock can be down to an hour a day. You have to move fast, get a shower, make a phone call, pick up your medication. There's a queue for the phone, what to do? You sit still, staring.

Officers calling 'movement' set the clock, split the day.

> *'Movement,' after morning unlock calls out freeflow to work or classes. 'Movement,' signals the end of morning session and time for lunch. 'Movement,' announces the end of lunchtime lock up and the start of afternoon activities.*
>
> *'Movement,' comes at the end of the working day before dinner and for free association on the wings before night-time lockup.*

The days go round and round, dull and dulling, hypnotizing. You forget who you are.

At night the distraction people are gone, including the doctor and the nurses and many of the people with the keys. Sometimes it's ok. You can stay in your room or talk to someone. Sometimes the threat people are around. They're looking for things to bargain, or just get, or they want to wind you up.

You tell them to leave you alone, you're not bothering them, but they don't listen. They set their own rules and you have to stand up for yourself or you really will end up with nothing.

The night-time lock up is when the trouble starts. It's in your head and in your heart.

"What if there's a fire, what if I need a doctor?" You wake and then you're up pacing, shouting and screaming.

"Help me."

And then you're on report or they've opened an ACCT[2] *on you.*

Arts and Justice

Looking at this through the lens of the arts you're in a dislocated world hidden from view. The setting is bland, the action is inaction, the struggle is internal. There are people locked up in their shame, officers lacking latitude to make the system better, families feeling powerless and set apart. You see conditions likely to compromise the health of residents and the workforce; everyone is either overstretched or undervalued. Will this place really help people to live better in the future?

Out of sight but not out of mind are victims of crime who want what happened to them never to be repeated. Can they rely on the system to deliver when it fails to see the humanity in people?

The Ambiguity of Health in Prisons

Looking at it through a lens with a health perspective is shocking. People in the criminal justice system represent only a small proportion of the total population, less than 1%, yet they experience significantly poorer physical and mental health. Involvement in the criminal justice system is associated with a higher relative risk of death from all causes, lowering

[2] The Assessment, Care in Custody and Teamwork (ACCT) is for prisoners identified as being at risk of suicide or self-harm. It is a planning and monitoring process requiring members of staff to report concerns and to comment on the person's progress towards recommended actions.

average life expectancy by as much as 20 years and there is evidence of increased risk of psychiatric morbidity including suicide and self-harm. More insidious in disentangling the impact of prisons on health is the pernicious bias and discrimination evident in the criminal justice system. Factors such as social class and ethnicity continue to be associated with an increased likelihood of arrest, harsher sentences and a greater chance of incarceration (Bromley Briefings 2013).

And, for people trying to cope with health issues in prisons, systemic problems are made worse by the lack of personal agency. Access to information on management of health conditions through the Internet is not allowed and there are few opportunities for self-care; stress relieving walks, access to fresh air, sunlight, fresh food and exercise are all limited (Centre for Mental Health 2011).

Yet, prisons are sometimes described as a public health opportunity. By providing health services, they offer health improvement to people who often feel unable to access care and prevention in the community. There are reports of people with mental health problems finding 'refuge' in the prison system having felt excluded from the care they needed in the community. For drug rehabilitation, prison health and care services can provide effective treatments especially where resources in the community have declined or reduced in scope (Condon et al. 2007).

But, in both cases, there is variability in the quality of care including a lack of measures to enable continuity on discharge from prison (Forrester et al. 2013). Services in prisons and the community are funded by different authorities and there are frequent reports of therapeutic pathways started in prisons being undermined by inconsistent or lack of support on the 'out' (Fazel and Baillargeon 2011).

Many studies have confirmed findings of poor health in the prison population but a national survey comparing mental health in prisons with the general population undertaken for ONS in 1998 (Singleton 1998) remains the standard for assessing the impact of healthcare policy and practice over time. The survey indicated that only 10% of those sampled had no evidence of any of the five main diagnoses under review and many people had two or more. The prevalence in prisons of personality disorders, psychosis, neurotic disorders and drug and alcohol dependence was significantly higher than in the general population. In some cases, this was by a factor of 10 times or more for sentenced people and even higher for those on remand.

These findings influenced an important policy move—the publication of the Department of Health guidance requiring that healthcare in prisons should have 'equivalence' with those in the general population (Bowden 2000). This led to the commissioning of health services in prisons moving from the Home Office to the NHS. It kicked off commissioning by the NHS with the establishment of nurse-led primary care practices in the prison estate and mental health in-reach teams provided by specialist mental healthcare trusts. Drug rehabilitation services became more widely available in most local prisons though they're still not fully integrated with NHS-funded health services. Despite these changes, there is little or no evidence that health has improved in the prison population (Till et al. 2014).

In fact, more recent research shows the continued scandal of significantly high levels of psychiatric morbidity (Rivlin et al. 2013). A recent systematic review of health in prisons found one in seven people in prisons has a serious but treatable mental illness. The pooled prevalence of psychosis was around 4%, major depression 10–12%, and personality disorder 40–70% (Fazel et al. 2016). The relative risk of death by suicide in male prisoners is now estimated to be about 3–6 times that of the general population. It's even higher in female prisoners, typically more than six times that of community rates (Fazel 2018).

Research demonstrates even further complexity with variations in the intensity of experience of mental illness by age and sentencing status (Fazel 2018). There are also widespread problems with depression and anxiety. High rates of mental illness now apply to an incarcerated population that has grown in size from just under 60,000 in the late 1990s to over 85,000 in 2018. Incarcerated people with mental illnesses continue to be housed in Victorian prisons lacking facilities for looking after them. Sentence length has increased over time and there are higher rates of recidivism (MOJ 2016).

The highest rates of mental illness occur in remand prisoners, detained but not yet sentenced. Among the rising numbers of older prisoners, O'Hara et al. (2016) found multiple health and social care needs, and more than half showed symptoms of clinical depression. Davoren et al.

(2015) found high rates of affective disorder and alcohol misuse among older remand prisoners with rates of psychotic illness and deliberate self-harm compared to younger remand prisoners.

Self-harm is a substantial cause of morbidity for people in prisons but is less studied than suicide. An epidemiological study (Hawton et al. 2014) based on 2004–2010 data in English and Welsh prisons found that in the previous 12 months in custody, 5–6% of men and 20–24% of women self-harmed. Risk factors include younger age and shorter sentences; self-harm seems to cluster in particular prison settings. Drug and alcohol problems are also common. A review of reception studies noted that 17–30% of men and 10–24% of women were diagnosed with alcohol misuse or dependence, 10–48% of men and 30–60% of women had a previous history of drug misuse or were dependent on illegal drugs (Fazel et al. 2017). Post-traumatic stress disorder is also thought to affect up to a fifth of prisoners and prisoners of both sexes report histories of severe trauma and abuse; women have higher rates of most psychiatric disorders than men (Baranyi et al. 2018).

There are significant differences in the physical health of people in the prison population with smoking, alcohol and illicit drug use contributing to a high relative risk of premature mortality from respiratory illness, cancers and vascular disease (Plugge et al. 2009). There is a higher relative risk of epilepsy, asthma and other respiratory illness, skin infections, gastrointestinal disease and dental problems, conditions also associated with poverty and homelessness (Harris et al. 2007), and the prison setting presents challenges for infectious disease.

The prevalence of HIV, TB and blood-borne viruses such as hepatitis C and hepatitis B is higher in the prison population than in the general population mainly because of the criminalisation of drug use leading to the detention of people who use drugs. Authors suggest that the most effective way of reducing the spread of infection is to reduce the incarceration of people who inject drugs (Dolan et al. 2016).

Managing public concern about the alarming incongruity of delivering health and healthcare to increasing numbers of vulnerable people with complex needs in a dehumanizing environment has created a plethora of supervisory overlords, scrutineers and special monitors who all have a stake in the governance of an increasingly perplexing prison system. Press reports, family interventions and lobbying from prison advocacy groups continue to inform reports from government select committees, Chief Inspectors of Prisons, and the Prison and Probation Ombudsman (PPO); they feature the need for urgent reform (Frater and Bartlett 2017).

Investigations into deaths in custody published by the PPO frequently list an individual's unaddressed poor health, its exacerbation by prison conditions, a lack of access to specialist health services and undue waits for emergency services as contributory factors in fatal incidents (PPO Annual Report 2016). Yet, to date, this has not encouraged a formal independent evaluation of the success of the policy on equivalence. Sustained implementation of initiatives such as health-promoting prisons, trauma informed training and quality initiatives promoted by the Royal College of Psychiatrists and others is difficult because of staff shortages. Arguably, an enhanced and more holistic approach to health is needed across the prison estate (Coid et al. 2002).

Arts, Health and Justice

The management challenge for governors to move away from a model of practice that merely increases confinement in the complex and often under-resourced prison system is significant. Yet by working with arts and sports, a number of governors are identifying interventions that offer a more lasting impact across a range of needs. Starting with personal experience of what works, they've enabled independent researchers to build a body of evaluation that can inform thinking about how best to go forward with policy and practice. While these are a group of governors with interest in the arts, their findings are consistent; they report similar effects for different people in a range of settings.

> "Employment and education create a daily rhythm of working" says Alli Black a governor with a lead role in Cumbria and Lancashire prisons, "though choices are limited and a workshop on safe plastering practice or gaining an entry level qualification in catering or cleaning is never going to have the kind of meaning for people's lives that will help them to come to

terms with what they've done and change ways of thinking and feeling. Arts programmes challenge at a personal level that's what makes the difference."

Talking about award-winning work from the art programme in HMP Send, a high-security women's training prison, the governor, Carlene Dixon notes the impact on mental well-being.

"It's an emotional reaction," she says, "but then they have to try to work out where these feelings have come from. It helps at least to try to resolve past experiences and relationships that are affecting them, or to work on particularly problematic thoughts and behaviours. For some people, well, it can change their lives."

There are also organisational impacts, effects that can counter the damaging and criminogenic culture of incarceration.

"People who are willing to explore deep seated emotions through the arts and express their vulnerabilities are more likely to resist risks associated with reoffending," says governor Ralph Lubowski, describing the wide reaching impact of the arts programmes he runs in HMP Stafford. Talking about his approach to developing a rehabilitative culture in this adult male category C prison he aligns personal observations of the intrinsic nature of creativity, the growing evidence base for individual change—and the need for a practical approach that can work in a prison.

"Arts," he says, appear to engage everyone according to the needs they have. It's low impact on prison resources but high value in delivering change. The arts are a means for people to consider their role in the world within the context of the story of their own lives. They're interpretive, they uncover underlying issues such as pain or fear or hurt that can explain personal histories and offending behavior. They inspire personal growth, insight and hope for possible new directions away from crime."

While the latitude for innovation is narrow in a hierarchical system, prison governors are increasingly able to draw on research to identify arts programmes that can motivate people in their care to develop goals associated with a better future for themselves and their families.

Starting with an emerging understanding of the positive relationship between arts and health, recent moves by an All Party Parliamentary Group on Arts and Health and the Royal Society of Public Health (Stickley et al. 2017) have secured an evidence-based Culture, Health and Well-being Alliance for the UK, now supported by Arts Council England (ACE). These efforts have been boosted by a report on the social impact of the arts from the WHO that sets out an agenda for evidence-based policy and practice (Fancourt and Finn 2019). There are also insights from arts therapy and specific evaluations of the arts in criminal justice settings. Findings demonstrate benefits from a range of interventions across all art forms, with different groups by age and ethnicity and especially for people with complex needs that have a significant mental health component.

Unsurprisingly, researchers endeavour to build the evidence base in terms of the health sector's standards producing epidemiological studies, economic analysis and systematic reviews (Daykin et al. 2008). In the clinical realm social prescribing for activities such as community singing leads to improvements in a range of conditions including mental health and breathing difficulties (Clift 2012), (Stickley and Hui 2012). A number of studies demonstrate benefits of participation in drawing and painting, music and dance for people affected by dementia or Alzheimer's, and their carers (Daykin et al. 2008), (Merom et al. 2016).

Beyond individual clinical outcomes, research is highlighting the potential value of the arts in identifying the nature of health in people's lives, a role in tackling the determinants of health. Studies show the value of arts in prevention and health promotion with outcomes demonstrating increased self-confidence and self-esteem. Examples include music (Parker et al. 2018), dance and visual arts (Stickley et al. 2015). Matarasso (1997) works with a definition of health and participatory arts that encompasses a range of individual benefits but also considers political dimensions for individuals within a community context. He examines the relationship between arts and health in enhancing social cohesion, fostering inclusion and cultural citizenship (Mccabe et al. 2007).

Evaluations of the impact of participation in the arts on people in prisons, and other criminal justice settings, find positive benefits for social connectedness and social capital (Ansdell and DeNora 2012) and employability (White and Angus 2003). Research on the effectiveness of arts-based programmes in prisons suggests they may improve individual psychological factors including giving individuals a sense of hope, the ability to build more equal relationships. Structured performance requires people to work as part of a team with a common goal where all members have to trust one another, sometimes for the first time (Anderson et al. 2011). The arts enable participants to develop new intrapersonal skills such as the need to negotiate or be altruistic. Through the arts, participants see themselves differently and begin to formulate the agency and self-direction needed to facilitate personal change (Cursley and Maruna 2015). There are reports of positive regulation of emotions and increased well-being (Caulfield and Wilkinson 2014), reductions in propensity for anger and aggression as an adjunct to anger management programmes (Blacker et al. 2008) and an increase in confidence and social skills (Caulfield et al. 2019). In a project with gang affiliated young men in HMP/YOI ISIS, researchers found that arts provided a safe environment to 'open up' and explore emotions; a way of understanding the impact of crimes (Meek et al. 2015); participants built empathy and victim awareness which, when combined with mentoring, enabled the development of skills in conflict resolution.

In an evaluation of a short-term music-based prison project, Cox and Gelsthorpe (2008) explored the impact of music on 71 male prisoners' mental health, behaviour and motivation to attend education courses. Data was gathered through questionnaires, interviews and focus groups from both participants and prison staff. Participants reported an increase in confidence and feelings of hope for the future. They said that participation in the arts made them feel differently both about themselves and others. On release from prison they were more able to make new connections and socially engaged relationships. The authors contend that there may be effects on the foundation of selfhood and human capital such as the capacity to co-operate, relate to others, negotiate and share.

Encouraging involvement in drama or in poetry and arts workshops can help people in prisons to understand their histories in a new light and to take control of their lives. Following a theatre-based project with women in prison, participants reported an enhanced sense of self and a newfound autonomy through freedom to express their emotions (McKean

2006). Performance enables validation by audiences often comprising peers, prison officers, family and sometimes members of the public. Anderson et al. (2011) argues that this kind of external validation is central to embedding the possibility of change in participants.

Drawing on an understanding of arts psychotherapies in forensic settings, supports the notion that there are intrapersonal and interpersonal effects that may have broad applicability across a range of risks to psychological health (Van Lith 2016). There is evidence that the arts: drama, music, visual arts, poetry, literature can map a different terrain to traditional concepts in health transcending a biomedical model and reaching into factors determining health.

The arts operate at a personal level and are uniquely able to meet diverse needs in different individuals. Evidence suggests that they enable recovery, creating conditions that help an unwell, damaged or traumatised self to reconnect with a former core (well) self. Working with people who have committed violent crimes or paraphilias, Collier and Stewart (2019) describe the value of arts as enabling personal growth because they reach into embedded experience and emotions related to the causes of crime. A number of authors note an increase in protective factors with significance for desistance from crime (Maruna et al. 2004) reducing antisocial behavior and risks of re-offending (Newman 2002).

Measuring Health in the Carceral System: An Interdisciplinary Agenda

Security issues, costs, chaos and loss to follow-up are just a few of the many practical difficulties involved in measuring health in prisons but there is also a more profound issue. The power imbalance in the carceral system may affect the way participants in a study respond to questions about their experience.

Addressing the question of complexity, many authors call for a more interdisciplinary approach to research that can draw insights from criminologists, sociologists, epidemiologists, arts and humanities specialists, prison and health service researchers, among others, with expertise in the criminal justice system. The recent publication of a generic outcome tool (Maguire et al. 2019) will boost opportunities for joint working by enabling data sharing, pooled estimates of effectiveness and comparative outcomes assessment.

At a population level, integrated joint approaches are needed to understand the acceptability and effectiveness of the arts by age, gender and ethnicity in different kinds of prisons and other criminal justice settings, including for prevention. There is a need to know how much we can rely on the childhood origins of behaviour to predict health outcomes and how these can be mediated; how psychotherapeutic effects can inform thinking about readiness for change over the life course; what the interaction is between criminogenic factors and motivation derived through initiatives such as sports and arts and how these influences play out against background factors affecting health and life chances.

Importantly, there are policy and practice questions: how might benefits be optimised, can individual and organisational effects foster the culture change needed to secure a step change in rehabilitation—and—how might a public health and humanities strategy impact at a population level, given the positive impact of the arts across a range of needs.

Successful collaboration will also benefit from a joint theoretical framework and the work of arts practitioners may offer consideration of a more inclusive rights-based approach. A possible theoretical basis for interdisciplinary working on these important questions arises from an understanding of the participatory nature of arts practice in prisons. Recognising the problems inherent in a rules-based prison environment, many arts practitioners draw on a theoretical foundation that treats everyone as peers or equals (Boal 2006). The aim is to release people from the restrictions of political or other constraints and generate a liberated but critically conscious thought. A central tenet of the approach is to enable people to participate from a culturally relevant point to them and not an imposed or anticipated baseline.

The intervention, the arts piece, creates a democratic perspective, a space between all the participants: residents in the prison, workers from the arts organisation and researchers. They work as equals posing and solving problems together. The result is a creative piece of high quality because of the authenticity of its broader more inclusive narrative. From the perspective of criminological or sociological evaluation, the method offers unique insights for qualitative analysis that can contextualise more formal, independent epidemiological or empirical studies. The participants tell stories, about their own lives. They reveal existential qualities such as emotional pain, despair, hope, grief, which may accompany or even constitute their state of health, and their ways of coping. It may explain behaviour and it may uncover a therapeutic way forward.

Artists Working in the Criminal Justice System

At the core of arts practice in the criminal justice system is a group of specialist arts practitioners working in arts organisations or as individual artists. Their specialism is characterised by facilitating arts exclusively or mostly with people affected by the criminal justice system including victims of crime, people convicted of or at risk of committing crimes, their friends and families, and staff or volunteers working in prisons or other criminal justice settings.

They take a responsive, interactive, participatory approach to arts encouraging improvisation and co-production of work. They value, understand, and enjoy working with people from a broad range of backgrounds, some with complex physical and mental health needs, all facing the psychologically demanding nature of the criminal justice system. These artists may not always focus on the crimes people have committed. Instead, they work with them to craft new ways of being; they inspire change.

The work of specialist arts practitioners, now well documented in impact assessments and evaluations held in the evidence library of the National Criminal Justice Arts Alliance (https://www.artsincriminaljustice.org.uk/evidence-library/) is found in all parts of the criminal justice system: for people at risk of crime in youth justice; in diversion schemes from the police or courts; for those remanded or sentenced in prisons and secure hospitals; for people in long-stay institutions or on short sentences, community orders, and on license following discharge from prison.

The National Criminal Justice Arts Alliance estimates that of 900 members in their network, about a third work exclusively or mostly in the criminal justice system. Many provide a bridge with arts organisations in community settings by fostering supportive networks, mentoring schemes, work placements, or apprenticeships for people on release from prison. The mode of working is usually through workshops, programmes, or short courses; with theatre and music the most frequent art form followed by creative writing. Visual arts, painting, and drawing is likely to be the predominant art form in prisons; it can be practised "in cell" and is the most usual art form offered in prison education.

The Policy Context

Investment in the arts in criminal justice settings has been largely from the insights and vision of philanthropic organisations and charitable trusts but now has increasing support from Arts Council England. The Ministry of Justice (MOJ) has been a consistent commissioner of specialist arts providers though with relatively small budgets and low-profile engagement indicative of some ambivalence, probably not so much with the value of the work, but with concern about public acceptability.

With evidence of a shift in public opinion and the added impetus of many new opportunities for employment in the UK's fast-growing creative industries, a bolder, more strategic vision is emerging. The MOJ now hosts an arts forum with the broad remit to deliver cross-government interests in the benefits of the arts including as a means to deliver rehabilitation through employment and education; the Department of Culture, Media and Sport (DCMS) has published a Culture White Paper (DCMS 2016) which explores the social impact of the arts, explicitly recognising the benefits in criminal justice settings, and a government response to a Select Committee Report (House of commons 2019) exploring the value of sports in prisons also noted the benefits of arts initiatives.

A review of education in prisons (Coates 2016), commissioned by Secretary of State for Justice, highlighted the value of arts as a bridge into learning for people who have been failed by more formal education.

"Many prisoners have had unsatisfactory experiences of the classroom," she said, "they will need … quality creative arts provision …"

As a result, access to the arts is supported by inclusion in the Prison Service Inspectorate's Expectations (HMIP 2017) by which they judge standards of care and the Justice Data Lab (MOJ 2016) has started to publish evaluations of arts programmes in prisons including their impact on rates of reoffending. Arts council England is now adding to its estimated £5 m investment portfolio, for arts organisations working in the criminal justice system, by providing funding for the NCJAA as a sector support organisation. This has a dual effect: recognising the need for a policy-influencing, strategic body capable of driving forward a vision for growth in the sector—and acknowledging the high quality of the work delivered.

Conclusions

A complex picture of health in prisons is presented that is consistent in demonstrating high levels of unmet needs yet little progress in finding solutions. Variation in health is a universal human pattern yet when socially produced and mediated should be amenable to change. When these kinds of disparities in health remain unaddressed, variations turn into unjust social inequalities. Arguably, this is especially true in the controlled environment of prisons where there is a duty of care.

Against this background of poor health, some mediated by the adverse consequences of incarceration, the discourse finds that the arts offer unique insights and, that the impact endures within the complexity of the carceral system. Arts shed light on the causes and consequences of incarceration and have a potentially powerful effect on individuals, improving health and well-being and transforming life chances. At a population level, wide-ranging benefit offers the potential for informing an inclusive new paradigm for rehabilitation.

An innovative research focus is needed that can generate new theoretical approaches and integrate insights from the range of disciplines embracing health, arts and criminal justice. At a very basic level, research is needed to understand how best to optimise the effects for individuals in order to guide policy and practice. An arts-informed public health and humanities model of change might be reliably expected to have a broad reach, given the impact across a range of health needs. Creative pathways for improving health and life chances may even drive reform of the prison concept.

References

Anderson, K., Colvin, S., McNeill, F., Nellis, M., Overy, K., Sparks, R., et al. (2011). Inspiring change: final project report of the evaluation team: University of Glasgow, University of Strathclyde, University of Edinburgh.

Annual Report 2016. (2016). *American Journal of Pharmaceutical Education, 80*(8), S9. https://doi.org/10.1007/s00234-016-1748-0.

Ansdell, G., & DeNora, T. (2012). Musical flourishing: Community music therapy, controversy, and the cultivation of wellbeing. In *Music, Health, and Wellbeing*. https://doi.org/10.1093/acprof:oso/9780199586974.003.0008.

Baranyi, G., Cassidy, M., Fazel, S., Priebe, S., & Mundt, A. P. (2018). Prevalence of posttraumatic stress disorder in prisoners. *Epidemiologic Reviews*. https://doi.org/10.1093/epirev/mxx015.

Blacker, J., Watson, A., & Beech, A. R. (2008). A combined drama-based and CBT approach to working with self-reported anger aggression. *Criminal Behaviour and Mental Health*. https://doi.org/10.1002/cbm.686.

Boal, A. (2006). The aesthetics of the oppressed. *The Aesthetics of the Oppressed*. https://doi.org/10.4324/9780203969830.

Bowden, P. (2000). The future organisation of prison health care. *The Journal of Forensic Psychiatry*. https://doi.org/10.1080/09585180050142697.

Bromley Briefings. (2013). Prison: The facts. *Prison Reform Trust*.

Caulfield, L., & Wilkinson, D. (2014). Good Vibrations: health and wellbeing of older offenders. *Full Report accessed from the National Criminal Justice Arts Alliance evidence library*. Bath Spa University; University of Worcester. http://www.artsevidence.org.uk/media/uploads/goodvibrations&olderprisonersreportfinal.pdf

Caulfield, L., Jolly, A., & Massie, R. (2019). An evaluation of The Irene Taylor Trust's Sounding Out programme (2016–2018). Institute for Community Research & Development, University of Wolverhampton, March 2019. Full Report accessed from the National Criminal Justice Arts Alliance evidence library. http://www.artsevidence.org.uk/media/uploads/sounding-out-evaluation-2016-2018.pdf

Centre for Mental Health. (2011). Mental health care and the criminal justice system. *Centre for Mental Health—Briefing, 39*. https://doi.org/10.1016/0022-4405(80)90019-9.

Clift, S. (2012). Creative arts as a public health resource: Moving from practice-based research to evidence-based practice. *Perspectives in Public Health*. https://doi.org/10.1177/1757913912442269.

Coates, D. S. (2016, May). Unlocking potential—A review of education in prison. *Ministry of Justice*, 1–13.

Coid, J., Bebbington, P., Jenkins, R., Brugha, T., Lewis, G., Farrell, M., & Singleton, N. (2002). The national survey of psychiatric morbidity among prisoners and the future of prison healthcare. *Medicine, Science and the Law*. https://doi.org/10.1177/002580240204200309.

Collier, J., & Stewart, P. W. (2019). Afterword. *The End of the Sentence*. https://doi.org/10.4324/9780429020728-13.

Condon, L., Hek, G., Harris, F., Powell, J., Kemple, T., & Price, S. (2007). Users' views of prison health services: A qualitative study. *Journal of Advanced Nursing*. https://doi.org/10.1111/j.1365-2648.2007.04221.x.

Cox, A., & Gelsthorpe, L. (2008). Beats and bars music in prisons: an evaluation. Institute of Criminology, University of Cambridge. Full Report accessed from the National Criminal Justice Arts Alliance evidence library. http://www.artsevidence.org.uk/media/uploads/evaluation-downloads/mip-beats-&-bars-2008.pdf

Cursley, J., & Maruna, S. (2015). A Narrative-Based Evaluation of 'Changing Tunes' Music-Based Prisoner Reintegration Interventions. *Full Report accessed from the National Criminal Justice Arts Alliance evidence library*. https://www.artsevidence.org.uk/.../narrative-based-evaluation-changing-tunes-music-ba/.

Davoren, M., Fitzpatrick, M., Caddow, F., Caddow, M., O'Neill, C., O'Neill, H., & Kennedy, H. G. (2015). Older men and older women remand prisoners: Mental illness, physical illness, offending patterns and needs. *International Psychogeriatrics*. https://doi.org/10.1017/S1041610214002348.

Daykin, N., Byrne, E., Soteriou, T., & O'Connor, S. (2008). The impact of art, design and environment in mental healthcare: A systematic review of the literature. *Journal of The Royal Society for the Promotion of Health*. https://doi.org/10.1177/1466424007087806.

DCMS. (2016). *The culture white.*

Dolan, K., Wirtz, A. L., Moazen, B., Ndeffo-mbah, M., Galvani, A., Kinner, S. A., Courtney, R., McKee, M., Amon, J. J., Maher, L., Hellard, M., Beyrer, C., & Altice, F. L. (2016). Global burden of HIV, viral hepatitis, and tuberculosis in prisoners and detainees. *The Lancet, 388*(10049). https://doi.org/10.1016/S0140-6736(16)30466-4.

Fancourt, D., & Finn, S. (2019). *WHO Health Evidence Synthesis Report-Cultural Contexts of Health: The role of the arts in improving health and well-being in the WHO European Region.*

Fazel, S. (2018). Editorial: Synthesizing the evidence on prisoner health—Taking stock and moving forward. *American Journal of Epidemiology, 187*(6), 1137–1139. Oxford University Press. https://doi.org/10.1093/aje/kwx375.

Fazel, S., & Baillargeon, J. (2011). The health of prisoners. *The Lancet, 377*(9769), 956–965. https://doi.org/10.1016/S0140-6736(10)61053-7.

Fazel, S., Hayes, A. J., Bartellas, K., Clerici, M., & Trestman, R. (2016). Mental health of prisoners: Prevalence, adverse outcomes, and interventions. *The Lancet Psychiatry, 3*(9), 871–881. Elsevier Ltd. https://doi.org/10.1016/S2215-0366(16)30142-0.

Fazel, S., Yoon, I. A., & Hayes, A. J. (2017). Substance use disorders in prisoners: An updated systematic review and meta-regression analysis in recently incarcerated men and women. *Addiction*. https://doi.org/10.1111/add.13877.

Forrester, A., Exworthy, T., Olumoroti, O., Sessay, M., Parrott, J., Spencer, S. J., & Whyte, S. (2013). Variations in prison mental health services in England and Wales. *International Journal of Law and Psychiatry.* https://doi.org/10.1016/j.ijlp.2013.04.007.

Frater, A., & Bartlett, A. (2017). Human cost of delivering healthcare in unhealthy prisons. *BMJ (Online)*. https://doi.org/10.1136/bmj.j1374.

Frater, A., Bartlett, A., & Tang, H. (2016). *Women in the criminal justice system in London: A health strategy.*

Harris, F., Hek, G., & Condon, L. (2007). Health needs of prisoners in England and Wales: The implications for prison healthcare of gender, age and ethnicity. *Health and Social Care in the Community*. https://doi.org/10.1111/j.1365-2524.2006.00662.x.

Hawton, K., Linsell, L., Adeniji, T., Sariaslan, A., & Fazel, S. (2014). Self-harm in prisons in England and Wales: An epidemiological study of prevalence, risk factors, clustering, and subsequent suicide. *The Lancet*. https://doi.org/10.1016/S0140-6736(13)62118-2.

HM Inspectorate of Prisons. (2017). Expectations: Criteria for assessing the treatment of and conditions for men in prisons. (Para 71, p. 40) Version 5, 2017.

House of Common. (2019). Department of Culture, Media and Sport Committee. Changing Lives: the social impact of participation in culture and sport. Eleventh Report of Session (2017–19). House of Commons, HC 734, May 2019.

Lammy, D. (2017). *The Lammy review: final report An independent review into the treatment of, and outcomes for Black, Asian and Minority Ethnic individuals in the criminal justice system*. Retrieved from https://www.gov.uk/government/publications/lammy-review-final-report.

Liebling, A., & Maruna, S. (2013). The effects of imprisonment. *The Effects of Imprisonment*. https://doi.org/10.4324/9781843926030.

Maguire, M., Disley, E., Liddle, M., Meek, R., & Burrows, N. (2019). *Developing a toolkit to measure intermediate outcomes to reduce reoffending from arts and mentoring interventions*. Retrieved from https://doi.org/ISBN978-1-84099-820-7.

Maruna, S., Lebel, T. P., Mitchell, N., & Naples, M. (2004). Pygmalion in the reintegration process: Desistance from crime through the looking glass. *Psychology, Crime and Law*. https://doi.org/10.1080/10683160410001662762.

Matarasso, F. (1997). Use or Ornament? The social impact of participation in the arts. *Comedia*. https://doi.org/10.1258/ce.2009.009009.

Mccabe, K., Summerton, R., & Parr, H. (2007). Mental health via cultural citizenship. *Journal of Public Mental Health*. https://doi.org/10.1108/17465729200700026.

McKean, A. (2006). Playing for time in 'The Dolls' House'. Issues of community and collaboration in the devising of theatre in a women's prison. *Research in Drama Education: The Journal of Applied Theatre and Performance*. https://doi.org/10.1080/13569780600900685.

Meek, R., Elisabeth, D., & Melissa, H. (2015). *Evaluation of the belong London PLAN A programme at HMP YOI/ISIS*. Retrieved from https://pure.royalholloway.ac.uk/portal/files/25727782/Belong_evaluation_Meek_et_al.pdf.

Merom, D., Grunseit, A., Eramudugolla, R., Jefferis, B., Mcneill, J., & Anstey, K. J. (2016). Cognitive benefits of social dancing and walking in old age: The dancing mind randomized controlled trial. *Frontiers in Aging Neuroscience*. https://doi.org/10.3389/fnagi.2016.00026.

MOJ. (2016). Justice Data Lab. Publication Summary (pp. 1–11), Ministry of Justice January 2016.

Newman, T. (2002). Promoting resilience: A review of effective strategies for child care services. Exeter: Centre for Evidence-Based Social Services, 2002.

O'Hara, K., Forsyth, K., Webb, R., Senior, J., Hayes, A. J., Challis, D., Fazel, S., & Shaw, J. (2016). Links between depressive symptoms and unmet health

and social care needs among older prisoners. *Age and Ageing, 45*(1), 158–163. https://doi.org/10.1093/ageing/afv171.
Parker, A., Marturano, N., O'Connor, G., & Meek, R. (2018). Marginalised youth, criminal justice and performing arts: Young people's experiences of music-making. *Journal of Youth Studies*. https://doi.org/10.1080/13676261.2018.1445205.
Plugge, E. H., Foster, C. E., Yudkin, P. L., & Douglas, N. (2009). Cardiovascular disease risk factors and women prisoners in the UK: The impact of imprisonment. *Health Promotion International*. https://doi.org/10.1093/heapro/dap034.
Rivlin, A., Hawton, K., Marzano, L., & Fazel, S. (2013). Psychosocial characteristics and social networks of suicidal prisoners: Towards a model of suicidal behaviour in detention. *PLoS ONE*. https://doi.org/10.1371/journal.pone.0068944.
Singleton, N., Meltzer, H., Gatward, R., Coid, J., & Deasy, D. (1998). *Psychiatric morbidity among prisoners in England and Wales*. London: The Stationery Office.
Stickley, T., & Hui, A. (2012). Social prescribing through arts on prescription in a UK city: Participants' perspectives (Part 1). *Public Health*. https://doi.org/10.1016/j.puhe.2012.04.002.
Stickley, Theodore, Paul, K., Crosbie, B., Watson, M., & Souter, G. (2015). Dancing for life: An evaluation of a UK rural dance programme. *International Journal of Health Promotion and Education*. https://doi.org/10.1080/14635240.2014.942438.
Stickley, Theo, Parr, H., Atkinson, S., Daykin, N., Clift, S., De Nora, T., Hacking, S., Camic, P. M., Joss, T., White, M., & Hogan, S. J. (2017). Arts, health & wellbeing: Reflections on a national seminar series and building a UK research network. *Arts and Health*. https://doi.org/10.1080/17533015.2016.1166142.
Till, A., Forrester, A., & Exworthy, T. (2014). The development of equivalence as a mechanism to improve prison healthcare. *Journal of the Royal Society of Medicine*. https://doi.org/10.1177/0141076814523949.
Van Lith, T. (2016). Art therapy in mental health: A systematic review of approaches and practices. *Arts in Psychotherapy*. https://doi.org/10.1016/j.aip.2015.09.003.
White, M., & Angus, J. (2003). Literature Review of Arts and Adult Mental Health Canadian Alliance for Healthy Hearts and Minds (CAHHM).

12

Pregnancy in Prison

Laura Abbot

Introduction

This chapter provides some background to women's imprisonment, particularly pregnant women in the UK and embeds anonymised quotes from research participants to highlight their experiences. The rights and entitlements of pregnant women are described and the recent qualitative research exploring the experiences of pregnant women in prison is introduced. To consider what makes the pregnant woman's experience of prison unique from other experiences of incarceration or, indeed, of other pregnancy experiences, has led to the formation of an important and original contribution to knowledge which spans several academic and health disciplines. My position as a Registered Midwife occupies an exceptional stance, with my professional expertise merging with sociology and prison research. My findings demonstrate: the complexity

L. Abbot (✉)
University of Hertfordshire, Hatfield, UK
e-mail: l.abbott@herts.ac.uk

© The Author(s) 2021

M. Maycock et al. (eds.), *Issues and Innovations in Prison Health Research*, Palgrave Studies in Prisons and Penology, https://doi.org/10.1007/978-3-030-46401-1_12

involved in navigating the prison system when entitlements are complex to access; the irregularity of provision of suitable basic requirements; the inattention within the system when considering the pregnant woman; the exceptionality of the shame experienced and the potential for pregnancy being a unique 'turning point' and 'catalyst for desistence' (LeBel et al. 2008; Maruna 2001; Sharpe 2015; Paternoster and Bachman 2017). The focus of the chapter concentrates on some of the findings of the current research, specifically: equivalence of health care; nutritional wellbeing; basic provisions (or lack of); changes in identity, and compassion and support for pregnant women in prison. The chapter also describes how prison can be a safe haven for some women and introduces the concept of pregnancy itself being a unique 'turning point' for desistance and health.

Background: Pregnant Women in Prison

Women and girls in prison make up approximately 2–10% of the global imprisoned population, and their numbers have doubled since the year 2000 (Walmsley 2013). The United States has the highest number of imprisoned women at 12 per 100,000 of the national population, and Denmark, at 2.6 per 100,000 of the national population, has the lowest (Walmsley 2013). The UK has the highest prisoner population in the European Union, with England and Wales having one of the uppermost figures at 6.7 per 100,000 of the national population (Gerry and Harris 2016). Numbers of female prisoners have been rising slowly since 2015, and generally represent 5% of the overall UK prison population. A review of women's prisons in 2006 found that most women prisoners were mothers, some were pregnant, and many came from deprived backgrounds (Corston 2007). Precise numbers of pregnant women held in UK prisons are not recorded, though it is estimated that 6% of the female prison population are at varying stages of pregnancy and around 100 babies are born to incarcerated women every year (Albertson et al. 2014; Prison Reform Trust 2017; Abbott 2015; Kennedy et al. 2016).

A considerable number of women in prison have been victims of crime and many have multiple complex needs and difficult lives. Current statistics suggest that: 46% have violent partners; 53% may have suffered sexual abuse and rape; 66% are substance abusers, and 80% suffer some form of mental-health disorder (Corston 2007; North et al. 2006; Gullberg 2013; Prison Reform Trust 2017; Baldwin et al. 2015; Baldwin and Epstein 2017). In 2006, the Home Secretary of the UK Labour government requested an evaluation of women in the criminal justice system following reports of six suicides over 13 months in one prison. Baroness Jean Corston undertook the review of the UK female prison estate over a period of nine months (Corston 2007). Analysis of the findings demonstrated that most women in prison were disadvantaged either through poverty, mental illness, historic abuse, addiction, or ill-health. It was reported that the majority had children, and several were pregnant. The Corston report made 43 recommendations, taking a 'radical new approach' to improve the criminal justice system for women including taking a holistic stance towards imprisoned women and the opening of more community centres to use as an alternative to prison sentences. Evidence suggests that women are more likely to commit non-violent crimes compared with men, and most women serve sentences of less than six months in duration (Carlen and Worrall 2004; Walklate 2004; Carrington 2014; Baldwin and Epstein 2017).

Women's Prisons in the UK

There are 12 women's prisons in the UK, of which six currently have Mother and Baby Units attached (MBU[1]), with 54 MBU places available nationally (Ministry of Justice 2020). Women prisoners may be held as one of four security categories: Category A, Restricted Status, Closed Conditions, or Open Conditions.[2] Ten of the female estates in the UK

[1] A mother and baby unit places women who have successfully applied for a place, with their babies up to 18 months of age.

[2] **Category A prisoners** are deemed the most dangerous prisoners who require the strictest security conditions. **Restricted status** is any woman on remand or sentenced who poses a serious risk to public safety. **Closed conditions** are for women who are too substantial a risk for open conditions although requiring less security. **Open conditions** are for women who can be trusted and are a minimal risk to the public. (PSI 39/2011)

are closed prisons,[3] holding women who are categorised as 'A', 'restricted status' and 'closed conditions'. There are two open prisons[4] (D Category) where women are sentenced if they meet the requirements or prior to resettlement into the community. Category D prisons have 'open conditions' where women can go towards the end of their sentences or if qualifying for open conditions. Many women enter the system already pregnant and this is often only discovered at the initial health assessment on reception to prison (Corston 2007; North et al. 2006; and Gullberg 2013). However, exact numbers are not known, nor, indeed, whether their pregnancies are unplanned or intentional.

The UK Prison Service has issued guidance for the treatment of pregnant women and new mothers in prison within a Prison Service Order (PSO).[5] There is no specific PSO for pregnant women, but they are mentioned in more generic guidance (National Offender Management Services 2014). It is specified that suitable nutrition and rest are required, that handcuffs should *not* be used after arrival at hospital or clinic appointments and women should not travel in cellular vans, due to potential risks inherent in being locked in a confined space. The guidance directs the Prison Service in making adequate provisions for women wishing to breastfeed their babies and suggests that careful planning should take place when women are being separated from their babies due to the risk to their mental health (ibid). The Royal College of Midwives (2016) and Abbott et al. (2020) recommend that all pregnant inmates should receive the same quality of care as if they were on the outside[6] and have issued guidance in relation to incarcerated pregnant women and new mothers. There is no specific direction from organisations such as the National Institute for Health and Care Excellence (NICE) in relation to pregnant prisoners. However, NICE guidance *does* refer to female pris-

[3] A closed prison is maximum security holding category A, restricted status, closed conditions and remand prisoners.

[4] An open prison is a minimum-security prison where women can undertake outside work and are trusted with minimal supervision.

[5] A Prison Service Order (PSO) or Prison Service Instruction (PSI) is guidance on how prison services are regulated.

[6] 'On the outside' is a phrase used to describe being away from or not inside an institution such as a prison.

oners in broader guidance relating to smoking cessation, substance misuse, alcohol addiction and complex social needs (NICE 2010, 2014). The recent confidential enquiry into maternal deaths in the UK—*Mothers and Babies: Reducing Risk Through Audits and Confidential Enquiries Across the UK* (MBRRACE-UK 2017)—found that two-thirds of the women who died had "pre-existing physical or mental health problems" and states that medication in pregnancy should not be stopped "without consulting a specialist". The importance of access to care for vulnerable women in society, adopting a multidisciplinary team approach, and having specially trained midwives for women with complex social needs is recommended (ibid).

Rights of the Pregnant Woman in Prison

In the UK, there is a statutory recognition that *all* prisoners should receive an equivalence of health care to that provided in the community (Council of Europe 2006; Rogan 2017). Furthermore, the United Nations (UN) Bangkok Rules (2013) states that women in prison should be given gender-specific care (UN 2013). Nonetheless, current conditions in prison can create barriers to delivering adequate care for pregnant women (North et al. 2006; Corston 2007; Kennedy et al. 2016). Economically, responsibility for health funding lies with the Department of Health (DH) and the Strategic Health Authorities (SHAs). More recently, private health care providers such as *Care UK*™ have been contracted as providers of prison health care for 21 prisons in England and Wales (Plimmer 2016). There is no known requirement for midwives to be positioned as permanent members of staff in health care departments in prison, but community midwives do visit women in prison to provide antenatal and post-natal care.

The Incarcerated Pregnancy Research

The aim of my research was to examine the pregnant woman's encounter with the English prison estate and their experience of the associated conditions, through:

- Semi-structured audio-recorded interviews with pregnant women, women who had experienced pregnancy in prison, and prison staff.
- Deconstructing the daily patterns and consideration of their impact upon the pregnant woman, including observation of the spaces, rooms and prison wings.
- Interactions with significant people and the milieu that the pregnant prisoner was exposed to.

The fieldwork was undertaken in three prisons: Prison A: a closed prison with no Mother and Baby Unit (MBU); Prison B: a closed prison with an MBU; and Prison C: an open prison with an MBU. Data collection methods consisted of fieldwork diaries and audio-recorded semi-structured interviews with women who were currently pregnant, those who had been imprisoned during pregnancy, and prison staff. Thematic analysis developed from the initial stages using basic analytical methods through to using the computer software package NVivo.

Negotiating Nutritional Well-Being as a Pregnant Woman in Prison

In relation to prison food, the literature suggests that the monotony and limited choice can feel like an extra layer of punishment when incarcerated (Smith 2002; Godderis 2006a, b; Smoyer 2015a, b). The evidence recognises that this is a concern for all prisoners (Godderis 2006a). The symbolism of food as power (Brisman 2008) and the theoretical link between food and violence in prison (Bohannon 2009) demonstrates the importance of understanding the impact of food for the pregnant woman.[7] There is limited, if any, research into the perinatal women's experience of food in prison. Specific recommendations for pregnant women in prison include: following national guidelines (Department of Health (DH) 2004; National Institute for Health and Care Excellence (NICE) 2010, 2014); considering gastro-intestinal discomforts associated with pregnancy and allowing for the exchange of acidic foods; access to food outside of the prison regime; and access to fresh water (Shlafer et al. 2017).

Nausea and vomiting can be a normal, albeit distressing physiological symptom in early pregnancy (Niebyl 2010). I was able to interview Abi five times during her pregnancy and her symptoms of nausea and vomiting were so extreme that she had been hospitalised twice. Each time I met Abi she sank down into a chair, arms held tightly around her body or with her head in her hands, looking pale and sad. Abi's nausea was a constant presence and therefore exacerbated any feelings of hunger and discussions around prison food. She told me: *"The smell of food just puts me right off and I can't* (eat it), *I can't. I hate it!"* Conversely, some women were able to ensure their nutritional needs were met through creative ways. Karis was in her fifth pregnancy and had been homeless and addicted to illegal drugs when she came into prison. All of her children had been removed at, or soon after birth and were looked after in the care system. Karis had been in and out of prison, but this was the first time she had been pregnant in prison. Determined to use her pregnancy as a 'turning point' (LeBel et al. 2008; Maruna 2001; Maruna et al. 2006), Karis was able to find ways to optimise her nutritional well-being despite the food being *"awful, like slop … its stodge"*:

> *I managed to get a job in the gym … I was exercising even though I was pregnant. I had salad, I was known for it, salad every single day, my friends in the kitchen would bring me an extra piece of chicken to put with the salad, that's why I got a job in the gym as well, the cross trainer was my best friend.* (Karis)

[7] The current spend on food per prisoner per day in England is £2.02 (MoJ, 2015, Freedom of Information request from Prison Reform Trust).

Karis used her experience of prison to prove that she could be a mother and demonstrated her tenacity while she used the environment to her advantage to ensure her optimal health. Karis was one of seven women interviewed for whom pregnancy was *their* 'turning point'. This change came from *"being given a chance"* and was subsequently a motivator for transformation.

Health Care Equivalence

A common cry from all women was the difficulties in getting medicine that they had been prescribed *"on the out"*. These medicines included antidepressants, anti-hypertensive drugs, and vitamins and remedies which would relieve minor disorders of pregnancy, such as creams and indigestion medicines: "*They won't let me have it* (anti-depressants) *because I'm pregnant"*; *"I have to wait for my anti-sickness"*; *"I don't know if you're allowed them when you're pregnant"*; *"I've got eczema and I'm still waiting for my cream"*; *"I've not had my aspirin"*; *"I reported heartburn to my midwife … I was prescribed Gaviscon*[8] *four weeks later"*; *"I haven't had any folic acid"*; *"I waited three days for paracetamol and I was in agony"*. Skye had been taking anti-hypertensive[9] drugs to prevent pre-eclampsia[10] but since arriving in prison she had not received her medication:

> *My Mum had a brain haemorrhage, through high blood pressure, so that's why I'm worried in here with my high blood pressure. They said they have to wait for confirmation from my doctor … you don't understand, I need it.* (Skye)

In the second interview with Skye, she told me she had started receiving her prescribed aspirin; however, she was being asked to swallow it without the tablet being dissolved—*"health care was giving me an aspirin tablet raw"*—against the approved formulary mode of administration. This poor access to medication was detrimental to the pregnant women's

[8] Gaviscon is a liquid medication available to buy over the counter for the relief of heartburn.

[9] Anti-hypertensive medication reduces blood pressure.

[10] Pre-eclampsia is a serious pregnancy complication characterised by high blood pressure and fluid retention which, if untreated, can lead to eclamptic fits and cerebral vascular accident (stroke).

physiological well-being. Lily was asthmatic, and told me of her experience of not getting the respiratory medication she relied upon:

> *I've had asthma since I was born, and my chest keeps getting tight … they don't know how long it's going to be until they'll give me one* (inhaler), *but I've got to wait and have another asthma test done.* (Lily)

Women in Prison A spoke about having to queue up outside the pharmacy building for medication that, in the community, they would have had in their possession. The 'hatch' was a window from the pharmacy where the women queue to receive their medicine; I would regularly see the women queuing outside in all weathers for medicine and at times tensions were fraught, with occasional fights breaking out between prisoners. If it was raining, women would get wet because umbrellas were not allowed in prison. For the pregnant woman, the frustration of not being able to have tablets in their possession led to further disempowerment, as Caroline describes:

> *I have four different blood pressure medications and iron … I was having to queue up outside in the rain … you are not allowed umbrellas here you can't have coats with hoods, so you literally have to queue up outside in the rain and whatever the weather. I was doing that three times a day to get my medication.* (Caroline)

Health Care Provision

Most research participants described situations that were linked to equivalence of health care (such as receipt of medication, access to timely midwifery advice and appropriate assessment by a trained midwife). The care put in place for pregnant women and new mothers was generally in the form of security protocols or procedures, such as opening ACCT[11] documents to keep women from self-harm. However, rather than this feeling like a support mechanism for women, being 'on suicide watch'—as one

[11] ACCT (Assessment, Care in Custody and Teamwork) is a series of documents opened in response to concern that a prisoner is at risk of self-harm or suicide.

woman exclaimed: *"having a light shone in my eyes every 15 minutes through the night"*—was distressing, especially for those returning to prison following separation. Women would sometimes talk about how they would 'mask' their emotions to avoid this process being applied. Jane explains what being on an ACCT was like:

> *When I was sentenced, I was so shocked I cried 'I prefer to be dead than go to prison' and you know when you say these things, they put me on suicide watch. I had to shake a leg every hour! Every hour for two weeks, I had to shake my leg every hour to show I was still alive.* (Jane)

Nonetheless, prison staff view an ACCT as a supportive process: *"They return, and they've got no baby, and they're automatically placed on suicide watch, to assist them through the first couple of days"*.

Access to Antenatal Classes and Resources

In the community, women can choose to access antenatal classes; in Prison A there were no such classes: *"They've not offered me any antenatal classes"*. The midwife stated that she did try to spend time discussing labour and birth: *"I think they need antenatal classes … I do try and spend some time discussing it"*. In Prison B, antenatal classes were facilitated by the MBU staff and health visitors, and in Prison C women could access classes in the community should they choose this: *"anything that they could access in the community they can access here"*. The findings demonstrate the inconsistencies for pregnant women across the female prison estate. Women who had accessed antenatal classes run by volunteers found them valuable:

> *It's not until you look back and see, the little groups were so important in there, just being able to talk to someone, just something little, you know, just like, how will I know I am in labour? Just to be able to ask someone that question.* (Frances)

Lack of Basic Provisions

Several women in this study described their experiences of discomfort caused by poor bedding, exacerbating muscle and joint discomfort. Lola described her first night in prison and how she was unaware that her allocated bedding would be stored in her pillowcase. Whilst this lack of knowledge may be a common occurrence for all prisoners on their first night, the pregnant woman appeared especially vulnerable to anxiety:

> *On the night time, they didn't tell me that my bedding was in my pillowcase, and I thought that I had no bedding. Until my friend told me the next day … I didn't know what to do. I didn't know, I thought that was the pillow.* (Lola)

When pregnant women could order clothes, they often had to wait for many months. It was a common perception that women had no rights, even if pregnant: *"you're just a prisoner, you have no rights"*. Receiving parcels and packages from outside was difficult for pregnant women who required larger clothes and maternity bras: *"I'm entitled to maternity clothes and they've been ignored"*. Prisoners sometimes felt that knowledge of entitlements was deliberately kept from them, with the system relying on prisoners not knowing their rights: *"It's like if we don't know, we can't ask"; "I get right pissed off and I'm thinking, why are they withholding this information from us?"* Clothes were often ill-fitting due to weight loss or incorrect sizing: "*I don't like wearing these* (baggy clothes) *when I've lost weight. I might have lost more than a stone*". Other women talked about the quality of the clothes: "*Because, obviously, you have to hand wash them, your knickers fall apart*". Women would use baggy clothes to hide their pregnancy and so blend in and not draw attention to themselves: "*When I've got my top off I can see a bump*", or to ensure they felt protected from harm from other prisoners.

Suppression of bodily functions was a common finding in all women who were lactating.[12] In Prisons A and B women were unable to access basic provisions to soak up excess milk: *"I just had to put tissue in my bra"; "I cut them* (sanitary towels) *in half and stick them in my bra"*. Sylvia,

[12] Lactation is the secretion of milk from the breasts.

sentenced at 41 weeks pregnant, went into labour whilst she was in court. She was sent straight from prison reception to hospital where she gave birth, was separated from her baby and returned to the prison, all within 24 hours. Skye described what she saw when Sylvia was received onto her wing:

> *A girl that's come on our wing, she was just sent here, without her baby, and all her breasts were leaking and everything … she didn't even have a bra … no one wants to even see that, let alone be that person and go through it. Everyone's sitting eating their food, and she's sitting there with big wet patches. I'm shocked. It's just like someone bleeding everywhere.* (Skye)

Skye's observations and subsequent astonishment that a woman could be left to seep breastmilk appeared to be something that prisoners noticed but staff overlooked. Caroline had been advised to use surgical gauze for her leaking breasts, though the seepage of milk was excessive; she told me about this in our sixth interview when she was five days post-birth:

> *Well, that woman* (nurse) *who gave me the gauze, there's no way she's had children … One of the girls told me that she used to have to use the new born nappies and put them in her bra. Because she used to leak that much, that even breast pads weren't enough, she used to have to put nappies in.* (Caroline)

A woman who is pregnant in prison, although in receipt of health care, has little or no choice over place of birth, birth partner or whether the baby remains with her (Albertson et al. 2014; Sikand 2017). An example of disempowerment for a woman in prison is when she attends hospital for an ultrasound scan. The ultrasound scan may be seen as a social occasion for women and families (Earle and Letherby 2003) or can also be viewed as an unnecessary observation which further medicalises pregnancy (Howson 2013). However, a woman in prison will not be told the date of her scan for security purposes and will be accompanied by Prison Officers rather than a partner or family member. Due to the limited number of female prisons, it is likely that a woman will give birth far away from her home in an unfamiliar hospital (Albertson et al. 2014;

Galloway et al. 2015). She may have some provisions for labour in place, but these will be vetted by the prison service prior to transfer.

Changes in Identity

Sharon had also been in prison previously and was pregnant with her first baby when she was interviewed; she spoke of how this differed:

> *I think last time I was quite loud, wild and gobby and I did what I wanted to do when I wanted to do it and this time I am quite quiet, just keeping my head down, doing my time.* (Sharon)

The changes in Sharon's identity from prisoner to pregnant prisoner appeared to be an incentive for a change in her behaviour, demonstrating a potential 'turning point' and 'catalyst for desistance' (Maruna et al. 2006; Sharpe 2015; Paternoster and Bachman 2017). Whether this was through restraint due to wanting to be given an opportunity to keep her baby or because simply being pregnant caused her to mature and quietly complete her sentence are concepts worth considering. Women who changed their status and identity as a pregnant prisoner to being a *normal prisoner* meant they could be just *like everyone else.* Being able to blend in more would offer some relief from the attention that a visible pregnancy would bring in prison. For many participants, their pregnancy was secondary to their identity as 'prisoner' (Abbott et al. 2020). Women would commonly try and block out their pregnancy, stating: "*I block it out*", or "*a part of you forgets*". The reasons for this were complex but, like Jane, pregnancy denial appeared as a way of coping with the "*horrible*" experience of being in prison for the first time:

> *You know, although you are pregnant, a part of you forgets that you are pregnant. Because you're in there because there's a lot to deal with. It's terrible really because you don't focus on what you should be focusing on. It all goes out the window.* (Jane)

Exclamations of: "*I'm not made for jail*"; "*someone else is in control of my life*" meant the identity as prisoner surpassed the identity as pregnant woman, who therefore tried to mentally block out the pregnancy:

> *Although I was pregnant in there and I knew I was pregnant. Because I was in prison, I shut it out … I just couldn't* (acknowledge pregnancy) *because I was in prison, I just couldn't.* (Pamola)

For those anticipating separation but then surprised at being allowed to keep their baby, being given a chance at motherhood was described positively:

> *I was just overcome with … I can't even describe it, it was just immense. Better than any fucking drug I've ever taken in my life.* (Ellie)

This prospect often appeared to signify a change in the woman to better herself, seizing the opportunity fully where being in prison was the catalyst to change. It is uncertain whether the threat of separation from their baby in prison uniquely encourages women to maximise opportunities despite being incarcerated or whether such women would have bettered themselves on the outside. However, this catalyst to change is worthy of deeper exploration.

Support and Kindness

During my fieldwork and interviews there was often a mention of a particular staff member from health care, prison officers to chaplaincy and charity volunteers. Kindness made a huge difference to women. The support of other women in prison also made an impact and the value in the relationships with pad mates and friends made in prison were helpful for the pregnant woman:

> *They're supporting you, they want you to go home and see your family, they want you to do well, they want you to be happy. I'm at that part of my sentence where I can make plans, I'm going home.* (Tracey)

Staff would also describe how they found value in working with women who hoped to turn their lives around through motherhood, especially on the MBU:

> *Building women's confidence, them feeling valued, and being nurtured and being told, 'You're a good mum, aren't you? Look at how he responds to you, look at that and you've just done that, that's brilliant!.* (Prison Officer)

Prison as a Safe Haven for Some

For a number of women, especially those who have led chaotic lives on the outside, prison can represent a place of safety (Baldwin and Epstein 2017). Women who are addicted to illegal substances may get the support required, have access to health care, routine, meals and shelter away from violent situations in the community. Jenna, a repeat offender was addicted to heroin. She spoke about how being in prison this time helped her, especially being pregnant:

> *I'm glad I've come in because I was on quite a bad road to destruction, and I did need this break; and especially with finding out that I was pregnant.* (Jenna)

The Birth Charter (Kennedy et al. 2016) recommends that appropriate and well-run community programmes are available so that women can get the help they need on the outside rather than seeing prison as the safer option when pregnant. Having been in prison a number of times, she spoke about the difficulties she faced on the outside:

> *As much as you've got good intentions, as soon as you step a foot out of that gate it's completely different. I'm hoping this time things have got to be different for me.* (Jenna)

Women who have been given support in prison and have been able to keep their babies with them, appear to sometimes seize the opportunity to change behaviour and often go on to lead productive lives, contributing to society through employment and motherhood post release. Women who are given a chance to change and are able to mother their babies on an MBU are more likely to breastfeed and less likely to reoffend. Karis had been able to keep her baby with her and was given the support and opportunity to change. Several years later, Karis is still clean from drugs, a full-time mother to her son and in fulltime employment, she reflected on her experiences:

> *Just being given a chance to let me prove that I could do it … but I also think I was ready to change.* (Karis)

Karis credited some of the support for her being able to change to the Birth Companions who helped her through her pregnancy and supported her during the birth: "*[*Birth Companion*] came in with his first teddy and that was just … That meant so much for him to just have his own little teddy*". When Karis was reflecting on her experience she spoke about being given a chance by her social worker demonstrating the impact that health and social care professionals can have on someone's life: "*I look at Christine* (pseudonym), *she was my social worker … now she's a woman that helped me change my life, because she gave me a chance.*" Karis demonstrates that being given opportunities at the right time with the right kind of support can make a long-term difference to an individual, their children and ultimately to society.

Theoretical Perspectives: Pregnancy as a 'Turning Point' and Catalyst for Desistance

Adaptation to prison life has been observed, with prisoners '*moving backwards as well as forwards*' through distinct phases of acclimatisation, with some remaining in the first, 'liminal stage' unable to move towards acceptance of the system (Harvey 2008: 58, 61). The experience of prison can lead to new, adapted identities—a phenomenon described by scholars where prisoners may redefine themselves, often in a religious context (Booker and Dearnley 2016; Maruna et al. 2006). The criminology literature also suggests that imprisonment can be a 'catalyst for desistance'[13] especially when life events (such as becoming a parent) elicit a 'turning point' in prisoners' lives (LeBel et al. 2008; Maruna 2001; Maruna et al. 2006; Sharpe 2015; Paternoster and Bachman 2017). The loss of liberty and autonomy has been labelled as a 'pain' of imprisonment from a sociological perspective (Sykes 1958/2007: 67). Crewe et al. (2017) found that loss of control was a greater 'pain' for imprisoned women than men. This may also trigger a sense of crisis and therefore impact upon stress levels, making it a struggle to retain mental well-being. Focusing upon the female estate, Rowe (2015) found that prisoners were creative in how they directed the system they were held within, 'navigating' ways to 'alleviate the pains of imprisonment'.

Criminology academics discuss various 'turning points' for prisoners being a 'catalyst for desistance'; for example, a male prisoner's partner being pregnant, or finding religion (LeBel et al. 2008; Maruna 2001; Maruna et al. 2006; Paternoster and Bachman 2017). My research found that pregnancy, too, is a 'catalyst for desistance', thus adding to this body of knowledge. Turning points are significant in terms of releasing one's potential contribution to society, with a real opportunity for reform through 'desistance' whereby a significant societal impact reduces the burden to society: a burden avoided if both mother and child bond and develop healthy relationships (Kennedy et al. 2016). For example, Karis, who had been in prison multiple times and had endured enforced removal of all of her children, admitted: "*I kinda go on a destructive, I've done it in the past … the worst thing they ever did was take my kids away*". Karis used the pregnancy experience to change her behaviour in order to be given a chance to keep a baby for the first time:

> *I told her* (social worker) … *I'll do anything … I'll jump through hoops if you want me to … if you want me to go for a drug test every day I'll do it.* (Karis)

It was acknowledged by women who were not allowed to keep their baby that keeping it could have been a catalyst for change, yet the forced separation meant that women felt despair that, sometimes, sent them

[13] Desistance is the termination of offending behaviour (Maruna et al. 2012).

into a negative spiral of self-destruction and despondency. Lola recognised that had she been given a chance to be a mother, which *could* have led to a turning point, and wanted to breastfeed her baby; however:

> *I poured my heart out to them saying I want another chance … and then all of them said no … I was going to breastfeed her, to have more bond with her while I'm in here, but, obviously, she's getting taken so there's no point.* (Lola)

The pain of separation for those who anticipated enforced removal co-exists with the joy of others being able to keep their baby. This divergence appeared to split the women's experiences of imprisonment into the pleasure of those given a chance to be with their baby from the unbearable suffering of those who were separating.

Conclusions

This chapter has explored some of the findings of the qualitative research exploring the experiences of pregnant women in prison. Embedded narratives of some of the research participants specifically relate to equivalence of health care, nutrition, entitlements and lack of basic provisions. Pregnancy in prison is described as a new 'turning point' for desistance, adding to the evidence as a unique opportunity for change as long as the appropriate support is in place.

References

Abbott, L. (2015). A pregnant pause: Expecting in the prison estate. In L. Baldwin (Ed.), *Mothering justice: Working with mothers in criminal and social justice settings* (1st ed.). England: Waterside Press.

Abbott, L., & Scott, T. (2020). Women's experiences of breastfeeding in prison. *MIDIRS Midwifery Digest, 27*(2).

Albertson, K., O'Keefe, C., Burke, C., Lessing-Turner, G., & Renfrew, M. (2014). Addressing health inequalities for mothers and babies in prison.

Health and Inequality: Applying Public Health Research to Policy and Practice, 39.

Baldwin, L., & Epstein, R. (2017). *Short but not sweet: A study of the imposition of short custodial sentences on women, and in particular, on mothers*. Leicester: De Montfort University.

Baldwin, L., O'Malley, S., & Galway, K. (2015). Mothers addicted: Working with complexity. In Chap. 10: 239–262: Baldwin, L. (2015). *Mothering justice: Working with mothers in social and criminal justice settings.*

Bohannon, J. (2009). The theory? Diet causes violence. The lab? Prison. *Science, 325*(5948), 1614–1616.

Booker, A., and Dearnley, H. (2016). *Faith and Identity in Prison. In Religion, Faith and Crime* (pp. 347–373). Springer.

Brisman, A. (2008). Fair fare: Food as contested terrain in US prisons and jails. *Georgetown Journal on Poverty Law and Policy, 15*, 49.

Carlen, P., & Worrall, A. (2004). *Analysing Women's Imprisonment*. London: Taylor & Francis.

Carrington, K. (2014). *Feminism and Global Justice*. New York: Routledge.

Corston, J. (2007). *The Corston report: A report by baroness Jean Corston of a review of women with particular vulnerabilities in the criminal justice system: The need for a distinct, radically different, visibly-led, strategic, proportionate, holistic, woman-centred, integrated approach*. Home Office.

Council of Europe. Committee of Ministers. (2006). *European prison rules*. Council of Europe. Recommendation Rec. 2 of the Committee of Ministers to member states on the European Prison Rules.

Crewe, B., Hulley, S., & Wright, S. (2017). The gendered pains of life imprisonment. *British Journal of Criminology, 57*(6), 20.

Department of Health. (2004). *National Service Framework for Children, Young People and Maternity Services, Standard 11: Maternity Services*. London: DH.

Earle, S., & Letherby, G. (2003). *Gender, identity and reproduction*. New York: Springer.

Galloway, S., Haynes, A., & Cuthbert, C. (2015). *All babies count—An unfair sentence: Spotlight on the criminal justice system*. London: NSPCC.

Gerry, F., & Harris, L. (2016). *Women in prison: Is the justice system fit for purpose?* Halsbury Law Exchange. Retrieved September 21, 17, from http://blogs.lexisnexis.co.uk/halsburyslawexchange/wp-content/uploads/sites/25/2016/11/SA-1016-077-Women-in-Prison-Paper-ONLINE-FINAL.pdf.

Godderis, R. (2006a). Dining in: The symbolic power of food in prison. *The Howard Journal of Criminal Justice, 45*(3), 255–267.
Godderis, R. (2006b). Food for thought: An analysis of power and identity in prison food narratives. *Berkeley Journal of Sociology, 50*, 61–75.
Gullberg, S. (2013). *State of the estate—Women in prison's report on the women's custodial estate 2011–12*. London: Women in Prison.
Harvey, J. (2008). An Embedded Multimethod Approach to Prison Research. In King, R., and Wincup, E. (Eds.), *Doing Research on Crime and Justice* (Part V: Chapter 18: pp. 487–500). Oxford University Press.
Howson, A. (2013). *The body in society: An introduction*. New York: John Wiley & Sons.
Kennedy, A., Marshall, D., Parkinson, D., Delap, N., & Abbott, L. (2016). *Birth charter for women in prison in England and Wales*. London: Birth Companions.
LeBel, T. P., Burnett, R., Maruna, S., & Bushway, S. (2008). The chicken and egg of subjective and social factors in desistance from crime. *European Journal of Criminology, 5*(2), 131–159.
Maruna, S. (2001). *Making Good: How ex-Convicts Reform and Rebuild their Lives*. Washington, DC: American Psychological Association.
Maruna, S., Wilson, L., & Curran, K. (2006). Why god is often found behind bars: Prison conversions and the crisis of self-narrative. *Research in Human Development, 3*(2-3), 161–184.
Maruna, S., McNeill, F., Farrall, S., & Lightowler, C. (2012). Desistance Research and Probation Practice: Knowledge Exchange and Co-Producing Evidence-Based Practice Models. *Irish Probation Journal, 9*, October 2012.
Mothers and Babies: Reducing Risk Through Audits and Confidential Enquiries Across the UK (MBRRACE-UK). (2017). *National perinatal epidemiology unit*. Oxford. Retrieved from https://www.npeu.ox.ac.uk/mbrrace-uk.
Ministry of Justice. (2020). *Population and Capacity Briefing*. London: Ministry of Justice.
National Institute for Health and Clinical Excellence (NICE). (2010). *Pregnancy and complex social factors: A model for service provision for pregnant women with complex social factors*. NICE. Retrieved September 13, 17, from http://www.nice.org.uk/guidance/cg110.
National Institute for Health and Clinical Excellence (NICE). (2014). *Pregnancy and complex social factors overview*. NICE. Retrieved September 13, 17, from http://pathways.nice.org.uk/pathways/pregnancy-and-complexsocialfactors.

National Offender Management Services. (2014). *Mother and baby units prison service instruction* (PSI) *49/2014 PI 63/2014*. Retrieved August 10, 15, from https://www.justice.gov.uk/downloads/offenders/psipso/psi-2014/psi-49-2014-mother-and-baby-units.pdf.

Niebyl, J. R. (2010). Nausea and Vomiting in Pregnancy. *New England Journal of Medicine, 363*(16), 1544–1550.

North, J., Chase, L., & Alliance, M. (2006). Getting it Right: Services for Pregnant Women, New Mothers, and Babies in Prison: Lankelly Chase.

Paternoster, R., and Bachman, R. (2017). The missing element in theories of desistance. *The Routledge International Handbook of Life-Course Criminology*, 29.

Plimmer, G. (2016, May 9). Care UK becomes biggest prison health care provider. *Financial Times*.

Prison Reform Trust. (2017). *Bromley briefings, prison: The facts*. Summer 2017. London: Prison Reform Trust. Retrieved August 10, 17, from http://www.prisonreformtrust.org.uk/Portals/0/Documents/Bromley%20Briefings/Summer%202017%20factfile.pdf.

Rogan, M. (2017). Human rights and correctional health policy: A view from Europe. *International Journal of Prisoner Health, 13*(1).

Rowe, A. (2015). 'Tactics', agency and power in women's prisons. *British Journal of Criminology, 56*(2), 332–349.

Royal College of Midwives. (2016). *Caring for childbearing prisoners: A position paper*. London: Position Statement for Women in Custody.

Sharpe, G. (2015). Precarious Identities: 'Young' Motherhood, Desistance and Stigma. *Criminology and Criminal Justice, 15*(4), 407–422.

Shlafer, R. J., Stang, J., Dallaire, D., Forestell, C. A., & Hellerstedt, W. (2017). Best practices for nutrition care of pregnant women in prison. *Journal of Correctional Health Care, 23*(3), 297–304.

Sikand, M. (2017). *Lost spaces: Is the current provision for women prisoners to gain a place in a prison mother and baby unit fair and accessible?* The Griffins Society University of Cambridge Institute of Criminology.

Smith, C. (2002). Punishment and pleasure: Women, food and the imprisoned body. *The Sociological Review, 50*(2), 197–214.

Smoyer, A. B. (2015a). Feeding relationships: Foodways and social networks in a women's prison. *Affilia, 30*(1), 26–39.

Smoyer, A. B. (2015b). Making fatty girl cakes food and resistance in a women's prison. *The Prison Journal, 96*(2), 191–209.

Sykes, G. M. (1958/2007). *The society of captives: A study of a maximum-security prison*. Princeton University Press.
United Nations. (2013). *The Bangkok rules*. Retrieved from http://www.penalreform.org/priorities/women-in-the-criminal-justice-system/bangkok-rules-2/.
Walmsley, R. (2013). *World prison population list*. World Prison Brief. Institute for Criminal Policy Research, International Centre for Prison Studies, Birkbeck, University of London.
Walklate, S. (2004). *Gender, Crime and Criminal Justice*. 2nd edn. London: Willan Publishing.

13

Transforming Ways of 'Doing' Masculinity and Health in Prisons: Performances of Masculinity Within the Fit for LIFE Programme Delivered in Two Scottish Prisons

Matthew Maycock, Alice MacLean, Cindy M. Gray, and Kate Hunt

Although the fluid, performed nature of gender is well established (cf. Butler 1990; West and Zimmerman 1987), constructions of masculinity have commonly been linked to practices that are 'toxic' to health (cf. Courtenay 2000; Verdonk et al. 2010), particularly in relation to 'hyper-masculine' ideals (cf. Mosher and Tomkins 1988; Toch 1998). In this chapter, we argue that masculinities can be aligned with positive health behaviours not exclusively the health practices which are damaging to health (Sloan et al. 2015). We consider how masculinities are performed

M. Maycock (✉)
Universtiy of Dundee, Dundee, UK

A. MacLean
University of Glasgow, Glasgow, UK

© The Author(s) 2021
M. Maycock et al. (eds.), *Issues and Innovations in Prison Health Research*, Palgrave Studies in Prisons and Penology, https://doi.org/10.1007/978-3-030-46401-1_13

over the course of pilot deliveries of a health promotion programme (Fit for LIFE) (Maycock 2018a), in a largely male environment, namely two Scottish prisons. We explore performances of hegemonic (Connell 1995; Connell and Messerschmidt 2005) and inclusive (Anderson 2008, 2009; Anderson and Mccormack 2018; Anderson and McGuire 2010) masculinities. In so doing, we aim to advance masculinities theory through moving from a binary, at times oppositional, orientation to a more nuanced reading of masculinity within a specific gendered context.

Additionally, we highlight aspects of change in the performance of prison masculinities within the context of the delivery of the Fit for LIFE programme, as in the men's weight management programme—Football Fans in Training (FFIT) which inspired it (Bunn et al. 2016; Hunt et al. 2013). This illustrates the potential for health promotion interventions to provide new opportunities for performances of masculinity that positively contribute to health. Before describing the collection and analysis of interview data on the experiences of participating in this programme, we provide an overview of developments in masculinities theories, and summarise findings from studies of masculinities within prisons in general.

Masculinities Theory

Connell's theory of hegemonic masculinity (Connell 1995; Connell and Messerschmidt 2005) was instrumental in popularising the idea that masculinities are both multiple and hierarchically structured, with one 'hegemonic' configuration prevailing over other forms (described as

C. M. Gray
School of Social and Political Sciences and Institute of Health and Wellbeing, University of Glasgow, Glasgow, UK
e-mail: Cindy.Gray@glasgow.ac.uk

K. Hunt
Institute for Social Marketing and Health, University of Stirling, Stirling, UK
e-mail: kate.hunt@stir.ac.uk

'complicit', 'subordinate', 'protest' and 'marginal'). This theory has been influential in the study of men and masculinities, including in relation to health (Gough 2006; Emslie et al. 2006; Knight et al. 2012; Schofield et al. 2000). Connell and others have discussed the role of homophobia in hegemonic masculinity theory, and in performances of masculinity more generally (Kimmel 2002; De Boise 2014). This is reflected in research describing the homophobic nature of many prison environments (cf. Richmond 1978). Critiques of Connell's theory as originally propounded (cf. Demetriou 2001; Wetherell and Edley 1999) led her to revisit the concept of hegemonic masculinity (Connell and Messerschmidt 2005), resulting in a greater focus on hegemonic masculinities at local, regional and global levels.

In studying changes in some performances of masculinity in the Global North, Anderson has subsequently developed the theory of inclusive masculinity (2009), in which he claims homophobia is less influential on performances of masculinity, and emotional intimacy between men is increasing. Anderson views Connell's theory of hegemonic masculinity as being insufficient to describe contemporary manifestations of masculinity. Anderson adopts an overtly positive perspective on masculine performances, with a focus on more horizontal or egalitarian manifestations, in which hierarchy is less apparent. He describes inclusive masculinity as

> ... based on social equality for gay men, respect for women, and racial parity and one in which fraternity men bond over emotional intimacy. (Anderson 2008, 604)

Similarly to Connell, Anderson foregrounds power relations in the development of inclusive masculinity theory. Critiques of Anderson's analysis have questioned the extent to which homophobia remains formative of performances of masculinity (De Boise 2014), but Anderson's alternative view of the declining importance of homophobia remains one of the main distinctions between theories of hegemonic and inclusive masculinities.

Our research considers the extent to which contemporary performances of masculinity (e.g. increasing emotional intimacy between men) resonate with hegemonic and/or inclusive theories of masculinity in the context of the delivery of the Fit for LIFE programme in two Scottish prisons.

Masculinities in Sport and Prison Gymnasia

Sport and prison gymnasia (cf. Meek 2013) have significance in many aspects of prison life, including performances of gender. The importance of sport within prison as a context for creating certain types of bodies (Maycock 2018a) and as a space of intense competition between men in prisons has been highlighted in several studies. For example, weight lifting has been shown to be an important focus of activity in prison (Baumer and Meek 2018; Frey and Delaney 1996). De Viggiani (2012, 278) observes that:

> … [most people in custody were] preoccupied with the use of weights to build muscle bulk. When individuals spoke of the 'gymnasium,' they were usually referring to the weights room.

Reflecting research on gymnasia more broadly (cf. Andrews et al. 2005), prison gymnasia can be positive *and* negative spaces for people in custody. In his study within HMP Wellingborough, Crewe (2009, 436) observed how "people in custody emphasized the importance of the gymnasium in 'releasing that aggression', relieving anxieties and aiding sleep" and the ways in which status influenced opportunity to use certain equipment within the gymnasium, noting that high-status people in custody were "first to choose" (Crewe 2009, 260).

Crewe et al. (2014, 66) link the focus on gymnasia as places to build strength to the broader emotional regime of the prison: "Since it was a place where strength could be built and demonstrated, the gymnasium was a place which seemed to exemplify the prison's intense emotional regime". Several researchers (cf. De Viggiani 2012) have commented that men recognise that gymnasia are sites where 'competitive one-upmanship' may prevail, reflecting a wider dominance of certain performances of masculinity within sport (Wellard 2009). De Viggiani describes the atmosphere of the prison gymnasium he observed as "intimidating …

with a distinctly macho atmosphere" (2012, 278). Age is one important axis of stratification influencing prison gendered hierarchies that have a particular resonance in prison gymnasia.

These descriptions of men within prison gymnasia, reflect more mainstream views of hegemonic prison masculinities, describing them as places of competition and hierarchy in which certain bodies are privileged. However, a small number of researchers consider the possibility that prison gymnasia and sport in prison more generally might be contexts in which inclusive, or 'softer', forms of masculinity are evident. Andersons's theory of inclusive masculinity creates a conceptual context within which to explore the ways in which men bond through emotional, and tactile, intimacy. Crewe et al. (2014, 66–67), for example, highlight some supportive and emotionally engaged performances of masculinity within the gymnasium and associated sporting activities within prisons:

> ...in the ways that people in custody 'spot' for each other, in their mutual support and encouragement, it was also possible to discern sublimated forms of intimacy. Certainly, the vivid and joyful ways in which people in custody engaged in collective exercise, and the sheer amount of physical horseplay among younger people in custody, pointed to submerged emotional sentiments.

Earle and Phillips (2012, 148) describe how practices with often contradictory implications for masculinity can also be seen in gymnasia:

> Gym facilities undoubtedly help men survive incarceration and are highly valued because they offer men avenues for self-respect, health, and exercise, but the practices they foster also tend to reinforce an embodiment laced with anxious, sometimes narcissistic, undertones of control.

Context: The Fit for LIFE Programme

Before describing our fieldwork methods, we provide a brief context for the research. Our fieldwork was conducted within two Scottish prisons in which we iteratively adapted the community-based weight management and healthy living programme (FFIT) (Gray et al. 2013) in collaboration with physical education instructors (PEIs) working within the prison gymnasia. When delivered in Scottish professional football clubs, FFIT was successful in engaging hard-to-reach men at high risk of future ill-health and supporting them to make sustained improvements to their weight, diet and physical activity (Gray et al. 2018; Hunt et al. 2014a, b). The work we report here was undertaken as part of an iterative adaptation of FFIT to the prison setting (Maclean et al., in preparation), which aimed to support people in custody who were not already using the sports and physical activity facilities in the prisons to engage with prison gymnasia staff and facilities and make changes to their daily lives to increase physical activity, improve diet and, if appropriate, lose weight.

Fit for LIFE is a group-based 10-week programme adapted and optimised for the prison setting over four phases (Maycock et al. forthcoming). The weekly 'classroom' elements of the sessions cover topics such as healthy eating, goal setting and participants' week-on-week progress in following an incremental pedometer-based walking programme to increase their daily steps. The 'classroom' sessions are followed by a group-based physical activity session led by the PEIs, including circuits, football games, use of gym equipment, competitions and indoor tennis. Participants are also given suggested exercise routines for 'in-cell workouts' designed to support them to increase their strength and flexibility whilst locked up in their cell. Recruitment to the programme in both prisons was undertaken by the PEIs, who are responsible for the use of prison gymnasia and sports facilities by people in custody.

Methods

The fieldwork reported here was conducted within two prisons (Prison A and Prison B) during the second iteration of the Fit for LIFE programme between September 2013 and May 2014. Ethical approval was obtained from the relevant West of Scotland NHS, University of Glasgow and SPS ethics boards.

Participants ranged in age from 19 to 55. One participant described himself as homosexual; other participants tended not to discuss their sexuality, perhaps reflecting the fact that prison contexts are often considered homophobic (Richmond 1978) and heteronormative (Jenness and Fenstermaker 2014) environments. None of the participants were from a black or ethnic minority. This reflects the low numbers of ethnic minorities in Scottish prisons; official figures indicate that over 90% of the male Scottish prison population were white (Carnie et al. 2017).

Our research took a reflexive qualitative approach (Alvesson and Sköldberg 2017). Data were collected through observations of the majority of the weekly session deliveries of the Fit for LIFE programme ($n = 9$ at Prison A; $n = 6$ at Prison B). These observations were undertaken with the permission of participants, mostly by a male researcher (MM), although three sessions were observed by other (female) researchers (CG and AM). In addition, semi-structured one-to-one interviews were undertaken with programme participants ($n = 12$ at Prison A; $n = 9$ at Prison B) immediately after the end of the programme deliveries to explore participants' experiences of taking part in the programme in the context of prison life. The interviews were conducted (by MM) in rooms within the sports facilities and small interview rooms in the Halls (the residential areas where the participants lived), with members of staff nearby but not within earshot to enable participants to express their views in private. All interviews were digitally recorded with participants' written permission, transcribed by an external agency, and all transcripts were checked for accuracy. Inevitably, the sub-sample of participants who took part in interviews was self-selected. A considered effort was made to try to interview participants who had dropped out of the programme ($n = 3$), but this proved only possible with one participant as the other former participants did not want to take part in an interview and one had been released.

The observations of session deliveries allowed us to compare what participants said in the interviews about their experiences of participating with other men in the programme with the apparent dynamics between participants, and between participants and the PEIs, during the educational and physical activity part of the sessions. Interviews were also conducted with the PEI facilitators, but these are not reported here. Detailed field notes were taken immediately after each prison visit. These textual data (field notes and interview transcriptions) were analysed using Nvivo

10 to facilitate the organisation and management of the material. Analysis was conducted using a thematic approach and was led by MM, in consultation with members of the research team who had all reviewed a sub-sample of the transcripts. Coding relevant to this chapter was structured around: 'doing' masculinity within the context of the Fit for LIFE programme; and aspects of the performance of hegemonic and inclusive masculinities.

The chapter includes illustrative extracts of interview or observation data. All names and places have been changed and participants have been given pseudonyms. Some biographical details of participants have also been changed to prevent deductive disclosure of participants' identity and, for similar reasons, only broad (decade of age) rather than exact participant ages are provided.

Findings

We consider the contrasting, but complementary, views of prison masculinities within emerging from our session observations and post-programme interviews. Below, we first examine the ways in which participants described their experiences of the more hegemonic forms of masculinity that dominate much of prison life. We then explore performances of inclusive masculinity, as evident at different times, by different participants in the Fit for LIFE programme. Lastly, we examine: *when* inclusive masculinities emerge within group settings; *who* performs these; and *for* whom. It is important to note that issues of coercion and consent within prison research are complex (cf. Mcdermott 2013; Moser et al. 2004); those participating in the Fit for LIFE sessions had chosen to do so, and were generally positive about the programme and keen to attend. However, there were instances in which it appeared that certain participants did not want to be at a particular session, perhaps reflecting a participant's wider disengagement and detachment from publicly performed aspects of prison life.

Hegemonic Prison Masculinities Within the Wider Prison Context

During both programme deliveries and the post-programme interviews, participants regularly commented on various aspects of their lives within prison, providing insights into normative performances of prison masculinities. Such comments illuminated aspects of competition, hierarchy, violence, 'banter' (teasing and/or joking) and humour (Terry 1997). This normative masculine core relates to a matrix of gendered expectations that many men fail to meet, but most aspire to. James (30s, Prison A) alluded to this during his interview and indicated how such expectations shape not only how people in custody move, but also how they speak:

> I think people know by maybe, maybe the way you walk, your—even the way you speak. If you coming in and you speak like that, and you speak like… like some of the people I was describing earlier [younger people in custody], you're going get no respect from anybody.[1]

Thus, ways of walking and talking appear to have a bearing on the level of respect bestowed by other people in custody. During programme observations, participants also talked about the ways in which the prison context could be hostile and how penalties were bestowed for not adhering to the normative ways of 'being a man' in prison. James went on to say:

> we're in a hostile situation here [in prison], eh? And people don't want to speak forward in case the boy, two boys down does like that, "He's a fucking idiot," excuse my French.

Participants recognised ongoing dangers and potential for violence in various forms, although they also suggested that the prison environment was not always overtly violent. When bullying did occur, it was dealt with (often by force) by other people in custody. For example, Bruce (40s, Prison B) described how this worked in the Hall where he lived:

[1] All quotes have been changed from colloquial English into standard English.

> There was one guy in our Hall that was bullying. People used to come down to the gym quite a lot and he was like a big muscle. And about ten people in custody all battered him in the middle of the Hall… He's getting too big for his boots, and at the end of the day, it's a small environment, anybody can get to you in here.

Again, this extract points to certain expectations about how men should behave, closely associated with hegemonic performances of masculinity, with harsh, often violent, consequences for those who overstep or fail to adhere to these. These shaped the interactions between participants, particularly during the early sessions of the programme, as the extract from an observation field note below illustrates:

> At session one, when the people in custody came up to the gym they sat in groups relating to their Halls (which is quite easy to see given that each Hall has its own colour [of sweatshirt]). The men were clearly very apprehensive as they didn't know most of the other participants; I noticed a lot of them looking down throughout the session, there was very limited eye contact between one another, some had quite white knuckles as they were clenching their fists and were clearly very guarded and apprehensive at this initial stage of the programme. It is difficult to know whether this is due to them starting a new programme, because they don't know the other participants, or most likely a combination of these two factors.

The expectations of what a man should be like in prison also extended to the sorts of interests people in custody were expected to have. Sport and involvement in certain prison activities (such as education) were consistently important, with football being the most popular sport to play, watch and discuss. As a non-football player, John (50s, Prison A) found this challenging, suggesting that lack of interest in football may raise questions about his masculinity:

> Oh, you're not playing football? Oh, you're not a real… you're not a real man then. Tennis is for poofs.

For many people in custody, keeping fit and having a certain body shape was about protecting themselves in a context in which they might be attacked, as discussed in more detail elsewhere (Maycock 2018a). This often emerged when Fit for LIFE participants talked about their reasons for participating in the programme, as described here by Scott (20s, Prison A):

> The reason's obviously to stay fit, take care of yourself, you know? If anybody attacks you, you've got the strength, you've got the flexibility, you can do what you want. I think, well to be honest it's all about protecting yourself.

Cumulatively, these comments and observations give an impression of participants' experiences of being a man in these prisons, including the gendered expectations that existed and the perceived consequences of not conforming to these expectations. It is within this context that many participants took part in the Fit for LIFE programme, which for many was their first experience of using the prison gymnasium or sports facilities (or indeed of gyms in any context, including in the community). For some, as described below, this resulted in the development of new relationships and alternative performances of masculinities within later sessions of the Fit for LIFE programme.

Hegemonic Masculinities in the Fit for LIFE Programme

Multiple hierarchies were evident within and between Fit for LIFE participants. During programme sessions, status appeared to be associated with physical prowess and strength, but reputations—associations to families and gangs on the outside—were also relevant. For example, in mentioning being 'higher up', Adam (40s, Prison B) describes how prison hierarchies relate to pre-prison lives on the outside:

> See you could be like, somebody outside could be a gangster, do you know what I mean? So when they came in, do you know, what I mean, they'll be a bit higher up.

Age and sexuality seemed to be two critical factors shaping hierarchies observed during Fit for LIFE sessions, and in this context it appeared that younger people in custody dominate. Age was influential in shaping the nature of interactions during the Fit for LIFE programme, the types of people who made more routine use of the gymnasia facilities. In his post-programme interview, one of the oldest participants, John (50s, Prison A), described problems in accessing the weights he wanted to use:

> Even going to the gymnasium now, a lot of the time you can't get on the weights you want to get onto because it's too busy.

John's views contributed to his feelings of discomfort in using the gymnasium. That he viewed the gymnasium as 'busy' was a reflection of his position (and in some sense exclusion) as a consequence of the age hierarchies within the gymnasium. Other older participants talked in a similar way about being less comfortable there, in a space occupied largely by younger men. For example, Lewis (50+, Prison B) said:

> So I set goals and I step—and sometimes I get to certain places [such as the gym] and I say, "Oh well it's too much for me, I'm too old now!" And I'm realistic, if you understand what I'm saying?

Looking good, or at least better, was another consistent theme to emerge during discussions about gymnasium use. Scott (60s, Prison A) said:

> Everybody wants to go to the gymnasium. It's recreational, you feel better, and you want to look better. So the more gymnasium you get, the better.

In an all-male environment, 'looking good' or losing weight took certain forms. 'Looking good' in anticipation of their release from prison was an important motivator for many who took part in the programme, and use of the weights in the gymnasium was one of the main ways of achieving the types of bodies and associated strength considered desirable (Maycock 2018a).

Reflecting long-standing research within criminology exploring the homophobic nature of prison environments (cf. Richmond 1978), 'gay' was widely used as a pejorative term, reflecting the heteronormativity within both prisons. John (50s, Prison A) discussed some of the difficulties he had as a consequence of being openly gay, which resulted in him getting 'hassle' and feeling marginalised:

> ...because I'm gay and they know that. So they don't expect me to be sporty and... I get hassle every day.

Thus, within the context of the programme and the prison context more broadly, homophobia remains an important component of the performance of hegemonic masculinity. We return to the questions this raises for 'inclusive' prison masculinities in the discussion, through considering the ways in which the prison context shapes a different type of inclusive masculinity.

Competition Between Participants

Although the programme emphasised that men should be working to their own goals, competition between participants during programme sessions was an expression of men trying to (re)negotiate their position relative to other participants. This was expressed through statements and references to physical capacity and strength. During an end of programme interview, Rory (30s, Prison B) consistently expressed more hegemonic-referencing masculinities, in the ways in which he viewed himself in competition with other members of the group:

> I was hammering [beating] everybody from the word go. I was far superior to them all... I'm the sort of person, see once I get up there I don't like anybody beating me, you know?

Paul (40s, Prison B) focused on his personal achievements but was also quite competitive. It was important for him to be the "best in the group":

> I lost the most weight out of everyone. Well I done the fitness test today and I was above average. But I was kind of determined to actually be the best in the group.

Observation fieldnotes indicate that during programme sessions, words with aggressive undertones (e.g. 'hammering', 'smash', 'beast') were regularly used by participants when discussing competition within the group. A number of sub-groups formed among the participants, often reflecting the Hall they lived in and, as Adam (40s, Prison B) describes, competition between these sub-groups was sometimes apparent during programme sessions:

> Yes, because we were and wanting to "right, come on, whose team are we going in, we'll beat you this week."

Such forms of competition within the group resonate with aspects of competition more broadly within the prisons, between different Halls and pre-prison associations, and with Connell's notion of hegemonic masculinity within which hierarchy and competition is formative.

Banter

Certain types of speech emerged as a critical factor in shaping prison masculinities. Participants and staff engaged in forms of 'banter' shaped by the prison context. Banter was frequently recorded during session observations:

> Angus [a PEI] was particularly good at talking with the participants and trying to engage them this week, he has a good way with the participants despite telling me that he was apprehensive at the start. Angus was the focus of a lot of banter [about his weight and losing a recent football match between staff and people in custody] but he didn't seem to mind this so much, he interacted quite easily with the participants. (Field note extract, October 2013)

Banter within the prison has several functions: it is an important part of everyday interactions and can be a positive and enjoyable part of daily life. For example, Jack (20s, Prison A) felt that banter was a means through which to feel comfortable with other people in custody:

> But that's a good thing because it's banter. It gets people comfortable with each other. They get to know, well he's not there just to sit and slag you, he's not there just try and bring you down, he's having a laugh.

However, more frequently participants indicated that, within the prisons, banter was a form of policing which enforced and emphasised hierarchies between people in custody. Adam (40s, Prison B) talked about the dangers of banter, and how it has the potential to escalate into violence:

> ...it's just, it's the way it goes in the jail, do you know what I mean? Everybody, you get a little laugh ...but you've got to watch with the banter in here. See a bit of banter could lead to, end up a fight. ... because people end up taking it the wrong way and they think "Are you taking the piss with me?" And it starts a lot of problems.

Harry (20s, Prison A, Exit interview) talked at some length about the negative consequences of banter for him and the difficulties he had with banter within the group whilst undertaking the programme. Ultimately, this banter resulted in him leaving the programme midway, before some of the dynamics of the group had changed (as described later):

> They used to just tease me, like "He can't do that" and everything, you know what I mean? And they'd laugh about it. Like I say, it wasn't anything about the course that made me leave. It was just a certain couple of boys and that—they would laugh at people that were not as fit as them and just childish things.

Here we see how banter can function as a way to marginalise participants who are 'not as fit' or as competent within a particular context. The quote illustrates that it is not only sporting competence, but also levels of fitness and men's bodies, that influenced the hierarchies evident amongst participants in the programme. Having explored aspects of hegemonic masculinities as evident or experienced during programme delivery, we now turn to consider the occasions in which men's accounts also included reference to contrasting, more inclusive, performances of masculinity.

Inclusive Masculinities Within the Fit for LIFE Programme

Many of the aspects of the performance of hegemonic masculinities within the Fit for LIFE programme appear to mirror what men said about daily life within other parts of the prisons. However, as the programme progressed, some differences in the ways that participants appeared to relate to and support each other, or relate to staff became evident, demonstrating more inclusive performances of masculinity.

Relationships Between Participants and PEIs During Fit for LIFE

The relationships between participants and PEIs were in some ways distinct from those they mentioned between people in custody and prison staff in other contexts within the prisons, and on the halls in particular. Warmth and encouragement between the participants and PEIs was evident. For example, if a participant made progress in relation to his fitness in some way, the PEIs often gave positive feedback and showed evident pride and satisfaction in this.

At times, the hierarchies between the participants and PEIs seemed relatively insignificant, although they were always evident in some way. For example, amongst themselves, the PEIs referred to one another (and other prison staff and the research team) using first names, whilst they always referred to participants by their surnames or nicknames. This subtle manifestation of the hierarchy between staff and people in custody was observed consistently throughout our visits to both prisons.

The atmosphere during the Fit for LIFE programme in some ways reflects the fact that the participants have chosen to spend time on a programme within the gymnasium; indeed time in the gymnasium is constructed generally, and recognised by both staff and inmates, as a privilege within the prison. Within the gymnasium during Fit for LIFE sessions, relatively harmonious and supportive relationships between staff and participants were consistently seen, although they were still expected to conform to appropriate codes of behaviour.

Relationships Between Participants

Participation in the programme and increasing use of the prison gymnasium and sports facilities also provided an opportunity for participants to develop more positive and supportive relationships between themselves. As Ben (20s, Prison B) observed:

> Down here man [in the gymnasia during FFL deliveries], it's a bit of a more relaxed atmosphere [than the rest of the prison], know what I mean?... the guys can get a laugh with each other, they can train together, things like that.

The use of sports facilities in prison provides an important means of passing time, keeping fit, trying to lose weight and achieving a certain body type. However, there was also a sense that, at certain protected times (such as during the Fit for Life programme), these facilities could be a space in which it was possible to both exercise and spend time with other men like them, who they may not normally be able to connect with in a relatively relaxed context. Alan (40s, Prison A) commented on this important incentive in going to the programme:

> ...you get a bit a camaraderie with other guys—guys I hadn't met before in the Hall that were in different flats [levels within a Hall], know?

For some participants, the relationships possible during the Fit for LIFE programme appear to be the main focus of their time there.

Within the Fit for LIFE programme, despite the individualistic and competitive responses which some participants expressed during the early weeks of the programme (see above), others recognised a greater degree of egalitarianism amongst group members. For Ethan (20s, Prison A), this was an important reason why he was able to 'fit in'; he viewed other participants as being at the 'same level':

> As I say it was just good that everybody was at the same level and everybody was doing the same thing. Everybody fitted in together, know what I mean?

This section has highlighted examples of more inclusive masculinities and supportive relationships that were evident during deliveries of the programme in both prisons. Contrasting Ethan's views here with Rory's more competitive and non-inclusive engagement with the group above, raises a number of questions about inclusive masculinity which we examine below.

When and for Whom Does Inclusive Masculinity Manifest Itself?

During the observations of the initial weeks of the delivery of the programme, participants appeared quite guarded and reticent to interact, both with the PEIs and their peers. However, over time this began to change. As Jack (30s, Prison A) noted when talking about future programmes, it took time for participants to feel comfortable within the group:

> …it'll take them a few weeks to get in to that role that everybody else is doing, to fit, feel that they're fitting in.

We illustrate the ways in which more inclusive performances of masculinity began to emerge as the programme progressed in relation to two participants, James and John. These two men both discussed in some detail their experiences of making a transition, through engaging with other programme participants, from a more typical and more guarded style of interacting with other men, to finding an acceptance amongst their co-participants that they had not experienced previously within the prison. John (50s, Prison A) talked about the isolation he experienced, particularly because of being open about his sexuality (he defined himself as gay). Taking part in the programme seemed particularly transformative for John. Despite finding prison life hard and being excluded from much of prison life, John found a kind of acceptance within the group that was mediated through banter:

> So… you see, when I first came in [to prison], they wouldn't have done that [included him]… although it's taking the piss, it's including me, you know? Which they would never have… I would just have been ostracised. And taking part in that group changed that quite a bit.

This again highlights the complexity of banter within the prison context. As a consequence of taking part in the programme, John experienced a new sense of inclusion and found a way to take part in physical activity in the prison sports facilities during the Fit for LIFE programme that he was at ease with, with other people in custody. In a post-programme interview, John said that this was initially through participation in the programme, and subsequently reinforced by participation in an over-40s exercise class. For John the gymnasium became somewhere he began to feel safe, allowing him to develop new friendships and in some way to find a 'place' within the prison. Positioned towards the bottom of the within-prison masculine hierarchy due to his sexuality, age, body shape, finding a place within the prison was something that John had previously struggled with. However, taking part in Fit for LIFE helped him to feel more accepted:

> I think I'm more included now. I think they've included me as one of the gang and, you know, still stop and talk to me, whereas before they might've just have walked right past me. Again, it's included me more because I've taken part so I'm one o' the gang.

For James (30s, Prison A), being part of a group with other participants was also influential in his transformation to interacting in ways that were more aligned with inclusive performances of masculinity. Prior to entering prison, James ran his own business, was very much the head of his household, and had not spent much time in groups of men. Through participation in FIT for LIFE, James said he felt more able to listen to others:

> Listening more and being content when people are speaking rather than just listening to my own voice. I was never, ever part of a—a group of lads when I was growing up.

Listening to other participants' views and opinions, in ways that he had not previously done on the Halls, was a new, and positive, experience for James and he went on to speak about the value to him of being in the group:

> I've never been in a group like this before. I thought it was great… when I was in this group I was listening to the others. I'm listening to Ryan, and I'm listening to Ethan, and then Peter would say something. I liked the environment. The environment was good. Well that's what I'm saying, it all goes back to the group. FIT Club's [colloquial programme name] brought me into the group situation… And [now] I'll sit and listen to somebody.

When a sense of a group identity had formed and participants had got to know each another better, they seemed to develop more trusting relationships (at least within the session deliveries). Their experiences illustrate that, for some men at least, taking part in the programme, and thereby engaging with other men in custody within a(n increasingly trusting) group context, was a meaningful experience with implications for the ways they performed masculinity within some contexts within the prisons.

Discussion

We have examined the ways in which the context of taking part in a group-based, PEI-led physical activity and healthy living programme (Fit for LIFE) over several weeks facilitated a wider range of performances of masculinity and relationships. Our findings illustrate the importance of different settings in shaping performances of prison masculinities. This research illuminates a complex, changing plurality of performances of masculinity, which included displays of hegemonic, marginal, complicit, subordinate (Connell 1995), as well as aspects of inclusive, masculinity (Anderson 2009). Both theories of masculinity have received criticism, leading to refinement (hegemonic masculinity by Demetriou (2001), Wetherell and Edley (1999), and inclusive masculinity by de Boise (2014)). Both theories recognise multiple masculinities, but differ in the extent to which homophobia is an organising principle in the establishment and maintenance of hierarchies of masculinity. In this prison-based research, we observed more hegemonic manifestations of masculinities as the group first met and participated in the programme, and some more inclusive manifestations as the group coalesced, facilitating semi-public displays of more trusting and relaxed interactions and greater acceptance of an openly gay man, at least in the experience described by participants who self-identified as homosexual.

We would argue that neither hegemonic nor inclusive masculinity theory fully accounts for the diversity of masculinities evident within these men's experiences of taking part in this group-based programme within two Scottish prisons. Anderson develops the notion of homohysteria (Anderson 2009), and views homophobia as having increasingly limited relevance to the performance of masculinity. However, in these prison contexts at least, homophobia remains part of the performance of prison masculinities. The aspects of inclusive masculinity which we observed or men themselves discussed focus on male bonding through emotional and physical intimacy, as opposed to Anderson's focus on reduced homophobia and homohysteria. The camaraderie and support mentioned by many participants is also described in the support, encouragement and intimacy, which Crewe et al. (2014) discuss in their analysis of interactions in an English prison gymnasium. For some participants in our study, the programme constituted a space in which the performance of more inclusive masculinities was possible, albeit alongside the competitive, hierarchical hegemonic masculinities that are initially more obvious in these spaces. Within the context of the 10 weeks of the Fit for LIFE programme, more inclusive forms of masculinity (expressed particularly through greater social and emotional intimacy) became more evident as the programme progressed.

Our data illustrate that prison gyms can be more or less intimidating and accommodating of a range of masculine performances, depending on the context. Our analysis suggests that health promotion interventions adapted specifically for prisons are potentially spaces in which it is possible to observe a wider range of masculinities being performed. This is consistent with other research; for example, in a study in a North American low-security prison, Buckaloo et al. (2009) highlight that prisoners who exercised regularly had lower reported levels of depression; Martos-García et al. (2009) in a two-year ethnographic study in a high-security Spanish prison explore diverse meanings of sport in prison, while Meek and Lewis (2014) in a study with women in the English prison state again highlight the positive impacts of engaging with physical activities in custody through promoting desistance from crime.

This chapter demonstrates the potential for programmes such as Fit for LIFE to offer positive social and emotional, as well as physical, interactions for some men in custody. The ability to express and experience a greater degree of social and emotional intimacy, perhaps only within limited contexts within prison life is important, given the evidence of the negative impact of incarceration for physical, mental and emotional health (Herbert et al. 2012; Schnittker and John 2007; WHO 2014).

Limitations

Earle and Phillips (2012) have discussed the limitations of prison research in relation to the degree to which participation or immersion in prison life is curtailed. Most of our time in the gymnasium was during the deliveries of the programme and, whilst some of the participant interviews were conducted in their residential Halls, there were very limited opportunities to observe how men behaved and interacted with others in custody outside the gymnasium. Accounts of prison masculinities outside of programme deliveries are thus largely second-hand, rather than directly observed, albeit conveyed through the accounts of the men themselves. Thus, in focusing on the context of the Fit for LIFE programme, this chapter can only provide a partial account of prison masculinities, which may not be generalizable to other men in custody, and in particular to performances of masculinity within prison halls where people in custody spend the majority of their time.

Initially, it was challenging to gain participants' trust at Prisons A and B; perhaps unsurprisingly they tended to be suspicious of anyone new, whose behaviour might deviate from what is considered 'normal' within a given prison. However, repeated visits to the prisons over several months, as well as being researchers not directly involved within the criminal justice system (at the time of the fieldwork), was an advantage. So while we were 'outsiders' (following Simmel's (1950) notion of the 'stranger'), this was within certain limits; we were neither people in custody nor members of staff. For many programme participants, we were located somewhere in-between their constructs of prison staff and people in custody, in a liminal space occupied by 'civvies' (civilians), which had implications for the conversations and relationships we were able to develop (these themes are explored in more detail in Maycock (2018b)). We had a good and close working relationship with the PEIs, which may have influenced the ways in which participants interacted and disclosed or concealed certain feelings or insights both in relation to the programme and wider prison lives. Liebling (2001) considers issues of 'taking sides' in prison research, which also has implications for our research and the research material we were able to collect.

As Sallee and Harris III indicate, the researcher's gender also has implications for "data collection and rapport building with male participants" (2011, 409). The research team consisted of three women and one man, with the latter undertaking most of the fieldwork and all of the interviews that constitute the data for analysis in this chapter.

Conclusion

This chapter has shown that a group-based physical activity and healthy living programme, Fit for LIFE, delivered by experienced physical education instructors in two Scottish prisons, appeared to be a context which facilitated the transformation of the performance of masculinity within prisons, at least during later programme session. Based on observations and interviews collected between September 2013 and May 2014, our findings illustrate a diversity of performances of masculinity in this context which contrasts with most existing prison masculinities literature which has tended to emphasise hegemonic, hypermasculinity in the prison environment (cf. Mosher and Tomkins 1988; Toch 1998). Our utilisation of both hegemonic and inclusive theories of masculinity to analyse the data contrasts with a more oppositional application of these theories. Our analysis of masculinities performed within the context of the FIT for LIFE programme illustrates how both hegemonic and inclusive masculinities can be evident in the same context, at different times.

Despite well-developed templates for various performances of masculinity, for example those associated with hierarchies around age and the building of certain bodies (Maycock 2018a), we argue that health promotion interventions can be spaces in which a greater diversity of masculine performances are evident, including more inclusive performances (see also (Hunt et al. 2013; Wyke et al. 2015) Our analysis illustrates how the prison context has the potential to shape specific manifestations of hegemonic and inclusive masculinity. We have described the evolution in the performance of masculinity over the FIT for LIFE programme, showing how such facilitated programmes may promote more positive supportive relationships between men in custody and constitute purposeful activity within custody.

References

Alvesson, M., & Sköldberg, K. (2017). *Reflexive methodology: New vistas for qualitative research*. Sage.

Anderson, E. (2008). Inclusive masculinity in a fraternal setting. *Men and Masculinities, 10*, 604–620.

Anderson, E. (2009). *Inclusive masculinity: The changing nature of masculinities*. London: Routledge.

Anderson, E., & Mccormack, M. (2018). Inclusive masculinity theory: Overview, reflection and refinement. *Journal of Gender Studies, 27*, 547–561.

Anderson, E., & McGuire, R. (2010). Inclusive masculinity theory and the gendered politics of men's rugby. *Journal of Gender Studies, 19*, 249–261.

Andrews, G. J., Sudwell, M. I., & Sparkes, A. C. (2005). Towards a geography of fitness: An ethnographic case study of the gym in British bodybuilding culture. *Social Science & Medicine, 60*, 877–891.

Baumer, H., & Meek, R. (2018). Sporting masculinities in prison. In M. Maycock & K. Hunt (Eds.), *New perspectives on prison masculinities*. Springer.

Buckaloo, B. J., Krug, K. S., & Nelson, K. B. (2009). Exercise and the low-security inmate: Changes in depression, stress, and anxiety. *The Prison Journal, 89*, 328–343.

Bunn, C., Wyke, S., Gray, C. M., Maclean, A., & Hunt, K. (2016). 'Coz football is what we all have': Masculinities, practice, performance and effervescence in a gender-sensitised weight-loss and healthy living programme for men. *Sociology of Health & Illness*, n/a–n/a.

Butler, J. (1990). *Gender trouble: Feminism and the subversion of identity*. New York; London: Routledge.

Carnie, J., Broderick, R., Cameron, J., Downie, D., & Williams, G. (2017). *Prisoner survey*. Scottish Prisoner Service.

Connell, R. (1995). *Masculinities*. Cambridge: Polity.

Connell, R. W., & Messerschmidt, J. W. (2005). Hegemonic masculinity: Rethinking the concept. *Gender & Society, 19*, 829–859.

Courtenay, W. H. (2000). Engendering health: A social constructionist examination of men's health beliefs and behaviors. *Psychology of Men & Masculinity, 1*, 4.

Crewe, B. (2009). *The prisoner society: Power, adaptation, and social life in an English prison*. Oxford: Oxford University Press.

Crewe, B., Warr, J., Bennett, P., & Smith, A. (2014). The emotional geography of prison life. *Theoretical Criminology, 18*, 56–74.

De Boise, S. (2014). I'm not homophobic, "I've got gay friends": Evaluating the validity of inclusive masculinity. *Men and Masculinities*. https://doi.org/10.1177/1097184X14554951.

De Viggiani, N. (2012). Trying to be something you are not: Masculine performances within a prison setting. *Men and Masculinities*. https://doi.org/10.1177/1097184X12448464.

Demetriou, D. Z. (2001). Connell's concept of hegemonic masculinity: A critique. *Theory and Society, 30*, 337–361.

Earle, R., & Phillips, C. (2012). Digesting men? Ethnicity, gender and food: Perspectives from a 'prison ethnography'. *Theoretical Criminology, 16*, 141–156.

Emslie, C., Ridge, D., Ziebland, S., & Hunt, K. (2006). Men's accounts of depression: Reconstructing or resisting hegemonic masculinity? *Social Science & Medicine, 62*, 2246–2257.

Frey, J. H., & Delaney, T. (1996). The role of leisure participation in prison. *Journal of Offender Rehabilitation, 23*, 79–89.

Gough, B. (2006). Try to be healthy, but don't forgo your masculinity: Deconstructing men's health discourse in the media. *Social Science & Medicine, 63*, 2476–2488.

Gray, C., Hunt, K., Mutrie, N., Anderson, A., Leishman, J., Dalgarno, L., & Wyke, S. (2013). Football fans in training: The development and optimization of an intervention delivered through professional sports clubs to help men lose weight, become more active and adopt healthier eating habits. *BMC Public Health, 13*, 232.

Gray, C. M., Wyke, S., Zhang, R., Anderson, A. S., Barry, S., Boyer, N., et al. (2018). Long-term weight loss trajectories following participation in a randomised controlled trial of a weight management programme for men delivered through professional football clubs: A longitudinal cohort study and economic evaluation. *International Journal of Behavioral Nutrition and Physical Activity, 15*, 60.

Herbert, K., Plugge, E., Foster, C., & Doll, H. (2012). Prevalence of risk factors for non-communicable diseases in prison populations worldwide: A systematic review. *The Lancet, 379*, 1975–1982.

Hunt, K., Mccann, C., Gray, C., Mutrie, N., & Wyke, S. (2013). "You've got to walk before you run". Positive evaluations of a walking programme as part of a gender sensitised weight management programme delivered to men through professional football clubs. *Heath Psychology, 32*, 57–65.

Hunt, K., Gray, C., Maclean, A., Smillie, S., Bunn, C., & Wyke, S. (2014a). Do weight management programmes delivered at professional football clubs attract and engage high risk men? A mixed-methods study. *BMC Public Health, 14*, 50.

Hunt, K., Wyke, S., Gray, C. M., Anderson, A. S., Brady, A., Bunn, C., et al. (2014b). A gender-sensitised weight loss and healthy living programme for overweight and obese men delivered by Scottish Premier League football clubs (FFIT): A pragmatic randomised controlled trial. *The Lancet, 383*, 1211–1221.

Jenness, V., & Fenstermaker, S. (2014). Agnes goes to prison: Gender authenticity, transgender inmates in prisons for men, and pursuit of "the real deal". *Gender & Society, 28*, 5–31.

Kimmel, M. S. (2002). Masculinity as homophobia. In E. Disch (Ed.), *Reconstructing gender: A multicultural anthology*. London: McGrawHill.

Knight, R., Shoveller, J. A., Oliffe, J. L., Gilbert, M., Frank, B., & Ogilvie, G. (2012). Masculinities, 'guy talk' and 'manning up': A discourse analysis of how young men talk about sexual health. *Sociology of Health & Illness, 34*, 1246–1261.

Liebling, A. (2001). Whose Side are We on? Theory, Practice and Allegiances in Prisons Research. *British Journal of Criminology, 41*(3), 472–484.

Martos-García, D., Devís-Devís, J., & Sparkes, A. C. (2009). Sport and physical activity in a high security Spanish prison: An ethnographic study of multiple meanings. *Sport, Education and Society, 14*, 77–96.

Maycock, M. (2018a). "They're all up in the gym and all that, tops off, fake tan." Embodied masculinities, bodywork and resistance within two British prisons. In M. Maycock (Ed.), *New perspectives on prison masculinities*. London: Palgrave.

Maycock, M. (2018b). 'What sort of jumper is that, your wife has terrible taste mate'. Exploring the importance of positionality within ethnographic research conducted alongside a public health programme in three scottish prisons. In E. Garnett, J. Reynolds, & S. Milton (Eds.), *Ethnographies and health: Reflections on empirical and methodological entanglements*. Cham: Springer International Publishing.

Mcdermott, B. E. (2013). Coercion in research: Are prisoners the only vulnerable population? *Journal of the American Academy of Psychiatry and the Law Online, 41*, 8–13.

Meek, R. (2013). *Sport in prison: Exploring the role of physical activity in penal practices*. London: Routledge.

Meek, R., & Lewis, G. (2014). The impact of a sports initiative for young men in prison: Staff and participant perspectives. *Journal of Sport & Social Issues, 38*, 95–123.

Moser, D. J., Arndt, S., Kanz, J. E., Benjamin, M. L., Bayless, J. D., Reese, R. L., et al. (2004). Coercion and informed consent in research involving prisoners. *Comprehensive Psychiatry, 45*, 1–9.

Mosher, D. L., & Tomkins, S. S. (1988). Scripting the macho man: Hypermasculine socialization and enculturation. *Journal of Sex Research, 25*, 60–84.

Richmond, K. (1978). Fear of homosexuality and modes of rationalisation in male prisons. *The Australian and New Zealand Journal of Sociology, 14*, 51–57.

Sallee, M. W., & Harris, F., III. (2011). Gender performance in qualitative studies of masculinities. *Qualitative Research, 11*.

Schnittker, J., & John, A. (2007). Enduring stigma: The long-term effects of incarceration on health. *Journal of Health and Social Behavior, 48*, 115–130.

Schofield, T., Connell, R. W., Walker, L., Wood, J. F., & Butland, D. L. (2000). Understanding men's health and illness: A gender-relations approach to policy, research, and practice. *Journal of American College Health, 48*, 247–256.

Simmel, G. (1950). *The sociology of Georg Simmel.* Trans. K. H. Wolff. Glencoe, IL: Free Press.

Sloan, C., Conner, M., & Gough, B. (2015). How does masculinity impact on health? A quantitative study of masculinity and health behavior in a sample of UK men and women. *Psychology of Men & Masculinity, 16*, 206.

Terry, C. M. (1997). The function of humor for prison inmates. *Journal of Contemporary Criminal Justice, 13*, 23–40.

Toch, H. (1998). Hypermasculinity and prison violence. In L. H. Bowker (Ed.), *Masculinities and violence*. Thousand Oaks: Sage.

Verdonk, P., Seesing, H., & De Rijk, A. (2010). Doing masculinity, not doing health? A qualitative study among dutch male employees about health beliefs and workplace physical activity. *BMC Public Health, 10*, 712.

Wellard, I. (2009). *Sport, masculinities and the body*. London: Routledge.

West, C., & Zimmerman, D. H. (1987). Doing gender. *Gender & Society, 1*, 125–151.

Wetherell, M., & Edley, N. (1999). Negotiating hegemonic masculinity: Imaginary positions and psycho-discursive practices. *Feminism & Psychology, 9*, 335–356.

WHO. (2014). *Prisons and health*. Copenhagen: WHO.

Wyke, S., Hunt, K., Gray, C. M., Fenwick, E., Bunn, C., Donnan, P. T., et al. (2015). Football Fans in Training (FFIT): A randomised controlled trial of a gender-sensitised weight loss and healthy living programme for men – End of study report. *Public Health Research*.

14

More Than Just a Game: The Impact of a Prison Football Team on Physical and Social Well-Being in a Welsh Prison

Jamie Grundy and Rosie Meek

Introduction

This chapter is inspired by and draws from a larger project which culminated in a series of semi-structured interviews with the players who represented HMP Prescoed FC in the Gwent Central Division Two for the 2018/2019 season, in South Wales. The interest in the original project was stimulated by the first author's own experience of playing as an amateur footballer in the 1990s against prison teams in the north of England. Although initially apprehensive about playing in prisons and against prisoners, it soon became clear through these early experiences that the prison

J. Grundy (✉)
Inside Out Support Wales, Wales, UK
e-mail: jamie@jamiegrundy.net

R. Meek
Department of Law and Criminology, Royal Holloway University of London, Surrey, UK
e-mail: r.meek@rhul.ac.uk

© The Author(s) 2021

M. Maycock et al. (eds.), *Issues and Innovations in Prison Health Research*, Palgrave Studies in Prisons and Penology, https://doi.org/10.1007/978-3-030-46401-1_14

teams contained players who tended to shared more similarities than differences to the players in the visiting team. The second author's introduction to the power of prison football came through her affiliation with Ian Wright's Football Behind Bars initiative at HMYOI Feltham (Sky TV 2009), which led to her involvement in evaluating the impact of the TV show's legacy project: using football to engage young men in a holistic programme providing preparation for their release from prison, supporting routes into education, training, work experience and other resettlement pathways (Meek 2012). For both authors, since those formative years, and now as professionals working in the field of criminal justice, we still see football in prison offering a common ground and a way, not only to break down barriers but to promote a wide range of additional other positive outcomes associated with prison sport, with the ultimate aim of supporting rehabilitation (Grundy 2019; Meek 2013, 2018). Indeed, in the foreword to the book that details HMP Prescoed's footballing endeavours, former Wales goalkeeper Neville Southall says: "… even when everything is taken from you, football is sometimes the only thing that remains…" (Grundy 2019, 3). As Southall says, exercise has often been used to help people with their mental health and this emerges as particularly true of football at Prescoed: "The prisoners playing the game may not know it, but they are being prepared for a life beyond the prison walls and football offers them tools to reintegrate successfully into the community" (Grundy 2019, 3). This ex-professional footballer's words reflect our broader conceptualisation of prison health, one which recognises the importance of the various forms of mental and physical health promotion that take place beyond a prison's healthcare department. The impacts of these forms of health promotion may not be obviously observed and measured as a traditional health outcome but they have the potential to have powerful and long-lasting effects both within and outside the prison walls.

Background to HMP Prescoed

HMP Prescoed was originally built in 1939, constructed by prison labourers and serving as an open borstal for the first years of its existence. It was only formally purchased by the Home Office in 1945, as it had previously been a farm. After this it became a detention centre in 1964 and then changed to an open youth custody centre in 1983. It became an open young offender institution in 1988, taking Category D adult males a few years later. Since 2004, it has been exclusively an open prison for adult males. HMP Prescoed currently has two grass football pitches, both hidden from the main prison camp and hidden from public view. The pitches are thought to be a historical remnant from its time as a post-war youth borstal where physical activity was very much a part of its daily routine. Prior to this, Prescoed was, like so much in the surrounding area, a farm and it is assumed the pitches were the previous pastures for grazing cattle. Now the only prisoner football team in Wales plays on a number of firsts. Prescoed's is the only grass pitch in a Welsh prison, and it is the only full-size pitch too, either grass or synthetic, in a Welsh prison. According to the men residing in the prison, this uniqueness does not go unnoticed: "It's interesting too where the football pitches are located. It's away from the camp, so that you can't see the prison when you are there. You forget where you are. I suppose you forget you're in prison" (Grundy 2019, 46).

The description of Prescoed from its senior staff is that it is a working prison and a lot of its current population are employed in various jobs within the jail to help it function, such as cleaning, catering, recycling and more. Some are released on daily licence (RoTL) for work placements in the community, giving the men valuable work experience, and an opportunity to experience the outside world, albeit temporarily, in efforts to prepare them for their imminent release. Whilst there is plenty of staff at Prescoed, in a variety of prison officer and civilian roles, they are not always as visible as they would be in a closed prison. In fact, at Prescoed, it is sometimes difficult to distinguish between prisoner and staff member. Often it is only the uniform or gender which helps.

The impression given—at least to the first author as a result of his extended time located within the prison—is that it is an establishment with less focus on punishment and more focus on rehabilitation, those two competing priorities of a modern prison. The men residing at HMP Prescoed tend to be within the last two years of their sentences and will inevitably have undergone numerous rehabilitative courses and programmes to get them to the status of a Category D prisoner. We know from broader prisons literature, hundreds of inspectorate reports, official data and first-hand accounts that prisons are notoriously unhealthy, brutal and pessimistic places. But the idea of a location or activity within a prison environment, where participants are able to feel, temporarily at least, some sense of freedom, some form of hope or an opportunity to celebrate positive identity is offered, is important and the impact of this beyond the pitch should not be underestimated.

Methodological Approach

The broader project from which this chapter has been based was supported by National Sporting Heritage, which sustains a range of community projects with the aim of commemorating different forms of sports heritage. The project aimed to celebrate the voices of the prisoner footballers and, with the approval of the Ministry of Justice and the prison governor, the first author immersed himself in the project: turning up to each weekly training session and on a Saturday to get a feel for the team for approximately 16 weeks. During this time, the author was at least a bi-weekly visitor to the prison, attending training sessions and league matches, and supporting the additional responsibilities that come with the operation of a football team. The staff and the players were equally intrigued by and supportive of the first author's presence, and through this regular contact, a sense of trust was established. Once the project aims were introduced, a total of 11 of the players expressed an interest in participating. Throughout the 2018–2019 season, the first author was able to share in the trials and tribulations of being an arms-length participant for many of Prescoed's games by immersing himself in that specific feature of the prison as best he could as a relative outsider. Uniquely for a researcher though, this involved spending time with the players in the changing room before and after games, as well as participating in running the line, appealing decisions, celebrating the goals scored and commiserating the goals conceded—and ultimately becoming a member of the team itself:

> So I was there each week and I waited until the time was right to start interviewing the players. Then when I turned up one Saturday and it looked like Prescoed were going to be short of players, one of the players greeted me warmly with the words, 'Get your fucking boots on Grundy, we're one short'. At that point I knew I was in! (Grundy 2019, 6)

Having established trust and rapport with the men who represented the team, and in order not to conflict with the prison's daily regime, players were invited to participate in individual semi-structured interviews during the evening and weekends, according to their work, family or other prison commitments. The research approach was sensitive to the first author's status as an 'outsider' who had not been deprived of his liberty and who could return home at the end of his working day (Drake et al. 2005) and yet something of an 'insider' in terms of his status within the team.

Interviews took place in semi-private interview rooms located within the prison and were digitally recorded and transcribed verbatim. The resulting interview transcripts were checked by the prisoners themselves for accuracy, and all identifying features and names were removed. The resulting narratives represent the stories of the players that make up HMP Prescoed FC, the only prisoner football team in Wales.

Why Focus on a Prison Football Team?

Although all six prisons in Wales engage in sport, physical education and recreation, in 2019 only HMP Prescoed had the ability to field a football team playing in a local league, primarily because it is Wales's only 'open' prison. Prison inspection reports, held every two to three years and which analyse and monitor all aspects of prison life, mention the presence of football at Prescoed only in passing, suggesting that the initiative aids with efforts to reintegrate into the community (Her Majesty's Inspectorate of Prisons and Estyn 2018). To date, the local press appears to have had no knowledge of the team or its results. There is as much information as one would imagine on the league website: fixtures, league tables and scores only.

The HMP Prescoed football team is thought to have first entered the Gwent Central League in the 1990s and has remained a member ever since. Recollections from players of other clubs from that time refer to the immaculate pitch as being one of the best they'd played on. At that time, permanent ground staff worked with prisoners on work placement to maintain the pitches. Now, it plays a significant part in the regime of the prison and goes some way in attempting to reflect the 'normality'[1] of the world outside.

The impact on the broader culture of the prison may also be what the football pitch and membership of a 'normal' league at Prescoed represents. As one player explained, "Football, they can't take that away from you." It also represents an area of choice in a place where being deprived of one's liberty comes with the removal of the ability to make personal decisions. In Prescoed, some of the players are able to get brightly coloured boots sent to them from a mail order catalogue or from family, rather than wear the prison-issued basic black ones. Through this, they are beginning to rediscover and practice their ability to make personal choices—funds permitting.

In reflection, beyond the simple logistical challenges that ethnographical research in a prison presents, this project presented a number of challenges in order for an effective research project to take place. Important to this was the knowledge and experience of the researcher of both the subject of football and of being a grassroots footballer, both of which allowed him to play a part and participate in some of the activities and football conversations that helped to build relationships which would aid the research process. He was aware there could be adverse reactions in

[1] "The principle of normality", advocated for in the Nelson Mandela Rules (United National Office on Drugs and Crime 2015) suggests that making prison feel as normal as possible helps make the transition back to the community easier.

shifting from 'the football guy' to asking to interview the prisoners themselves because, for all the men, potentially the last time they had been interviewed was by the police. In line with the requirements of the National Research Committee, the participants would be issued with a time-bound, voluntarily informed Research Consent Form and Participant Information Sheet giving further information on the research project. This process was shown to be successful because an additional participant came forward with whom the author had not cultivated a relationship similar to the other participants. However, when this person saw the words "Ministry of Justice" on these documents, he chose not to participate. This was the only research participant withdrawal. The author therefore felt that the decision to immerse himself in the life of the football team over a sustained period of 16 weeks was instrumental in the success of the project.

Findings

The following text is comprised of research notes and quotes accumulated by the first author, developed into a narrative. The material seeks to demonstrate how football appears to mean different but important things to the individual players. These individuals come together as a unit, participating in both training and football each week and the motivations of doing so may vary according to the different players, but they operate as a team, even though they are thrown together, not by strategic design or tactical team selection, but by the simple fact of being footballers serving a prison sentence in the same jail. These extracts are a combination of field notes, direct quotes and material reproduced from Grundy's original publication (Grundy 2019), all of which serve to highlight the multifaceted purpose and features of the prison football team. In particular, this narrative highlights and develops the primary themes generated by the research, including those of collaboration and team skills, respect, hope and emotion.

Each Saturday, several non-footballers come to act as ball boys and de facto supporters at every game. Alan[2] takes pride in ensuring that the kit is washed after each game and hangs the shirts up on their pegs on Saturday mornings. Joe, who had been waiting for a while to play up front, goes in goal with no questions asked when the goalkeeper was injured early in a game. Sam asks every new arrival at the prison if they can play football and explains how to get involved. Paul, the ex-pro, quietly encourages the younger new players who are nervous about playing to get the best out of them. John spends all week checking to make sure the players are ready for Saturday. All these actions are those of people who want their team to win.

Sam's seniority, his easy-going demeanour, and his friendliness belied his status as a first-time prisoner and Induction Orderly. He would ask everyone coming through the unit if they played football and to what standard. Several players came to training and match days directly as a result of his intervention. His impact especially is symptomatic of the role football plays at Prescoed. Working as an Orderly, he welcomed newly arrived prisoners to where they stay for their first night, before being allocated a more permanent room in one of ten accommodation units. Officially the purpose of Induction is to inform prisoners about prison life, the regime and their responsibilities and privileges, and to begin to prepare them for their return to the community. This may include information on Chaplaincy, Healthcare (if individuals need access to medication for example), Samaritans, Listeners, Disability Services, and much more. It doesn't necessarily say anything about football, but to Sam catching people early was all part of being a member of the team.

Football also helped the time to pass more quickly, especially when combined with the frequency of games. Several players were able to count down their sentences by looking at the fixture list. They would keep Saturdays for football and Sundays for family visits which, when combined with work during the week on or off camp, helped their sentences pass more quickly for them.

The appeal of football to the players is a mixture of love for the game and the opportunity to keep fit. In any prison the gym is a focal point for a lot of male prisoners, which is the same at Prescoed. For some of the footballers they acknowledge that the game plays a part in their weekly workouts, such as by giving them an extra aerobic fitness session. For these players, they would

[2] All names have been changed.

regularly top up their training with a session after the game in the gym to give themselves a full body workout.

This attention to physical fitness unsurprisingly gave the players a significant edge over their competitors and was a reason they felt they won so many games, and it's hard to disagree. Added to this the players are without things like beer and takeaway food that they acknowledge was a big part of their lives before prison. Deprived of these distractions and many others, the players jump head first into physical fitness and healthy eating to fill the void. For some, such as Bailey, this sobriety helps them get their focus back to where they were before drugs took hold and they started on a path into prison. For others, like Alex, Neil, and John, there is a clear distinction being made that healthy body equals healthy mind, in terms of their plans for a crime-free life after prison. No one plans to return to prison of course.

John felt it more than most. "I don't understand it? How the fuck can they turn us over like that? We battered them for ninety minutes and yet we couldn't score more than once? What the fuck!" His red shirt was thrown into the middle of the room, the number seven barely legible from the mud and grass stains that covered all his kit. His frustration matched his tackling and intensity in a central midfield role. He struggled to take his boots off with hands shaking from the experience. Fingers clawing at rain soaked laces. As Captain, he would always be the last one to leave the game behind.

John looked down at the floor. Searching for an answer that had passed. Paul, the other senior player and an ex-pro, had seen it all before. He spoke up. "John, you're right. We were all over them. Two shitty goals, both headers. That fat fuck as well, how did he get his head on it? We got to be first to it, clear your lines. We'll do them the next game. We'll batter them and score a ton of goals." Other players nodded and murmured in agreement.

*Calum spoke up, which was rare. He wasn't having the criticism pointed at the defence for conceding from headers. "Thing is boys, if we didn't keep giving away stupid free kicks in the middle of the park, they wouldn't have scored, see? Every fucking time we got the ball every c*** would bomb forward wanting to score and we kick it long. Then we lose the ball and they're on the break. You've got to keep your shape boys. Play football. That's how we win these games."*

One of the quietest on and off the pitch, Calum had an ally in his fellow defender Tom. "You know we get fuck all off the ref. You can't go in trying to take the man out as well. The ref's looking to give it and all their lot on the side will shout for anything. They've come off there looking like they won the fucking cup final."

"Too right. Fucking high fivin' each other they was. What's that all about? It's not fucking Premier League," chipped in Neil.

John quickly stood up to his six foot plus height and wide frame of muscle and tattoo. He was furious and hurt in equal measure. The loss still carried in the adrenaline coursing through his blood stream. He held a boot in one hand and shin pad in the other, using both to illustrate his point aggressively. Neil, chilled from vaping outside the changing room, was also bare chested, his strong tattooed torso emphasising his commitment to both strength and fitness. The two locked eyes and their team mates looked down. Neither was to be trifled with. The ball boys, normally full of wise cracks and banter, like Saturday court jesters, knew better than to get in the way. Instead, they craned their heads round the door to see what was unfolding. The two prisoners had the hardened experience of at least five prison sentences between them and were clearly a match for anyone, if it came to that. But everyone in the changing room knew that it wouldn't.

Still, Neil had poked at John's pride and so he replied. "I wait all fucking week for this game. I know it ain't Premier League but it's about pride. You got to do it on the pitch. Our fucking heads went down and they think they're better than us. We've got to do it in training on a Tuesday and we've got to fucking do it here in the games. In the summer there's twenty, thirty boys up here wanting to play. Today we had the bare eleven. That's fucking shit! No wonder they turned us over. What the fuck! I'll go round them up for next week. I'm not having it." He sat down to struggle with his second boot. Neil went back out for a vape. There was nowhere to sit anyway.

Watching it all from the side, the PE Officer stepped forward. Experienced and understanding of the men's characters, now was the right time to interject. The air was clearer. His words of calm reassurance were listened to by each player and sowed the seeds of recovery for the return fixture, which Prescoed won seven nil. For the rest of the season the team remained undefeated.

Deprived of their liberty, Prescoed FC's players were unable to do their arguing over tactics and dodgy decisions in the car home or down the pub after the game. The Officer understood the importance of the men having their say and blowing off, even if it got a little heated, to get it out of them.

By the time they went back to their cells in twos and threes thirty minutes later, each player was in a better frame of mind and there would be no incidents that night in the prison.

Prescoed FC had just lost their first game in three years.

Conclusion

Football at HMP Prescoed—and in other prisons—doesn't just represent something done previously, before prison. It may also represent an alternative future for the players, such as wanting to play for a team again when released, or the opportunity to claim an identity beyond that of 'an offender'. For several men, particularly those with children, football was a way to re-engage with peers or children and family after making the transition from custody to community. For some it even represented the possibility to work or volunteer in the sector or to study sport or an affiliated discipline at a further or higher level. In this way, football continued to be a positive thread that runs through the men's lives before, during and after their sentence.

The good disciplinary record of HMP Prescoed, where there were only three incidents reported in the prison in the previous 12 months and where the prison is recognised positively on safety and respect (Her Majesty's Inspectorate of Prisons and Estyn 2018), is reflected in the good order record of the Prescoed football team where the number of red or yellow cards received by players is also low. Prisoner football teams in film or in print may be portrayed as being overtly physical, violent even, but this is not the case at Prescoed. Several players and staff noted that just to play the men have to abide by three sets of rules: those of the prison, those of the staff, and the laws of the game. This is before any consideration of tactics or team selection to win a game.

To the players, the effect on them of this triple whammy of rules is that it teaches them self-control, especially in the face of perceived or actual provocation, which may come from the opposition, a team member or even a referee. In fact, in the face of provocation, several of the players state that it pushes them to try harder to win the game, rather than react. They talk about 'biting their tongue', 'learning to be calm' or behaving in 'a calm and controlled manner'. There is an acknowledgement that the players as individuals are a part of something that matters to them and they do not want to lose the opportunity to play football, as they understand it could easily affect not only their chances of playing, but also increase the likelihood of being sent back to closed conditions, to another prison. Back to square one.

Allied to the role of helping them improve their behaviour, the players realise they are part of a team. Being part of a team often can mean putting one's personal considerations aside for the team performance to be optimised. This is certainly a common theme for the players at Prescoed, where the players realise that they need to come together as a team to get results. The team evolves regularly, with new players coming into the jail or prisoners being released midway through the season, sometimes at little or no notice. This would pose a challenge for any team in any league, but in this setting it merely reflects the 'churn' of prison life, which has an impact on education, programmes, cell-sharing arrangements, and in this case—the membership of the team.

Prescoed may not sound like a typical prison and the accounts relayed in this chapter may not reflect the reality of life for those residing in other prisons, or indeed the reality of life for other men residing in Prescoed. At the very least though we hope that these accounts firstly show us that the often limited 'traditional' notion of prison 'health' can manifest in many different ways in different parts of our prisons, beyond that recognised in the healthcare unit. Secondly, and perhaps more importantly, we hope to have demonstrated that investing time in building up rapport and trust, finding some common ground, and maybe even pulling on a pair of boots can be a valuable research tool in our efforts to uncover a more nuanced understanding of prison cultures.

References

Drake, D., Earle, R., & Sloan, J. (2005). General introduction: What ethnography tells us about prisons and what prisons tell us about ethnography. In D. Drake, R. Earle, & J. Sloan (Eds.), *Palgrave handbook of prison ethnography*. Basingstoke: Palgrave Macmillan.

Grundy, J. (2019). *90 minutes of freedom*. Poland: Amazon Fulfilment.
Her Majesty's Inspectorate of Prisons and Estyn. (2018). Report on an unannounced inspection of HMP Usk and HMP & YOI Prescoed. Retrieved February 28, 2020, from https://www.justiceinspectorates.gov.uk/hmiprisons/wp-content/uploads/sites/4/2018/02/Usk-and-Prescoed-Web-2017.pdf.
Meek, R. (2012). *The role of sport in promoting desistance from crime*. Bristol: Second Chance Project.
Meek, R. (2013). *Sport in prison: Exploring the role of physical activity in correctional settings*. Abingdon: Routledge.
Meek, R. (2018). *A sporting chance: An independent review of sport in youth and adult prisons*. London: Ministry of Justice.
Sky TV. (2009). *Football behind bars*.
United National Office on Drugs and Crime. (2015). The United Nations standard minimum rules for the treatment of prisoners. Retrieved August 7, 2020, from www.unodc.org/documents/justice-and-prison-reform/Nelson_Mandela_Rules-E-ebook.pdf.

Index[1]

[1] Note: Page numbers followed by 'n' refer to notes.

© The Author(s) 2021

M. Maycock et al. (eds.), *Issues and Innovations in Prison Health Research*, Palgrave Studies in Prisons and Penology, https://doi.org/10.1007/978-3-030-46401-1

I

The manufacturer's authorised representative in the EU is Springer Nature Customer Service Centre GmbH, Europaplatz 3, 69115 Heidelberg, Germany. If you have any concerns regarding our products, please contact ProductSafety@springernature.com

Printed and bound by CPI Group (UK) Ltd, Croydon, CR0 4YY
30/09/2026
02225494-0011